African States

SUNY series, James N. Rosenau series in Global Politics
—————
David C. Earnest, editor

African States

Domestic and External Security Challenges

Edited by

Abu Bakarr Bah

SUNY
PRESS

Published by State University of New York Press, Albany

© 2025 State University of New York

EU GPSR Authorised Representative:
Logos Europe, 9 rue Nicolas Poussin, 17000, La Rochelle, France
contact@logoseurope.eu

For information, contact State University of New York Press, Albany, NY
www.sunypress.edu

Library of Congress Cataloging-in-Publication Data

Name: Bah, Abu Bakarr, 1969– editor, author.
Title: African states : domestic and external security challenges / edited
  by Abu Bakarr Bah.
Description: Albany : State University of New York Press, [2025]. | Series:
  SUNY series, James N. Rosenau series in global politics | Includes
  bibliographical references and index.
Identifiers: LCCN 2024029902 | ISBN 9798855801361 (hardcover : alk. paper) |
  ISBN 9798855801385 (ebook) | ISBN 9798855801378 (pbk. : alk. paper)
Subjects: LCSH: National security—Africa. | Internal security—Africa. |
  National security and globalization—Africa. | Democracy—Africa. |
  Globalization—Africa. | Africa—Politics and government—21st century.
Classification: LCC JZ5584.A35 A377 2025 | DDC
  327.172096—dc23/eng/20240701
LC record available at https://lccn.loc.gov/2024029902

Contents

Introduction

The Glocal Security Challenges of the African State

ABU BAKARR BAH

Introduction: State and Security

The state in Africa has increasingly been subjected to domestic and external pressures geared toward changing it. From civil society–driven pro-democracy activism to armed rebellions and international humanitarian and military interventions, the African state has been the object of modification.[1] These domestic and external cross-pressures on the African state put it in a delicate glocal situation. Indeed, the African state has been the object of modification because of its precarious situation in terms of delivering the human security and human development needs of its citizens, notably physical security, political freedom, and economic well-being.[2] This failure is rooted in various domestic problems and external forces. Too often, African states have been characterized as failing or failed, and at best underdeveloped or developing.[3] These labels capture the problematic nature of the state in both the socioeconomic and the political and security dimensions. Notably, African states that have been deemed to be failing or failed attract a lot of attention as they are diagnosed by internal and external actors and subjected to varying forms of humanistic and subversive actions. As such, understanding the African state requires a glocal lens that interrogates the intersection of the domestic and the external dynamics.

The challenges of the African state are most evident in the prevalence of violent conflicts that destabilize African countries. Since African countries gained independence around 1960, too many of them have experienced major forms of political violence, including civil wars.[4] In the immediate postindependence period, civil wars raged in countries such as Congo, Nigeria, Angola, and Mozambique. Most of those wars became entangled in Cold War geopolitics. Right after the end of the Cold War, civil wars related to governance and ethnicity raged in countries such as Rwanda, Sierra Leone, Liberia, Uganda, and Cote d'Ivoire. More recently, the Global War on Terror has fused with civil wars in countries such as Libya, Mali, and Chad. In the horn of Africa, Sudan, South Sudan, Somalia, and Ethiopia have all been experiencing protracted civil wars.

Indeed, African states have been characterized by violent political conflicts. A critical issue in studying the African state is understanding the causes of the conflicts. African countries, especially those that have experienced civil wars, tend to be characterized by varying forms of dictatorship and poor governance that generate political grievances, especially along ethnic lines. These issues form the domestic drivers of conflicts that are manifested in election-related violence, violent street demonstrations, and in worst cases civil wars.[5] Efforts to combat domestic drivers of conflicts include various policies, often externally driven ones, aimed at instilling multiparty democracy, decentralizing the state, promoting inclusive government, and reducing corruption and poverty. However, success has been minimal, as too many African countries continue to suffer from political oppression, poor governance, and poverty. Violent conflicts have also been driven by external factors, especially the supply of arms and exploitation of natural resources.[6] These problems are compounded by globally induced environmental factors that undermine livelihoods; the very colonial root of the African state, which has created a history of ethnic political tensions; and the fusion of the Global War on Terror into African issues.[7] Many of the conflict drivers tend to generate significant international interventions, albeit often with unanticipated problems for the African state.[8]

The political violence that characterizes African countries along with the domestic and external conflict drivers raise critical questions about the African state, namely: What is the nature of the African state? How do domestic and external conflict drivers affect the state? How can African states transform into more stable forms? These questions require a critical look into the genesis of the state and its contemporary security challenges through a glocal lens. This book addresses these issues through various chapters that examine the colonial roots of the African state and its entanglement in geopolitical and external security issues. The chapters point to specific issues related to domestic and external conflict drivers through case studies on Sierra Leone, Cameroon, Mali, Nigeria, and Somalia. Overall, the chapters point to an interesting intersection of domestic and external issues in a way that captures the glocalized security situation shaping the African state.

The studies in this book revolve around key concepts related to the state and its security that need to be clarified from the outset. Notions of state, nation, security, and glocalization repeatedly emerge as they are further developed and applied to the cases. At the heart of these concepts is the state, which is a political entity that claims authority over a defined territory that is internationally recognized as a country. This is rooted in the Weberian and Westphalian notions of state.[9] As Max Weber notes, the state claims exclusive authority over the means of violence. However, this claim is also constrained by broader principles of human rights and democratic governance. Such principles of global liberal governance are anchored in both domestic struggles for power and international security and humanitarian norms and interests.[10] In that sense, the state becomes of a contested terrain for power among domestic actors and a geopolitical space for regional and global powers, including violent non-state actors. In Africa, states are the countries that emerged out of colonial rule. As such, the state in Africa is also a postcolonial political entity within a defined territory and the global system of states. It is precisely the colonial roots of African states and their neocolonial dependency that make them peculiar states within the international system.[11] Indeed, African states have the trappings of modern states, such as territorial boundaries and bureaucratic and security apparatuses for exercising authority.[12] However, as postcolonial political entities, African states are not neatly formed as nations. The postcolonial state in Africa, especially in sub-Saharan Africa, is a multiethnic state rather than a nation that has been molded into a nation-state.[13]

A key problem for the postcolonial state is nationhood, which is due to the multiethnic character of the state and the stratagem of divide and rule employed during colonial rule.[14] A nation is an identity that connects people to a territory and a sense of common political belonging to the specific territory within the international system of states. Such identities are rooted in objective, organic, and socially constructed features that shape common historical experiences that are woven into narratives of belonging and collective memories, including imagined ones.[15] The survival of nations in the international system rests on the establishment of a state, which becomes a nation-state. Nationhood fosters cohesion among the people of a state and reduces existential group differences, especially through common language, religion, and culture. As such, states seek to foster nationhood just as nations seek to gain statehood. If historical and political factors neatly align, the nation-state emerges as the nation establishes a state or when the state successfully creates a sense of nationhood.[16] However, such symbiosis of state and nation is very difficult to achieve and sustain. African states have been uniquely challenged in fostering nationhood because of the way Africa was carved into states without regard for the ethnic and cultural identities of the people.[17] This led to states that are composed of too many ethnic groups located in different areas of the state. Given the relative infancy of African states, as most of them only became independent around 1960, African countries have not yet really fostered nations out of their states. Nationhood remains a work in progress that constantly breeds political conflicts over resources, power, and proper representation in the state.

As is all too familiar, security is a major challenge for African countries. In many ways, security is a matter of order and well-being for the state and the citizens. Security dovetails with the forms and nature of conflicts in a country. While all states are characterized by some form of conflict, the issue of security is directly connected to violent conflicts.[18] Extant security studies literature makes a distinction between low-intensity and high-intensity conflicts, which undermine security at varying levels. A third form of violent conflict is terrorism, which can take the form of high- or low-intensity conflict. However, terrorism has emerged as a unique form of violent conflict. All of these are manifested in varying forms of civil wars, ranging from guerrilla wars to new wars and terrorism warfare.[19] Violent conflicts lead to two forms of security problems—state security and human security. State security is about the authority of the state and its claim to monopoly over the use of violence. When dissidents take up arms, they effectively challenge the authority of the state and legitimacy of the government. This undermines state security. Human security refers to the physical well-being of the people within a state, especially in relation of the ability of the state to ensure law and order. When there is significant breakdown of law and order, the lives and property of the masses become insecure, generating humanitarian problems. Human security issues become acute as violence increases and the state's ability to exert order significantly declines, especially in civil war situations.[20] In African countries, state security and human security have been undermined mostly by civil wars. Interestingly, African security issues are often glocal because of the intersection of domestic and external elements in African civil wars. While Africa has rarely faced conventional interstate wars, violent conflicts in Africa often take the form of civil wars and terrorism warfare that are regional in their operations. Even more, African conflicts often attract external military interventions from regional and global powers. As such, what may seem local can essentially be glocal in nature.

The glocality of African security issues speaks to the intersection of domestic and external conflict drivers and the application of global liberal governance to African conflicts. Glocality has been used as a critique of the notion of globalization, which captures the way countries and societies have been connected and absorbed into various transnational processes ranging from issues of trade to culture and security. However, globalization is rooted in homogenization into Western-dominated systems.[21] This homogenization leaves a significant lacuna in the way we understand local adaptations and resistances to globalization. As such, the notion of glocalization has been used to refer to the fusion of local factors with global factors in a way that does not reduce the local to the homogenization of the global. Rather, glocalization produces a new reality. We use the notion of glocalization to refer to the fusion of domestic and external drivers of conflicts in Africa. This fusion produces new war dynamics that make African conflicts anchored in fundamental domestic issues, but also firmly tied to external networks of war logistics, interests, and global liberal governance.

The African State and Its Glocal Challenges: From State Decay to Securitization

Efforts to theorize the African state often gravitate between colonialism and prebendalism. While colonialism-related works expose the structural and geopolitical conditions that impede proper functioning of African states and render them into dependency,[22] prebendalism examines the nature of power and governance in postcolonial Africa in ways that expose the problems of poor leadership, corruption, and nepotism, which often lead to state failure.[23] Clearly, the African state is a bit different from the Westphalian state, despite the manifest similarities. Indeed, African states are based on defined boundaries and the idea of sovereignty along with a bureaucratic apparatus, which make them resemble Westphalian states.[24] However, African states lack a critical feature of Westphalian states, especially those characterized as nation-states, which continues to undermine the manifest dismissions of Westphalian statehood in Africa. Notably, African states lack a deep-seated national identity rooted in shared culture and common language to generate and foster nationhood. This is largely because African countries are mostly multiethnic in ways that there are hardly clear majority groups, as most countries are composed of too many ethnic groups, which were pitted against one another under colonial divide-and-rule.[25] Even in the case of Somalia, clan identity has created a de-factor ethnicity problem.[26] Indeed, Westphalian states in Europe emerged out of empires that were diverse. However, the process of state formation entailed significant efforts at creating a common culture, especially language. This common culture became the linchpin for the development of a national identity associated with the state as minority groups were assimilated or pacified.[27] Shared national identity fosters a sense of nationhood, which creates better conditions for the development of a legitimate system of authority and political stability, albeit one that may be oppressive to minorities.[28] In Africa, shared sense of national identity has been problematic, as the state tends to be characterized by ethnic divisions that breed prebendalism.[29]

Indeed, postcolonial multiethnic countries have tried to forge a common national identity as a way to promote peace and economic development. Perhaps the best examples are in Southeast Asia, especially in Singapore, Malaysia, and Indonesia. In Malaysia, the state has effectively forged a nation by granting political power to the majority Malay, who are considered the Bumiputera, in return for citizenship recognition for the minority Chinese and Indian populations. While this arrangement has been challenged for its inherent discrimination toward minorities, it has somehow sealed a common Malaysian national identity that has become critical for stability and economic development—effectively making it a real state in the Westphalian sense.[30] In Singapore, careful statecraft has resulted in delicate ethnic engineering that simultaneously recognizes diversity while promoting ethnic integration into a Singaporean city-state-cum-nation-state. Notably, ethnicity has been technocratically managed through visionary political leadership so as to ensure peace and foster a common belonging.[31] In Indonesia, national identity has been forged through the inculcation of a national doctrine of Pancasila and a national language (i.e., Bahasa Indonesia) that dovetail with a dominant Islamic identity. Through these processes, diverse ethnic groups have been woven into a postcolonial Indonesian nation-state that has become the lynchpin for stability and development.[32] In Africa, Tanzania stands out as a unique case of national identity engineering rooted in the promotion of a common language and an African socialist ideology. Notably, Swahili and Ujamaa, under the leadership of Julius Nyerere, created a strong sense of national identity that somehow fosters ethnic harmony in Tanzania.[33]

For most countries in Africa, the state still is not connected to a solid sense of national identity.[34] Indeed, there are organically germinating features of shared identity. Notably, some African countries have a language that is widely spoken, such as Creole in Sierra Leone, Wolof in Senegal, Pidgin in Nigeria, and Swahili in Kenya. However, these are too often not well developed as written languages; and in most cases they are subordinated to the official (colonial) language, especially English and French (with the notable exception of Swahili). Moreover, they are secondary languages, as most people have their native language as their primary language and the one through which they identify. As such, these nascent common languages have not yet yielded a collective national identity that culturally ties the people to the state. This is because other languages tied to specific ethnic groups continue to be primary identities, and there is an ongoing connection between political power and ethnic domination. Overall, African countries continue to suffer a significant dissonance between statehood and nationhood.[35] As such, African countries are multiethnic states in which ethnic identity either competes with or dominates the national identity, thereby undermining a shared sense of nationhood. In this setting, ethnicity becomes a problem precisely because of its politicization. This generates ethnic grievances over marginalization, thereby undermining the cohesion of the state, as most evident in the various ethnically driven civil wars across Africa.

Studies on Africa continue to point to the problem of ethnicity. As Mahmood Mamdani notes, ethnicity goes back to colonial rule.[36] Ethnicity is still a source of political conflict as it is manipulated by the political elite.[37] The fundamental problem of ethnicity is that it undermines the state, putting it at constant risk of political violence. The problem of ethnicity leads to the issue of poor governance. Indeed, African countries made a fundamental decision right at the dawn of independence to maintain the colonial boundaries instead of trying to create ethnically homogenous state boundaries. With the rare cases of Sudan and Ethiopia, which are still multiethnic, African states have refused to break up. As such, the solution to ethnicity has mostly moved in two directions: a) democratization of the postcolonial state, including federalism and decentralization and b) regional and pan-African integration. Unfortunately, progress on either front is very limited.

The democratization of the state is connected to the discourse of prebendalism. As various studies have shown, postcolonial African countries have been characterized by what Robert Jackson and Carl Rosberg refer to as personal rule. The notion of personal rule captures the authoritarian and corrupt nature of the state that continues to undermine its security.[38]

Notably, elite interests intersect with ethnicity, fostering nepotism and a propensity to political violence under varying forms of military regimes, one-party states, and pseudo-democracies.[39] As Abu Bakarr Bah notes, these kinds of problems lead to state decay and in worst cases state failure.[40] It is within this contest of state decay and state failure that democratization and good governance emerge as ways to fix African states.[41]

There have been two major waves of democracy in Africa. The first was around the immediate postcolonial period and the second was at the end of the Cold War. The first democracy wave ended in failures as multiparty democracies increasingly degenerated into ethnic struggles for power. By the 1980s, African democracies had been replaced with one-party and military regimes.[42] The second democracy wave started as a promising effort to revive multiparty democracy and instill good governance under the banner of Western liberalism during the 1990s.[43] So far, the results of Africa's second democracy wave have been mixed. Indeed, there are countries that continue to hold multiparty elections in which power shifts to opposition parties, such as in Nigeria, Ghana, Senegal, Malawi, and Kenya. There are also countries that continue to combat corruption and instill good governance, such as Rwanda, albeit under conditions of overwhelming authoritarian power.[44] However, the second wave of democracy has been characterized by ethnic political violence, improper prolongation of presidential term limits, and manipulated election victories, as most evident in countries such as Cote d'Ivoire, Sierra Leone, Uganda, South Sudan, and Rwanda.[45] In some countries, this nascent democracy has collapsed as the military has seized power, such as in Mali, Burkina Faso, Guinea, Sudan, Niger, and Gabon.

African countries continue to struggle with fixing the authoritarianism and corruption that plague the state through civil and subversive efforts that gravitate between democratization and social disorder. Successful efforts to fix the state through grassroots civic activism buttressed by pan-African and Western pressure for good governance and election integrity tend to enhance the state. In Kenya, for example, civic activism along with devolution is enhancing democracy, albeit in a way that is not entirely free from violent protests. The African Union took a proactive stance by creating protocols for good governance and multiparty democracy. Notably, these include the New Partnership for Africa's Development, the African Charter on Democracy, Elections and Governance, and the Lomé Declaration (July 2000) on the Framework for an OAU Response to Unconstitutional Changes of Government. The African Union has been observing and certifying elections as a way to enhance election credibility. The pan-African vision for integration has also been viewed as a way to moderate ethnicity within African countries. If materialized, pan-African citizenship can free people from the state in which they are oppressed as a marginalized group since it will be easier to join co-ethnics in other parts of Africa. However, this vision of integration and pan-African citizenship is far from actualized. Even more, the pan-African democracy and good governance mechanisms increasingly have been weakened by electoral and constitutional malpractices and coups.

Efforts to fix African states are not limited to pan-Africanism and African agency, but are more deeply connected to the external factors that shape African states. In a way, the domestic challenges of the African state are connected to the external problem in two notable ways: a) colonial roots of the state and b) dependency. These issues have not only complicated the domestic issues undermining the African state but also have led to varying forms of securitization of the African state through international military interventions in the forms of humanitarian missions and geopolitical military initiatives. Unfortunately, the securitization of the African states feeds into state decay.

Indeed, contemporary African states are colonial creations both in the way territories were defined and in the forms of administration and political authority instituted in them. By its very nature, colonialism was rooted in the interests of the colonial power, as people were reduced to subjects whose resources and labor were exploited in the service of the colonial power. As such, the primary concern of the colonial powers in African countries was ensuring stability through pacification of dissent and co-optation.[46] This form of government resulted in authoritarian and ethnically divisive forms of rule, which continued into the postcolonial states of Africa. Independence in Africa did not mean the restoration of precolonial states. Rather, it simply meant the transformation of colonial territories into neocolonial states in the hands of African elite. Moreover, the postcolonial states remained in dependency to the colonial power through the capitalist world system into which they were absorbed and the geopolitical configuration of the world that emerged out of the second World War.[47] A key problem of the colonial root of the state is that it instilled personal rule, first in the form of colonial rule and later in the form of African dictatorship, which often lead to political violence. The critical link between colonial rule and the instability of the African state happened through the entrenchment of personal rule. Under such conditions, political oppression, ethnic marginalization, corruption, and poverty became hallmarks of the African state.[48] Clearly, such states fell into a path of deterioration wherein they are increasingly unable to meet the basic needs of their citizens, which puts them into economic and political turmoil.

Unfortunately, state decay and state failure have made African countries more dependent on external powers, making them prime targets for benevolent and cynical international interventions.[49] Dependency takes varying forms in Africa—from economic dependency to securitization.[50] Ultimately, dependency undermines sovereignty and makes African security a truly glocalized problem. In a way, the African state becomes an object of action from external powers. While the governance problems of the African state are addressed through the application of neoliberalism, the security challenges are supposed to be fixed through securitization under global liberal governance. Neoliberalism became the template for democratization and good governance, which were intended to end personal rule and lead to democratic and economically progressive states.[51] Securitization also happens as African states fall into decay and failure. Securitization is rooted in the need to restore the core Westphalian elements of statehood, notably the ability of the state to control the use of violence within its territory.[52] The state must maintain both state security and human security. As such, when African states are challenged by armed rebel groups or terrorist organizations in ways that destabilization them, external powers intervene militarily.

Securitization in cases of civil wars rooted in domestic governance issues occurs through peacekeeping missions under AU and UN authorizations. Peacekeeping missions are based on international humanitarian morality and regional security considerations.[53] Such cases include the peacekeeping missions in Sierra Leone, Liberia, Cote d'Ivoire, Democratic Republic of the Congo (DRC), Burundi, and South Sudan. In these cases, securitization evolves from small peacekeeping missions mainly tasked with monitoring ceasefires to robust missions with peace enforcement mandates under Chapter VII of the UN Charter. Such missions culminate with the implementation of security-sector reforms and developmental programs geared toward rebuilding the state, which had once failed.[54] In Sierra Leone and Liberia, for example, the UN missions evolved into elaborate postwar reconstruction missions, which attracted significant Western humanitarian and military involvements to rebuild the state.[55]

In other cases, securitization occurs through the Global War on Terror. Notably, this happens in countries that are experiencing terrorism warfare or places where global terrorist networks have infiltrated. Such interventions typically take the form of counterterrorism and special military operations by Western powers.[56] Mali stood out as a case of terrorism warfare and robust

French intervention, which ended in distrust as Mali descended into more terrorism warfare.[57] Counterterrorism programs have also been implemented in countries such as Niger, Somali, Nigeria, Chad, and Libya.[58] In these cases, securitization is deeply tied to the security and geopolitical interests of Western powers, which see African countries as incapable of fulfilling their responsibilities to the global security order. Ironically, securitization in these kinds of cases hardly results in the strengthening of the African state. Rather, it reinforces dependency and, in some cases, attracts more terrorism, further undermining the state, as most evident in Mali, Burkina Faso, and Niger. Even more, these states become hotly contested geopolitical spaces as Russia's military operators enter the securitization fight.

The domestic and external drivers of conflicts and securitization point to the glocal nature of the African state. African states are faced with glocalized security situations in which the security of the state is driven by domestic problems of governance and external forces rooted in global liberal governance. All of these go back to the very colonial roots of the state that created conditions for prebendalism and dependency. African security has been glocalized precisely because of the very nature of the African state, which requires constant remaking. Moreover, African security becomes a dialectical problem in which domestic and external issues generate contradictions. Untangling these contradictions require a deeper understanding of the fusion of the domestic and external challenges of African states.

A useful entry point for understating the fusion of the domestic and external challenges of African states is through the notion of glocalization, which is used in the various chapters to capture the glocal nature of the security challenges of African states. A key figure in the development of the notion of glocalization is Roland Robertson, who alluded to it in his article "Globality and Modernity."[59] Working with others, he continued to push the concept of glocalization in a series of articles that capture the ways local issues are tied to global processes and networks.[60] Ulrich Beck also critiqued the homogenizing nature of globalization through a cultural relativism standpoint as he pointed to the importance of the local through the notion of contextual universalism.[61] However, the initial critiques of globalization and framings of glocalization were in the realms of business, culture, and social movements, especially as a discourse on the homogenization of time and space.[62]

Though the concept of glocalization has been used in studies of social movements, culture, and globalization generally, it is hardly used in relation to security issues. Interestingly, Samuel Marfo et al. tried "to make a case for a 'glocalized peace and security architecture,' a comprehensive peace and security design which is both domestically or inward-looking relevant and internationally or outside-looking practicable."[63] As they argue, a glocalized peace and security architecture "attempts to suggest an approach which can foster a peaceful co-existence among states without necessarily endangering domestic politics in a seemingly chaotic global environment."[64] In this book, the notion of glocalized security is used to weave the domestic and external dimensions of (in)security, akin to the way the notion of glocalization has been used to examine the intricacies of global homogenization and local resistances.[65]

Scope and Themes: The State, Governance, and Security

In examining the African state and its security challenges, this book examines three issues that show the intersection of the domestic and external forces that render the African state as a glocal problem. These are a) the colonial roots of the state, b) problems of governance, and c) international and regional security imperatives. These themes emerge from the various chapters in ways that connect to the domestic and external drivers of African conflicts and the glocalized nature of African security. The themes not only dovetail with extant theories on the African state, but also tie neatly with a glocalized security lens into the African state.

First is the nature of the African state, which emerges in all the chapters. In chapter 1, Ian Spears takes on the fundamental question of the colonial nature of the state by underscoring how the boundaries of current African states, especially in sub-Saharan Africa, do not create conditions for the development of stable states. Spears raises two basic questions: Why does Africa fail to escape the cycle of low-intensity conflict and instability? What could be so hard about instilling democratic values or sidelining those who fail to follow its principles? In his analysis, Spears addresses various ideas about leadership and democracy in Africa, but ultimately argues that the permanent colonial borders initiate a dynamic that limits Africa's ability to escape patronage politics and embrace democratic rule even if regimes have undergone institutional reforms. For Spears, these are structural problems for the African state that inhibit the fostering of nationhood, which plays into ethnic politics, nepotism, and prebendalism. The problems of the African state go far beyond the issue of leadership, as too many African leaders have failed throughout the continent. For Spears, this is not accidental. Rather, the structure of the state precludes democracy, especially in a neoliberal sense.

The nature of the state emerges again in chapter 2 on Cameroon by Walters Samah. For Samah, the colonial legacies of the African state produce political marginalization of minorities that makes the state inherently unstable. He illustrates this with the Anglophone secessionist movement in Cameroon. Anglophones feel marginalized in ways that even democratization or federalism cannot fix precisely because the very ethnic and cultural composition of the state inhibits a sense of common belonging. The colonial baggage of the state also emerges in the chapters on Sierra Leone and Mali. As Abu Bakarr Bah and Kassandra Gonzalez show in chapter 3 on Sierra Leone, the postcolonial state has been plagued by deep ethnic divides, which continuously lead to deterioration and the eventual demise of democracy. Just as Spears argued, the colonial structure of the state makes neoliberal democracy practically unworkable in Sierra Leone. As Matthew Pflaum also notes in chapter 5 on Mali, the neocolonial vulnerability of the state becomes most vivid in the French military intervention, which exceeded the mandate and infringed on Mali's sovereignty. The precarious nature of the colonial state shows up again in chapter 4 on Nigeria by Mary Fox and chapter 6 by Keunsoo Jeong on Somalia, where the states are unable to ensure proper security as terrorists and pirates openly operate. Chapter 7 by Sebastian Paalo and John-Paul Banchani shows the neocolonial vulnerabilities of the state as the number of foreign military bases grows across Africa under dubious geopolitical security frameworks.

The second theme is governance, which emerges in many of the chapters, especially those on Cameroon, Sierra Leone, Mali, and Somalia. A key factor that renders the African state insecure is poor governance. The problematic colonial boundaries of the state are compounded by poor governance. As Samah shows in Cameroon, the state breeds oppressive rule that undermines democracy and creates a sense of disenfranchisement. In Sierra Leone, Bah and Gonzalez show how poor governance, driven by ethnic politics, resulted in state decay and civil war. Similar problems emerge in Mali where democracy collapsed under the weight of poor governance, which worsened the civil war. Mali's democracy was unable to withstand the problems of state failure and terrorism warfare. In Somalia, poor governance rendered the state into failure, which opened the country to conditions that make piracy thrive. Jeong shows several features of poor governance that are implicit in explaining the rise of piracy in Somalia. Notably, he points to issues such as poverty, the demise of legitimate authority, and lack of adequate policing.

The third theme relates to regional and international security, ranging from wars in Sierra Leone and Mali to piracy in Somalia and terrorism in Nigeria. In each case, the African state is an object of action. As Paalo and Banchani show, the securitization of Africa is increasingly happening through geopolitically induced military bases and outposts across Africa. While these may seem like voluntary collaborations to enhance security in Africa, in reality they are externally imposed outfits that undermine the development of more Indigenous and harmonious pan-African security architecture. In that sense, the African state becomes the object of glocalized security. Securitization also occurs through direct military intervention. As Bah and Gonzalez show, in Sierra Leone, international military intervention was driven by regional security considerations and the doctrine of the responsibility to protect (R2P). In Pflaum's chapter on Mali, international military intervention was mostly tied to the Global War on Terror, which was brought to Mali as a result of the destabilization of Libya. International security considerations emerge in Nigeria and Somalia as well. In Nigeria, Mary Fox shows how terrorism proliferates in terms of recruitment strategies that have been used by Boko Haram in Nigeria. A major issue that concerns Western power is piracy. As Jeong shows, Somalia has been under the international spotlight for piracy as Western powers try to connect piracy to terrorism under the Global War on Terror. However, Jeong notes that piracy in Somalia is more rooted in domestic issues of state failure, despite its global implications.

Conclusion: The State and Glocalized Security

The basic question of security in Africa goes back to the nature of the state. The state is rooted in colonialism and continues to exhibit the prebendal form of rule that was ingrained during colonialism. The postcolonial state, especially in sub-Saharan Africa, continues to be plagued by violence because of its authoritarian and corrupt nature, which pits ethnic groups against one another. However, efforts to fix the state through neoliberal democracy always run into the problems of ethnic and elite interests that make democracy unworkable. At the same time, the postcolonial state continues to suffer from dependency and adverse conditions of geopolitics, which make it continuously vulnerable to violence. Postcolonial dependency makes the African state an object of action under global liberal governance. The convergence of these domestic and external pressures has created conditions under which the African state will be inherently unstable and in need of external intervention, which happens through benevolent and cynical global humanitarian and security frames. As this work shows, the instability of the African state is not accidental. However, efforts to fix the African state tend to be bifurcated along the lines of domestic or external drivers of insecurity. This work shows the need for a more holistic approach that understands the glocal nature of the problems that plague the African state. We see this issue of glocalized security in the ethnic marginalization and corruption that led to civil wars in Sierra Leone and Cameroon, the terrorism warfare in Mali and Nigeria, the collapse of the state in Somalia, and the proliferation of external military bases and outfits across Africa.

In sum, glocality provides a lens for examining the African state through the domestic and external drivers of violent conflicts in the continent. A key marker of a state is its obligations to ensure state and human security. However, the ability of the state to provide such forms of security is conditioned by the intersection of domestic and external factors in a way that makes security a glocal problem. It is this glocality of the state and security that makes the African state not only an object of modification, but also a fertile issue for theorizing and an intriguing policy puzzle. Works ranging from critiques of colonialism to liberal peace, collective security, and human security all find the African state to be peculiar and a challenge to theorize. In large part, this is due to the bifurcation of the domestic and the external, which produces a lacuna in our understanding of the African state and its security challenges. The chapters in this book show the need for a glocal lens in examining the African state and issues of security. A glocal lens provides unique insights that bridge a variety of factors in the way we see the colonial baggage of the African state, the problems of governance, and the regional and global security problems of the African state.

Notes

1. Abu Bakarr Bah, "Changing World Order and the Future of Democracy in Sub-Saharan Africa," *Proteus: A Journal of Ideas* 21, no. 1 (Spring 2004): 3–12; Abu Bakarr Bah, "Civil Non-State Actors in Peacekeeping and Peacebuilding in West Africa," *Journal of International Peacekeeping* 17, no. 3–4 (2013): 313–36; Munzoul A. M. Assal, "Forging the Juba Peace Agreement: The Role of National, Regional, and International Actors," *African Conflict & Peacebuilding Review* 12, no. 2 (2022): 5–22; Abu Bakarr Bah, "People-Centered Liberalism: An Alternative Approach to International State-Building in Sierra Leone and Liberia," *Critical Sociology* 43, no. 7–8 (2017): 989–1007; Abu Bakarr Bah, ed., *African Security: Local Issues and Global Connections* (Athens, OH: Ohio University Press, 2024).

2. Commission on Human Security, *Human Security Now* (New York: United Nations, 2003); United Nations Development Programme (UNDP), *Human Development Report 1990* (New York: Oxford University Press, 1990).

3. Abu Bakarr Bah, "State Decay: A Conceptual Frame for Failing and Failed States in West Africa," *International Journal of Politics, Culture, and Society* 25, no. 1–3 (2012): 71–89.

4. Elizabeth Schmidt, *Foreign Intervention in Africa: From the Cold War to the War on Terror* (Cambridge: Cambridge University Press, 2013).

5. Michael Bratton and Nicholas Van de Walle, *Democratic Experiments in Africa: Regime Transitions in Comparative Perspective* (Cambridge: Cambridge University Press, 1997); Robert H. Jackson and Carl Gustav Rosberg, *Personal Rule in Black Africa: Prince, Autocrat, Prophet, Tyrant* (Berkeley: University of California Press, 1982); William Reno, *Corruption and State Politics in Sierra Leone* (New York: Cambridge University Press, 2008); Kimo A. Adiebo, "Resource, Economic, and Financial Management in South Sudan: Taking Stock of Chapter IV of the R-ARCSS," *African Conflict & Peacebuilding Review* 11, no. 2 (2021): 39–63.

6. Paul Collier and Anke Hoeffler, "On Economic Causes of Civil War," *Oxford Economic Papers* 50, no. 4 (1998): 563–73; Lansana Gberie, *A Dirty War in West Africa: The RUF and the Destruction of Sierra Leone* (Bloomington: Indiana University Press, 2005); Michael Beevers, "Natural Resource Reforms in Postwar Liberia and Sierra Leone: Contradictions and Tensions," in *Post-Conflict Institutional Design: Peacebuilding and Democracy in Africa*, ed. Abu Bakarr Bah (London: Zed Books/Bloomsbury Press, 2020), 136–63.

7. Mahmood Mamdani, *Citizen and Subject: Contemporary Africa and the Legacy of Late Colonialism* (Princeton, NJ: Princeton University Press, 1996); Abu Bakarr Bah, ed., *International Security and Peacebuilding: Africa, the Middle East, and Europe* (Bloomington: Indiana University Press, 2017); Michael Nwankpa, "Understanding the Local-Global Dichotomy and Drivers of the Boko Haram Insurgency," *African Conflict and Peacebuilding Review* 10, no. 2 (2020): 43–64.

8. Bah, *International Security and Peacebuilding*; Adekeye Adebajo, *Building Peace in West Africa: Liberia, Sierra Leone, and Guinea-Bissau* (Boulder: Lynne Rienner, 2002).

9. Edward Newman, "Failed States and International Order: Constructing a Post-Westphalian World," *Contemporary Security Policy* 30, no. 3 (2009): 421–43; Charles Tilly and Gabriel Ardant, *The Formation of National States in Western Europe* (Princeton, NJ: Princeton University Press, 1975); Max Weber, *Max Weber: Essays in Sociology*, trans. and ed. H. H. Gerth and C. Wright Mills (New York: Routledge, 2009).

10. Mark Duffield, *Global Governance and the New Wars: The Merging of Development and Security* (London: Zed Books, 2014); Bah, *International Security and Peacebuilding*.

11. Tilly and Ardant, *The Formation of National States in Western Europe*; Immanuel Wallerstein, *The Capitalist World-Economy* (Cambridge: Cambridge University Press, 1979); Christopher S. Clapham, *Africa and the International System: The Politics of State Survival* (Cambridge: Cambridge University Press, 1996); Joseph Reese Strayer, *On the Medieval Origins of the Modern State* (Princeton, NJ: Princeton University Press, 2005); Ali A. Mazrui, *Africa's International Relations: The Diplomacy of Dependency and Change* (London: Routledge, 2019); Michel-Rolph Trouillot, "The Anthropology of the State in the Age of Globalization: Close Encounters of a Deceptive Kind," *Current Anthropology* 42, no. 1 (2001): 125–38; Arjun Appadurai, *Fear of Small Numbers: An Essay on the Geography of Anger* (Durham, NC: Duke University Press, 2006).

12. Gianfranco Poggi, *The State: Its Nature, Development, and Prospects* (Stanford: Stanford University Press, 1990); Weber, *Essays in Sociology*.

13. Kwame Anthony Appiah, *In My Father's House: Africa in the Philosophy of Culture* (New York: Oxford University Press, 1992); Basil Davidson, *The Black Man's Burden: Africa and the Curse of the Nation-State* (New York: Times Books, 1992).

14. Mamdani, *Citizen and Subject*; Abu Bakarr Bah, *Breakdown and Reconstitution: Democracy, the Nation-State, and Ethnicity in Nigeria* (Lanham, MD: Lexington Books, 2005).

15. Anthony D. Smith, *Nationalism and Modernism* (London: Routledge, 2013); Johann G. von Herder, *Reflections on the Philosophy of the History of Man* (Chicago: University of Chicago Press, 1968); Florian Znaniecki, *Modern Nationalities: A Sociological Study* (Westport, CT: Greenwood Press, 1973); Jean-François Bayart, *The Illusion of Cultural Identity* (Chicago: University of Chicago Press, 2005); Benedict Anderson, *Imagined Communities: Reflections on the Origin and Spread of Nationalism* (London: Verso Books, 2006); Charles Taylor, *Multiculturalism: Examining the Politics of Recognition* (Princeton, NJ: Princeton University Press, 1994).

16. Znaniecki, *Modern Nationalities*; Anderson, *Imagined Communities*.

17. Mamdani, *Citizen and Subject*; Davidson, *The Black Man's Burden*; Appiah, *In My Father's House*.

18. Abu Bakarr Bah, "The Contours of New Humanitarianism: War and Peacebuilding in Sierra Leone," *Africa Today* 60, no. 1 (2013): 3–26.

19. Lotta Themnér and Peter Wallensteen, "Armed Conflict, 1946–2010," *Journal of Peace Research* 48, no. 4 (2011): 525–36; Bah, *International Security and Peacebuilding*.

20. Bah, "The Contours of New Humanitarianism"; Abu Bakarr Bah and Nikolas Emmanuel, *International Statebuilding in West Africa: Civil Wars and New Humanitarianism in Sierra Leone, Liberia, and Côte d'Ivoire* (Bloomington: Indiana University Press, 2024).

21. Roland Robertson, "Globalisation or Glocalisation?," *Journal of International Communication* 1, no. 1 (1994): 33–52; Roland Robertson, "Glocalization:

Time-Space and Homogeneity-Heterogeneity," *Global Modernities* 2, no. 1 (1995): 25–44; Ulrich Beck, *What Is Globalization?* (Cambridge: Polity Press, 2000).

22. Mazrui, *Africa's International Relations*; Wallerstein, *The Capitalist World-Economy.*

23. Patrick Chabal and Jean-Pascal Daloz, *Africa Works: Disorder as Political Instrument* (Bloomington: Indiana University Press, 1999); Richard A. Joseph, *Democracy and Prebendal Politics in Nigeria* (New York: Cambridge University Press, 1987); Bah, "State Decay"; Jackson and Rosberg, *Personal Rule in Black Africa.*

24. Newman, "Failed States and International Order"; Tilly and Ardant, *The Formation of National States in Western Europe*; Weber, *Max Weber: Essays in Sociology.*

25. Mamdani, *Citizen and Subject.*

26. Markus Virgil Hoehne et al., "Somali and Ethiopian Diasporic Engagement for Peace in the Horn of Africa"; Mahdi Abdile, "Customary Dispute Resolution in Somalia," *African Conflict and Peacebuilding Review* 2, no. 1 (2012): 87–110.

27. Znaniecki, *Modern Nationalities*; Herder, *Reflections on the Philosophy of the History of Man*; Anderson, *Imagined Communities.*

28. Weber, *Max Weber: Essays in Sociology.*

29. Joseph, *Democracy and Prebendal Politics in Nigeria.*

30. Zawawi Ibrahim, "Globalization and National Identity: Managing Ethnicity and Cultural Pluralism in Malaysia," *Growth and Governance in Asia* (2004): 115–36; Chee-Beng Tan, "Ethnic Identities and National Identities: Some Examples from Malaysia," *Identities Global Studies in Culture and Power* 6, no. 4 (2000): 441–80; Vejai Balasubramaniam, "A Divided Nation: Malay Political Dominance, Bumiputera Material Advancement and National Identity in Malaysia," *National Identities* 9, no. 1 (2007): 35–48.

31. Michael D. Barr and Zlatko Skrbiš, *Constructing Singapore: Elitism, Ethnicity and the Nation-Building Project* (Copenhagen, Denmark: Nias Press, 2008); John Clammer, "The Institutionalization of Ethnicity: The Culture of Ethnicity in Singapore," *Ethnic and Racial Studies* 5, no. 2 (1982): 127–39.

32. Lucy R. Montolalu and Leo Suryadinata, "National Language and Nation-Building: The Case of Bahasa Indonesia," in *Language, Nation and Development in Southeast Asia*, ed. Lee Hock Guan and Leo Suryadinata (Singapore: ISEAS, 2007), 39–50; Peter H. Lowenberg, "Language Policy and Language Identity in Indonesia," *Journal of Asian Pacific Communication* 3, no. 1 (1992): 59–77; Josef Errington, "Language, Religion, and Identity in Indonesia," *ISIM Newsletter* 3, no. 1 (1999): 16.

33. Marie-Aude Fouéré, "Julius Nyerere, Ujamaa, and Political Morality in Contemporary Tanzania," *African Studies Review* 57, no. 1 (2014): 1–24; Mrisho Malipula, "Depoliticised Ethnicity in Tanzania: A Structural and Historical Narrative," *Afrika Focus* 27, no. 2 (2014): 49–70; John Campbell, "Nationalism, Ethnicity and Religion: Fundamental Conflicts and the Politics of Identity in Tanzania," *Nations and Nationalism* 5, no. 1 (1999): 105–25.

34. Bah, *Breakdown and Reconstitution*; Abu Bakarr Bah, "Reconciling Ethnic and National Identities in a Divided Society: The Nigerian Dilemma of Nation-State Building," *Democracy & Development: Journal of West African Affairs* 4, no. 2 (Harmattan Edition 2004): 27–43; Abu Bakarr Bah, "Democracy and Civil War: Citizenship and Peacemaking in Côte d'Ivoire," *African Affairs* 109, no. 437 (2010): 597–615.

35. Davidson, *The Black Man's Burden*; Mamdani, *Citizen and Subject*.

36. Mamdani, *Citizen and Subject*.

37. Bah, "Democracy and Civil War"; Bah, *Breakdown and Reconstitution*; Onigu Otite, *Ethnic Pluralism, Ethnicity, and Ethnic Conflicts in Nigeria* (Ibadan, Nigeria: Shaneson, 2000); Rok Ajulu, "Politicised Ethnicity, Competitive Politics and Conflict in Kenya: A Historical Perspective," *African Studies* 61, no. 2 (2002): 251–68.

38. Jackson and Rosberg, *Personal Rule in Black Africa*.

39. Bah, "Changing World Order and the Future of Democracy in Sub-Saharan Africa"; Abu Bakarr Bah and Ibrahim Bangura, "Landholding and the Creation of Lumpen Tenants in Freetown: Youth Economic Survival and Patrimonialism in Postwar Sierra Leone," *Critical Sociology* 49, no. 7–8 (2023): 1289–1305.

40. Abu Bakarr Bah, "State Decay and Civil War: A Discourse on Power in Sierra Leone," *Critical Sociology* 37, no. 2 (2011): 199–216; Bah, "State Decay: A Conceptual Frame of Failing and Failed States in West Africa."

41. Bah and Emmanuel, *International Statebuilding in West Africa*; Bah, "People-Centered Liberalism"; Bratton and Van de Walle, *Democratic Experiments in Africa*.

42. Claude Ake, *Democracy and Development in Africa* (Washington, DC: The Brookings Institute, 1996); Claude Ake, *The Feasibility of Democracy in Africa* (Dakar, Senegal: CODESRIA, 2000); Samuel E. Finer, "The One-Party Regimes in Africa: Reconsiderations," *Government and Opposition* 2, no. 4 (1967): 491–509; Samuel Decalo, "Military Coups and Military Regimes in Africa," *Journal of Modern African Studies* 11, no. 1 (1973): 105–27.

43. Bah, "Changing World Order and the Future of Democracy in Sub-Saharan Africa"; Bratton and Van de Walle, *Democratic Experiments in Africa*.

44. de Dieu Basabose, *Anti-Corruption Education and Peacebuilding: The Ubupfura Project in Rwanda* (New York: Springer, 2019).

45. Denis M. Tull and Claudia Simons, "The Institutionalisation of Power Revisited: Presidential Term Limits in Africa," *Africa Spectrum* 52, no. 2 (2017): 79–102.

46. Peter P. Ekeh, "Colonialism and the Two Publics in Africa: A Theoretical Statement," *Comparative Studies in Society and History* 17, no. 1 (1975): 91–112; Mamdani, *Citizen and Subject*.

47. Mazrui, *Africa's International Relations*.

48. Chabal and Daloz, *Africa Works*; Bah, "State Decay"; Jackson and Rosberg, *Personal Rule in Black Africa*.

49. Adebajo, *Building Peace in West Africa*; Adekeye Adebajo and Ismail Rashid, eds., *West Africa's Security Challenges: Building Peace in a Troubled Region* (Boulder, CO: Lynne Rienner, 2004); Bah, "The Contours of New Humanitarianism."

50. Abu Bakarr Bah and Nikolas Emmanuel, "Migration Cooperation between Africa and Europe: Understanding the Role of International Incentives," in *The Oxford Research Encyclopedia of International Studies* (Oxford: Oxford University Press, 2022); Abu Bakarr Bah, "African Agency in New Humanitarianism and Responsible Governance."

51. Bah, "People-Centered Liberalism"; Duffield, *Global Governance and the New Wars*.

52. Weber, *Max Weber: Essays in Sociology*; Charles Tilly, "War Making and State Making as Organized Crime," in *Bringing the State Back In*, ed. Peter Evans, Dietrich Rueschemeyer, and Theda Skocpol (Cambridge: Cambridge University Press, 1985), 169–91.

53. Adebajo, *Building Peace in West Africa*; Bah, "The Contours of New Humanitarianism"; Bah, *International Security and Peacebuilding*.

54. Abu Bakarr Bah and Nikolas Emmanuel, "Positive Peace and the Methodology of Costing Peacebuilding Needs: The Case of Burundi," *Administrative Theory & Praxis* 43, no. 3 (2020): 299–318.

55. Bah, "People-Centered Liberalism"; Bah and Emmanuel, *International Statebuilding in West Africa*.

56. Thomas A. Dempsey, *Counterterrorism in African Failed States: Challenges and Potential Solutions* (Carlisle, PA: Strategic Studies Institute, US Army War College, 2006).

57. Mathieu Bere, "Armed Rebellion, Violent Extremism, and the Challenges of International Intervention in Mali," *African Conflict and Peacebuilding Review* 7, no. 2 (2017): 60–84.

58. Caroline Varin, "No Opportunity Lost: The ISWAP Insurgency in the Changing Climate of Lake Chad Region," *African Conflict and Peacebuilding Review* 10, no. 2 (2020): 141–57.

59. Roland Robertson, "Globality and Modernity," *Theory, Culture & Society* 9, no. 2 (1992): 153–61.

60. Roland Robertson, "Globalisation or Glocalisation?," *Journal of International Communication* 1, no. 1 (1994): 33–52; Roland Robertson, "Glocalization: Time-Space and Homogeneity-Heterogeneity," *Global Modernities* 2, no. 1 (1995): 25–44; Richard Giulianotti and Roland Robertson, "The Globalization of Football: A Study in the Glocalization of the 'Serious Life,'" *British Journal of Sociology* 55, no. 4 (2004): 545–68; Richard Giulianotti and Roland Robertson, "Glocalization, Globalization, and Migration: The Case of Scottish Football Supporters in North America," *International Sociology* 21, no. 2 (2006): 171–98; Roland Robertson and Kathleen E. White, "What Is Globalization?," in *The Blackwell Companion to Globalization* (Hoboken, NJ: Blackwell, 2007), 54–66.

61. Beck, *What Is Globalization?*; Ulrich Beck, Natan Sznaider, and Rainer Winter, eds., *Global America? The Cultural Consequences of Globalization*, vol. 8 (Liverpool: Liverpool University Press, 2003).

62. Saskia Sassen, *The Global City: New York, London, Tokyo* (Princeton, NJ: Princeton University Press, 2013); Robertson, "Glocalization: Time-Space and Homogeneity-Heterogeneity"; Bettina Köhler and Markus Wissen, "Glocalizing Protest: Urban Conflicts and the Global Social Movements," *International Journal of Urban and Regional Research* 27, no. 4 (2003): 942–51; Dannie Kjeldgaard and Søren Askegaard, "The Glocalization of Youth Culture: The Global Youth Segment as Structures of Common Difference," *Journal of Consumer Research* 33, no. 2 (2006): 231–47; Giulianotti and Robertson, "The Globalization of Football"; Beck, *What Is Globalization?*

63. Samuel Marfo, Halidu Musah, and Dominic DeGraft Arthur, "Beyond Classical Peace Paradigm: A Theoretical Argument for a Glocalized Peace and Security," *African Journal of Political Science and International Relations* 10, no. 4 (2016): 47–55.

64. Marfo et al., "Beyond Classical Peace Paradigm."

65. Thomas L. Friedman, *The World Is Flat [Updated and Expanded]: A Brief History of the Twenty-First Century* (New York: Macmillan, 2006); Beck et al., *Global America? The Cultural Consequences of Globalization*; Robertson, "Glocalization: Time-Space and Homogeneity-Heterogeneity."

References

Abdile, Mahdi. "Customary Dispute Resolution in Somalia." *African Conflict and Peacebuilding Review* 2, no. 1 (2012): 87–110.

Adebajo, Adekeye. *Building Peace in West Africa: Liberia, Sierra Leone, and Guinea-Bissau*. Boulder, CO: Lynne Rienner, 2002.

———, and Ismail Rashid, eds. *West Africa's Security Challenges: Building Peace in a Troubled Region*. Boulder, CO: Lynne Rienner, 2004.

Adiebo, Kimo A. "Resource, Economic, and Financial Management in South Sudan: Taking Stock of Chapter IV of the R-ARCSS." *African Conflict & Peacebuilding Review* 11, no. 2 (2021): 39–63.

Ajulu, Rok. "Politicised Ethnicity, Competitive Politics and Conflict in Kenya: A Historical Perspective." *African Studies* 61, no. 2 (2002): 251–68.

Ake, Claude. *Democracy and Development in Africa*. Washington, DC: The Brookings Institute, 1996.

———. *The Feasibility of Democracy in Africa*. Dakar, Senegal: CODESRIA, 2000.

Anderson, Benedict. *Imagined Communities: Reflections on the Origin and Spread of Nationalism*. London: Verso Books, 2006.

Appadurai, Arjun. *Fear of Small Numbers: An Essay on the Geography of Anger.* Durham, NC: Duke University Press, 2006.

Appiah, Kwame Anthony. *In My Father's House: Africa in the Philosophy of Culture.* New York: Oxford University Press, 1992.

Assal, Munzoul A. M. "Forging the Juba Peace Agreement: The Role of National, Regional, and International Actors." *African Conflict & Peacebuilding Review* 12, no. 2 (2022): 5–22.

Bah, Abu Bakarr. "African Agency in New Humanitarianism and Responsible Governance." In *International Security and Peacebuilding: Africa, the Middle East, and Europe,* edited by Abu Bakarr Bah, 148–69. Bloomington: Indiana University Press, 2017.

———, ed. *African Security: Local Issues and Global Connections.* Athens, OH: Ohio University Press, 2024.

———. *Breakdown and Reconstitution: Democracy, the Nation-State, and Ethnicity in Nigeria.* Lanham, MD: Lexington Books, 2005.

———. "Changing World Order and the Future of Democracy in Sub-Saharan Africa." *Proteus: A Journal of Ideas* 21, no. 1 (Spring 2004): 3–12.

———. "Civil Non-State Actors in Peacekeeping and Peacebuilding in West Africa." *Journal of International Peacekeeping* 17, no. 3–4 (2013): 313–36.

———. "The Contours of New Humanitarianism: War and Peacebuilding in Sierra Leone." *Africa Today* 60, no. 1 (2013): 3–26.

———. "Democracy and Civil War: Citizenship and Peacemaking in Côte d'Ivoire." *African Affairs* 109, no. 437 (2010): 597–615.

———, ed. *International Security and Peacebuilding: Africa, the Middle East, and Europe.* Bloomington: Indiana University Press, 2017.

———. "People-Centered Liberalism: An Alternative Approach to International State-Building in Sierra Leone and Liberia." *Critical Sociology* 43, no. 7–8 (2017): 989–1007.

———. "Reconciling Ethnic and National Identities in a Divided Society: The Nigerian Dilemma of Nation-State Building." *Democracy & Development: Journal of West African Affairs* 4, no. 2 (Harmattan Edition 2004): 27–43.

———. "State Decay: A Conceptual Frame for Failing and Failed States in West Africa." *International Journal of Politics, Culture, and Society* 25, no. 1–3 (2012): 71–89.

———. "State Decay and Civil War: A Discourse on Power in Sierra Leone." *Critical Sociology* 37, no. 2 (2011): 199–216.

———, and Nikolas Emmanuel. "Migration Cooperation between Africa and Europe: Understanding the Role of International Incentives." In the *Oxford Research Encyclopedia of International Studies.* Oxford: Oxford University Press, 2022.

———. *International Statebuilding in West Africa: Civil Wars and New Humanitarianism in Sierra Leone, Liberia, and Côte d'Ivoire.* Bloomington: Indiana University Press, 2024.

———. "Positive Peace and the Methodology of Costing Peacebuilding Needs: The Case of Burundi." *Administrative Theory & Praxis* 43, no. 3 (2020): 299–318.

Balasubramaniam, Vejai. "A Divided Nation: Malay Political Dominance, Bumiputera Material Advancement and National Identity in Malaysia." *National Identities* 9, no. 1 (2007): 35–48.

Barr, Michael D., and Zlatko Skrbiš. *Constructing Singapore: Elitism, Ethnicity and the Nation-Building Project.* No. 11. Copenhagen, Denmark: Nias Press, 2008.

Bayart, Jean-François. *The Illusion of Cultural Identity.* Chicago: University of Chicago Press, 2005.

Beck, Ulrich. *What Is Globalization?* Cambridge: Polity Press, 2000.

———, Natan Sznaider, and Rainer Winter, eds. *Global America? The Cultural Consequences of Globalization.* Liverpool: Liverpool University Press, 2003.

Beevers, Michael. "Natural Resource Reforms in Postwar Liberia and Sierra Leone: Contradictions and Tension." In *Post-Conflict Institutional Design: Peacebuilding and Democracy in Africa*, edited by Abu Bakarr Bah, 136–63. London: Zed Books/Bloomsbury Press, 2020.

Bere, Mathieu. "Armed Rebellion, Violent Extremism, and the Challenges of International Intervention in Mali." *African Conflict and Peacebuilding Review* 7, no. 2 (2017): 60–84.

Bratton, Michael, and Nicholas Van de Walle. *Democratic Experiments in Africa: Regime Transitions in Comparative Perspective.* New York: Cambridge University Press, 1997.

Campbell, John. "Nationalism, Ethnicity and Religion: Fundamental Conflicts and the Politics of Identity in Tanzania." *Nations and Nationalism* 5, no. 1 (1999): 105–25.

Chabal, Patrick, and Jean-Pascal Daloz. *Africa Works: Disorder as Political Instrument.* Bloomington: Indiana University Press, 1999.

Chee-Beng, Tan. "Ethnic Identities and National Identities: Some Examples from Malaysia." *Identities Global Studies in Culture and Power* 6, no. 4 (2000): 441–80.

Clammer, John. "The Institutionalization of Ethnicity: The Culture of Ethnicity in Singapore." *Ethnic and Racial Studies* 5, no. 2 (1982): 127–39.

Clapham, Christopher S. *Africa and the International System: The Politics of State Survival.* No. 50. New York: Cambridge University Press, 1996.

Collier, Paul, and Anke Hoeffler. "On Economic Causes of Civil War." *Oxford Economic Papers* 50, no. 4 (1998): 563–73.

Commission on Human Security. *Human Security Now.* New York: United Nations; UNDP *Human Development Report 1990.* New York: Oxford University Press, 2003.

Davidson, Basil. *The Black Man's Burden: Africa and the Curse of the Nation-State.* New York: Times Books, 1992.

Decalo, Samuel. "Military Coups and Military Regimes in Africa." *Journal of Modern African Studies* 11, no. 1 (1973): 105–27.

de Dieu Basabose, Jean. *Anti-Corruption Education and Peacebuilding: The Ubupfura Project in Rwanda.* New York: Springer, 2019.

Dempsey, Thomas A. *Counterterrorism in African Failed States: Challenges and Potential Solutions.* Carlisle, PA: Strategic Studies Institute, US Army War College, 2006.

Duffield, Mark. *Global Governance and the New Wars: The Merging of Development and Security.* London: Zed Books, 2014.

Errington, Josef. "Language, Religion, and Identity in Indonesia." *ISIM Newsletter* 3, no. 1 (1999): 16.

Friedman, Thomas L. *The World Is Flat [Updated and Expanded]: A Brief History of the Twenty-First Century.* New York: Macmillan, 2006.

Ekeh, Peter P. "Colonialism and the Two Publics in Africa: A Theoretical Statement." *Comparative Studies in Society and History* 17, no. 1 (1975): 91–112.

Finer, Samuel E. "The One-Party Regimes in Africa: Reconsiderations." *Government and Opposition* 2, no. 4 (1967): 491–509.

Fouéré, Marie-Aude. "Julius Nyerere, Ujamaa, and Political Morality in Contemporary Tanzania." *African Studies Review* 57, no. 1 (2014): 1–24.

Gberie, Lansana. *A Dirty War in West Africa: The RUF and the Destruction of Sierra Leone.* Bloomington: Indiana University Press, 2005.

Giulianotti, Richard, and Roland Robertson. "The Globalization of Football: A Study in the Glocalization of the 'Serious Life.'" *British Journal of Sociology* 55, no. 4 (2004): 545–68.

Herder, Johann G., von. *Reflections on the Philosophy of the History of Man.* Chicago: University of Chicago Press, 1968.

Hobsbawm, Eric. *On History.* London: Hachette, 2011.

Hoehne, Markus Virgil, Dereje Feyissa, and Mahdi Abdile. "Somali and Ethiopian Diasporic Engagement for Peace in the Horn of Africa." *African Conflict and Peacebuilding Review* 1, no. 1 (2011): 71–99.

Jackson, Robert H., and Carl Gustav Rosberg. *Personal Rule in Black Africa: Prince, Autocrat, Prophet, Tyrant.* Berkeley: University of California Press, 1982.

Joseph, Richard A. *Democracy and Prebendal Politics in Nigeria.* New York: Cambridge University Press, 1987.

Ibrahim, Zawawi. "Globalization and National Identity: Managing Ethnicity and Cultural Pluralism in Malaysia." *Growth and Governance in Asia* (2004): 115–36.

Kjeldgaard, Dannie, and Søren Askegaard. "The Glocalization of Youth Culture: The Global Youth Segment as Structures of Common Difference." *Journal of Consumer Research* 33, no. 2 (2006): 231–47.

Köhler, Bettina, and Markus Wissen. "Glocalizing Protest: Urban Conflicts and the Global Social Movements." *International Journal of Urban and Regional Research* 27, no. 4 (2003): 942–51.

Lowenberg, Peter H. "Language Policy and Language Identity in Indonesia." *Journal of Asian Pacific Communication* 3, no. 1 (1992): 59–77.

Malipula, Mrisho. "Depoliticised Ethnicity in Tanzania: A Structural and Historical Narrative." *Afrika Focus* 27, no. 2 (2014): 49–70.

Mamdani, Mahmood. *Citizen and Subject: Contemporary Africa and the Legacy of Late Colonialism*. Princeton, NJ: Princeton University Press, 1996.

Mazrui, Ali A. *Africa's International Relations: The Diplomacy of Dependency and Change*. London: Routledge, 2019.

Montolalu, Lucy R., and Leo Suryadinata. "National Language and Nation-Building: The Case of Bahasa Indonesia." In *Language, Nation and Development in Southeast Asia*, edited by Lee Hock Guan and Leo Suryadinata, 39–50. Singapore: ISEAS, 2007.

Newman, Edward. "Failed States and International Order: Constructing a Post-Westphalian World." *Contemporary Security Policy* 30, no. 3 (2009): 421–43.

Nwankpa, Michael. "Understanding the Local-Global Dichotomy and Drivers of the Boko Haram Insurgency." *African Conflict and Peacebuilding Review* 10, no. 2 (2020): 43–64.

Otite, Onigu, *Ethnic Pluralism, Ethnicity, and Ethnic Conflicts in Nigeria*. Iba-dan, Nigeria: Shaneson, 2000.

Poggi, Gianfranco. *The State: Its Nature, Development, and Prospects*. Stanford: Stanford University Press, 1990.

Reno, William. *Corruption and State Politics in Sierra Leone*. New York: Cambridge University Press, 2008.

Robertson, Roland. "Glocalization: Time-Space and Homogeneity-Heterogeneity." In *Global Modernities*. 1st ed., edited by Mike Featherstone, Scott Lash, and Roland Robertson, 24–44. London: Sage, 1995.

———. "Globalisation or Glocalisation?" *Journal of International Communication* 1, no. 1 (1994): 33–52.

———. "Glocalization: Time-Space and Homogeneity-Heterogeneity." *Global Modernities* 2, no. 1 (1995): 25–44.

Samuel Marfo, Halidu Musah, and Dominic DeGraft Arthur. "Beyond Classical Peace Paradigm: A Theoretical Argument for a Glocalized Peace and Security." *African Journal of Political Science and International Relations* 10, no. 4 (2016): 47–55.

Schmidt, Elizabeth. *Foreign Intervention in Africa: From the Cold War to the War on Terror*. No. 7. New York: Cambridge University Press, 2013.

Smith, Anthony D. *Nationalism and Modernism*. London: Routledge, 2013.

Strayer, Joseph Reese. *On the Medieval Origins of the Modern State*. Princeton, NJ: Princeton University Press, 2005.

Taylor, Charles. *Multiculturalism: Examining the Politics of Recognition*. Princeton, NJ: Princeton University Press, 1994.

Themnér, Lotta, and Peter Wallensteen. "Armed Conflict, 1946–2010." *Journal of Peace Research* 48, no. 4 (2011): 525–36.

Tilly Charles. "War Making and State Making as Organized Crime." In *Bringing the State Back In,* edited by Peter Evans, Dietrich Rueschemeyer, and Theda Skocpol. New York: Cambridge University Press, 1985.

———, and Gabriel Ardant. *The Formation of National States in Western Europe.* Princeton, NJ: Princeton University Press, 1975.

Tull, Denis M., and Claudia Simons. "The Institutionalisation of Power Revisited: Presidential Term Limits in Africa." *Africa Spectrum* 52, no. 2 (2017): 79–102.

Trouillot, Michel-Rolph. "The Anthropology of the State in the Age of Globalization. Close Encounters of a Deceptive Kind." *Current Anthropology* 42, no. 1 (February 2001): 125–38.

Varin, Caroline. "No Opportunity Lost: The ISWAP Insurgency in the Changing Climate of Lake Chad Region." *African Conflict and Peacebuilding Review* 10, no. 2 (2020): 141–57.

Wallerstein, Immanuel. *The Capitalist World-Economy.* New York: Cambridge University Press, 1979.

Weber, Max. *Max Weber: Essays in Sociology.* Translated and edited by H. H. Gerth and C. Wright Mills. New York: Routledge, 2009.

Znaniecki, Florian. *Modern Nationalities: A Sociological Study.* Westport, CT: Greenwood Press, 1973.

1

The Stability of Instability in Africa

Glocalization, Colonial Borders, and the Limits of Conflict Resolution

IAN S. SPEARS

In voicing his country's rejection of the February 2022 Russian invasion of Ukraine, Martin Kimani, the Kenyan representative to the UN Security Council, acknowledged what every student of African politics knows: that Africa's borders "were not of our own drawing. They were drawn in the distant colonial metropoles of London, Paris, and Lisbon, with no regard for the ancient nations that they cleaved apart." Nonetheless, Kimani concluded, Africa had moved on and felt little inclination to change African borders as Russia was in the process of doing: "We agreed that we would settle for the borders that we inherited . . . not because our borders satisfied us, but because we wanted something greater, forged in peace." Undoubtedly, the decision to keep Africa's colonial borders was informed by a fear that an absence of alternative guiding principles for statehood would result in a wider and violent struggle for territory. As Kimani himself observed, "had we chosen to pursue states on the basis of ethnic, racial or religious homogeneity, we would still be waging bloody wars these many decades later."[1]

Recent scholarship has indeed claimed that Africa has found ways to overcome the challenges long associated with arbitrary borders and internal diversity. Posner and Young, for example, claimed that since the 1990s

Africa has become increasingly institutionalized and that these institutions are providing the foundations for more predictable political life for the continent.[2] In a similar argument, Nic Cheeseman and colleagues present evidence that appears to refute claims that the African state was a mere "Hollywood set" devoid of content. Leaders, in their view, have become increasingly rule bound in their behavior: "formal institutions," they say, "shape the decisions made by leaders in contemporary Africa."[3]

If local leaders are able to do their part to overcome challenges associated with Africa's arbitrary borders, the advancement of democratization and order will also benefit from the global community's willingness to do theirs. Democracy advocates concede that, in spite of this tendency to ever-greater institutionalization, governments are still prone to "rig" elections. Nic Cheeseman and Brian Klass present contemporary political rulers as a binary, consisting of genuine democrats, who are more or less permanently committed to respecting institutional rules, and corrupt and nefarious "counterfeit democrats," who seek only to undermine democracy for their own self-interest. Advancing institutionalization and defending democracy, this perspective argues, requires "closing off one avenue of rigging after another until counterfeit democrats have nowhere left to turn."[4] In short, this positive trend toward political stability is contingent on good leaders continuing their embrace of political institutions and the international community sidelining those who refuse to play by the rules.

My own analysis, by contrast, marks both a reaffirmation of an earlier body of literature that is pessimistic about Africa's prospects as well as a departure from this more recent scholarship that argues that states in Africa are becoming increasingly institutionalized and predictable. I argue that an intolerance of a reconfiguration of African territory on the part of both the continent's leaders and the international community more broadly, while understandable, has not necessarily been good for Africa. Across the continent, politicians remain challenged by the procrustean task of keeping their often large and diverse states orderly and under control. In most cases, this requires patrimonial politics of the kind once described by Carl Rosberg and Robert Jackson and, later, Patrick Chabal and Jean-Pascal Daloz, and in more pervasive social variants as recently shown by Abu Bakarr Bah and Ibrahim Bangura.[5] While patrimonialism is a means of avoiding wider or more intense violence, the competition for scarce resources and the tendency to "instrumentalize" violence—either against the state or societal sources of wealth—means that stability and institutionalization are elusive.

The level and nature of violence are relevant here. Scholars such as Arjun Appadurai have made compelling arguments about the confluence of global processes, the nature of the state, and ethnocidal violence that have relevance to the theme of "glocalization" that is central to this volume.[6] While my analysis does not exclude instances of extreme violence, including ethnocide, it is not clear that ethnic purification and an ideological commitment to it is the normal endgame on the continent. Perhaps this is because, comparatively speaking, and unlike, say, India under the current BJP government or the developed countries of the West, there are fewer pretensions that African states are anything other than colonial creations. While groups have employed violence to take power (coups in Nigeria or in the Sahel) or engaged in practices of coercive assimilation (Cote d'Ivoire, Liberia) or exclusion (Rwanda, Burundi), violence and instability in Africa are less ritualistic in form and more often directed toward more prosaic tasks of increasing access to resources for themselves or denying access to others. In the majority of cases in Africa, groups coexist, tolerate, and occasionally merge with each other but, perennially unable to escape the competitive environment in which they exist, they instrumentalize disorder to draw attention to themselves, increase their prominence relative to others, and secure material benefits. While extreme violence does occur, the nature of violence specific to Africa is persistent instability as different groups compete for power and resources. To focus only on the conflagrations would be to miss the instability that is more characteristic of the African political scene.

Indeed, the postcolonial experience of Africa shows that few states depart from (or are resistant to) cycles of low-intensity conflict and instability—suggesting that internal behavior is a consequence of the unchanging nature of state structure.[7] Four decades ago, Rosberg and Jackson urged policymakers in the West to disabuse themselves of the idea that patrimonial states could be *fixed* or that they represented a transition to more advanced or rational political systems. Instead, they said, the personal rule that is common throughout Africa represents a *type* of governance; a default that emerges and consolidates itself when there are no significant institutional means to maintain regime coherence.[8] The markers of this type of rule were "conspiracy, factional politics and clientelism, corruption, purges and rehabilitations, and succession maneuvers." To the extent that these characterizations remain in place, and in spite of occasional signs of good leadership in Africa, they argued, the unstable nature of contemporary politics is here to stay. Indeed, since independence, Africa has consistently failed to escape this cycle of low-intensity conflict and instability. As Larry Diamond has observed, "there is not a single country on the continent where democracy is consolidated and secure."[9]

This chapter explores both the limits and possibilities for change in a world that has more or less permanent borders and inalienable sovereignty. In doing so, it takes a novel approach to the idea of "glocalization."[10] Following the framework originally outlined by Roland Robertson, the portmanteau "glocalization" refers to processes of homogenization and heterogenization.[11] One process involves the manner in which global conventions and norms impose themselves downward and produce common local outcomes. The other process involves the manner in which political elites both conform to global norms and adapt them to their own particular needs. While the norms of statehood and its juridical bases were nearly universally embraced by political elites in Africa, the attachment to these norms has manifested themselves in an inability to consolidate authority within their states. To be sure, the contemporary modern state was European in origin, and its extension to other regions was well intended and has been defended by political elites everywhere;[12] yet in Africa (and perhaps elsewhere in the once-colonized world), the attachment to a seemingly attractive global norm has produced a thorny outcome: that of persistent instability and conflict.

My argument is that permanent borders set in motion a dynamic that limits Africa's ability to escape patronage politics and embrace democratic rule even if regimes have undergone institutional reforms purported to produce more benevolent rule. If the challenge confronting Africa begins with deeper *structural* factors related to Africa's borders, the inability to advance democracy or to preclude violent conflict is not a failure to find "good" leaders. Nor is it a question of external powers holding local leaders to their democratic promises, as is sometimes suggested.[13] Indeed, the claim that all that stands in the way of democratic rule is a combination of self-interested leaders and an international community that is reluctant to hold them to account is a fundamental misunderstanding of political life in Africa and elsewhere in the once-colonized world. Instead, the most significant obstacle to political development lies in the nature of Africa's colonial borders and the state it produces, both of which are upheld by the confluence of conservative global and local forces that are at the heart of the concept of glocalization.

Africa's Stubborn Struggle with Political Instability

To argue that the African territorial state and its borders have been the source of weak or ever-weakening domestic political institutions, one needs to demonstrate that African countries have been experiencing steady decline and decay since independence. Moreover, it would be important to demonstrate that the problems are widespread and consistent in nature, varying only in degree of severity. Finally—and in accordance with theory on glocalization—one needs to show that all actors—domestic, regional, and international—tolerate the existing system and all of its dysfunctions rather than seek a more promising political dispensation. Support for each of these claims is not difficult to find.

To be sure, there are African states that have been held up as promising demonstrations of democratic rule—though in 2024 only five of the mainland continent's countries are said to be "free" by Freedom House, and virtually all of these states could be regarded as so only with qualification.[14] Ghana's seven elections have been characterized by instances of electoral fraud, vote buying, corruption, and the persistent risk of violence and vigilantism. Namibia's democratic credentials remain untested as it has been ruled by the same political elite since independence in 1989. In Botswana, the Botswana Democratic Party (BDP) has also dominated political life without serious opposition since independence in 1966. Given Freedom House's restrained endorsement of democratic life in these countries, the comparative stability they currently enjoy reflects not an absence of, or transition from, patrimonialism but rather its effective functioning.

Even countries that had a head start insofar as they emerged from relatively well-institutionalized (albeit racially exclusive) foundations show a tendency to break down. Zimbabwe is no longer seriously regarded as a democracy, though it was once assumed to possess sufficient "stateness" to become one.[15] Instead, Zimbabwe's elections since 2002 have been characterized by varying degrees of violence and repression. While South Africa is ostensibly institutionalized and democratic, the trend since the end of apartheid in 1994 is decidedly toward the erosion of these institutions rather than their strengthening.[16]

More troubling are the setbacks from once stable or democratic polities. Even countries that were thought to be relatively safe from conflict have revealed themselves to be no different from other countries. In 2006, the former American ambassador declared that, against all odds, Mali was proving to be "one of the most successful democracies in Africa."[17] But this optimism, too, proved premature. In 2012, a graduate of a US-led military training mission overthrew the government, and Islamists took over the north of the country. By 2015, Mali had become the world's most dangerous peacekeeping mission and is currently described by Freedom House as "not free."[18] Kenya and Ivory Coast were also once regarded as stable states that, if not democratic, were at least led by reasonably benevolent dictators. The undoing of both of these countries over the last two decades revealed that there was limited institutional basis to either their authoritarian or democratic rule.[19] Perhaps they also revealed that no countries were safe from the violence of the continent's ethnic politics.

Ethiopia, too, has become an unlikely humanitarian problem. Not long ago, however, it appeared to fulfill many of the aspirations of those who believed in a more promising future for the continent. Prime minister Abiy Ahmed was described as a peacemaker, having been awarded the Nobel Peace Prize in 2019 for his role in addressing the decades-long conflict with Eritrea. But violence and civil war have occurred in other parts of the country, most notably Tigray province, where the government sought to suppress an insurrection, as well as the neighboring provinces of Afar and Amhara. The initial violence appears to have been a consequence of an incremental process of liberalization and inclusion that began with the ascension of Abiy Ahmed to the country's highest office in 2018. Ethiopia had advantages reinforcing its move toward a more peaceful society: it has had one of the fastest growing economies in Africa, it hosts the headquarters of the African Union, and it has been an important ally to the United States. Recent violence reveals, however, that even liberalization cannot reliably be translated into political stability and peace in Africa's multiethnic states.[20]

The most worrying trends have been among countries that have been unable to escape persistent violence. In Chad, observers have lamented that "conflict has simply become more complex and entrenched, and agreements have not led to peace." Chad's problem has not been an absence of peace agreements but that the settlements have done so little to end ongoing conflict. "As soon as a peace agreement has been inked, its requiem has commenced," observed Siphamandla Zondi and Charles Nyuykonge. Unfortunately, "Chad has become a morgue rather than a laboratory of peace agreements."[21] Burundi's postindependence history, too, has been marked by "repeated cycles of intense violence, including between ethnic communities." Again, the problem has not been that no agreements have been reached but that they are so easily undone. "Repression has become less open, more under the radar, more difficult to trace, but is more systematic and is increasing," observed one United Nations report, which further noted that "The accountability mechanisms are exceedingly weak and impunity is endemic, which allows cycles of violence to continue unabatedly."[22]

Finally, the violent experiences of the Horn of Africa and across the Sahel reveal that persistent instability, war, or coercive government cannot be alleviated merely by installing new leaders or drawing new borders. Eritrea has avoided internal war (though not interstate war with Ethiopia) and perhaps even the most overt forms of ethnic violence. But it also remains one of the most repressive states in the world. On the other end of the scale, Somalia (with the notable exception of the self-declared northern region of "Somaliland") has been characterized either by its warlord politics or Islamic insurgency for more than three decades. The most egregious violence between Christians and Arabs in Sudan may have been alleviated by South Sudan's once-celebrated independence, but conflict there has now merely been reoriented (again) to one between Nuer and Dinka. In Sudan itself, even the excitement that accompanied the downfall of Omar al Bashir's thirty-year reign was not enough to stave off a brutal crackdown, a return to military rule, and an ensuing civil war.[23] Indeed, the coup in Sudan would be only one of a spate of successful or attempted military takeovers across the Sahel region from 2020 to 2023.

James O'Connell's 1967 treatise on the "Inevitability of Instability" portrayed relations among "African tribal communities" as akin to relations "among foreign states" but assumed that with time, a common sense of belonging might emerge.[24] But even if skeptics were to concede that the postindependence outcomes have varied across the continent, it has been hard to make the case that African states have experienced a convergence of identities or that institutional development has been advanced in the postcolonial era. Identities have remained strong because, unlike Appadurai's reflections on India, groups are less often in a position to become dominant or even contest power. African leaders and foreign observers alike did not anticipate the broad challenges that would come with statehood, and would never have believed that the nature of the state could be a source of conflict. Colonialism was seen at the time as the principal source of African conflict and instability. With independence came renewed confidence that prosperity and national solidarity were a matter of time and sensible policy decisions. Few considered the slow, corrosive effects of statehood itself.

But, indeed, observers of African politics have become dismayed and frustrated by the inability of African states to develop a governing capacity of their own, in spite of "plans of action" that called for "professionalizing," "building," or "enhancing" state capacity. The issue is not that progress has been slow; it is that it is regressive. A quarter century ago, a 1996 World Bank report titled *Partnership for Capacity Building in Africa* despaired at the profound weakness of institutions throughout Africa. "Almost every African country has witnessed a systematic regression of capacity in the last thirty years; the majority had better capacity at independence than they now possess," observed the report's authors, who further noted that "Many countries have lost professionals with valuables skills to more prosperous neighbors or to the developed world because of poor motivational practices, poor governance, internal conflicts, and civil wars."[25] As usual, the authors of the World Bank report placed a large portion of the blame for these failings on African leaders themselves. As they argued, "Very often, power became not an instrument for the accomplishment of collective national goals but rather the personal fiefdom of individual rulers, maintained to safeguard their political careers. In any event, long-term investments for *good governance and capacity* were largely forgotten, leaving Africa deprived of the *human and institutional bulwarks*" necessary to confront its many challenges.[26]

The 1996 World Bank report was not unusual in this respect. Democracy and good governance (and their counterparts: conflict and corruption) are routinely assumed by advocates to be merely *choices* that neither the local elites nor outside peacebuilders fully exercise. In most cases, the origins and subsequent nature of the state itself does not even feature in these discussions.[27] The assumption is that there is nothing fatally wrong with the colonial state, that the process of state formation is irrelevant to contemporary outcomes, and that, if corruption and violence persist today, it can only be the fault of leaders or the international community who will not hold them to account.

Thus, for the last two decades, Western scholars have persisted in their declarations that action on democracy requires sidelining Africa's most notorious leaders and ensuring that the international community fulfil its moral obligation to promote democratic rule. In 2004, for example, the author and former diplomat Michael McFaul argued that the desire for democracy was widespread and equated polling data that demonstrated a near-universal preference for democracy with the ability to achieve it.[28] Consequently, McFaul argued, intervention for the sake of promoting human rights and democracy was a legitimate means to an end. The obstacle remained the leaders themselves: "Obviously, the norm of democracy promotion is not universal," he wrote, "*because* autocrats still control major chunks of the world." The problem was "the autocrats" and "the dictators"; there was no suggestion that the dictators are symptomatic of some other underlying condition.

Similarly, in an assessment of the failures of African democracy, Peter Lewis described the "tactical cunning" of Joseph Kabila in the Democratic Republic of the Congo, the "presidential guile" of Senegal's Macky Sall, and a political class that "treats party affiliations and elections as transactions to be exploited for personal gain" in Nigeria.[29] A 2019 analysis of Sudan claimed that progress toward democracy was in jeopardy only because many of the elites in the now-deposed president's regime "have retained high positions," overlooking the fact that Sudan's size and ethnic complexity have never been favorable to Western-style liberal democracy.[30] Even Larry Diamond once attributed Africa's failure to achieve freedom and democracy to "bad governance" and corruption, not allowing for the possibility that these attributes could be symptoms rather than sources of a problem.[31] The message of all of these reports is that there are those who practice "good governance" and there are those greedy individuals who engage in undesirable activities such as "predation" or "corruption" and are, therefore, the obstacles to good governance. *If only* these nefarious obstacles to good governance could be managed or removed—that is, if only African leaders would commit to their democratic pledges—then states in Africa and elsewhere would benefit from democratic rule.

Critics, however, have focused not just on the autocratic leaders themselves but also on the timidity of misguided local "peacebuilders" and foreign governments, and regard momentary inattention to the project at hand as jeopardizing peaceful political development. For them, the international community should be held to account for failing to press harder for democratic change. These authors allude to (and lament) the triumph of cautious political realists over liberals within the foreign policy community who are unwilling to advance incipient democratic processes through to their completion. The means to bring about positive change *are* there in the form of material resources or the threat to withdraw peacekeeping forces, writes Christoph Zürcher, "yet peacebuilders almost never use this leverage."[32] Instead, a weak-kneed or ill-informed foreign policy community allows itself to be bullied or persuaded into believing unfounded claims that liberal reforms undermine security and therefore jeopardize precarious peace processes. Zürcher writes that "when confronted with local elites' resistance to democracy, the local peacebuilders usually gave in, choosing stability over potentially disruptive liberal reforms, and cooperation with status quo-oriented elites over the vagaries of possible regime change."[33]

Even when promising interventions and assistance are undertaken, critics cite the international community's failures of implementation or strategy. When things went wrong in Mali in 2013, for example, General Carter Ham of the United States Africa Command (Africom) claimed that its forces had failed to adequately train Malian troops on "values, ethics and a military ethos" that respected democratic rule.[34] The implication was, again, the unfalsifiable conviction that, *if only* proper attention had been paid to this objective, then the problem would have been avoided—as if, by way of a proper education or more training on the merits of civil military relations, the structural forces of the state could have been overcome.

To be sure, this democracy-building agenda is glocalization insofar as it speaks to the failure of local and foreign interests and policies. But it overlooks the possibility that the problems are rooted in the state system rather than individuals or, as noted by Chabal and Daloz, that these practices are regarded as a means to survive in environments that thwart the consolidation of a common identity and encourage winner-takes-all competition. Nor is there recognition of the idea, first identified by Robert Jackson and Carl Rosberg, that personal rule is a *type* of rule rather than a mere transitional inconvenience or reformable obstacle to democratic rule. More generally there is little awareness that the political instability, corruption, and authoritarian rule that comprise personal rule are dependent variables or *symptoms* of the once-colonial state. Democracy or its less liberal alternatives may be choices, but they are highly conditioned and limited by a prior and rational decision to privilege Africa's colonial borders.

Forces Conspiring against Stable Democratic Rule in Africa

Peacebuilders routinely assume that an alleged near-universal desire for democracy is reason enough for its realization.[35] On the basis that democratic rule has now become a "world value" and an "international norm," advocates say, half of the battle has been won, and the transition to sustained democracy should be relatively easy.[36]

But advocates and peacebuilders are wrong to take for granted that abstract aspirations for democratic rule will be translated into practice or that their own insistence on democratic rule can be converted into a form of governance in the image that outsiders imagine. Nor is it correct to assume that all that stands in the way of democratic rule are intransigent non-democratic rulers who refuse to leave office. The circle of those inclined to resist democratic rule extend beyond a given country's leadership and indeed can be found on every level of the political and social hierarchy from citizen to president. Three interrelated explanations help account for this failure to realize sustained peaceful democratic rule or even to construct a stable institutional basis for governing. They have their origins in the fact that borders are arbitrary and produce states where the common sense of purpose exists only as an abstract aspiration:[37] 1) citizens in such diverse states have little choice but to restrict their voting preferences to candidates from their own ethnic group; 2) Western constitutional remedies are too often inappropriate or irrelevant to African contexts; and 3) establishing consensus on the legitimacy of common institutions is too difficult in states with a plurality of political traditions.

The first explanation is that in ethnically diverse countries where there is no single cultural or political tradition, voting preferences are essentially fixed.[38] Even if it is agreed that identity is a construction, it remains a remarkably durable one that withstands state efforts to suppress it.[39] This is because the effect of borders that encircle identity groups is to increase competition among them, thereby politicizing and reinforcing respective identities and limiting possibilities for assimilation. As with any competitive process, the task of each party is less to *resolve* the conflict or to ensure fairness than it is to win what can be won—particularly if a group's minority status already places it at a disadvantage. Consequently, even if citizens *want* democratic rule in the abstract, the desire is subverted by the fact that in most cases a given voter cannot afford to vote for anyone but his or her own identity group.[40] Likewise, political leaders face powerful pressures and incentives to look after their own by providing them with resources and protection. In this way, the desire for democracy (that is, a political system where voter preferences *change* from election to election) cannot be acted on. People desire electoral politics if it serves their relative demographic weight or if they can be assured that voters will make choices based on policies. But they will resist, cheat, or otherwise subvert democracy if they are fearful that their minority status will permanently exclude them from power.

The attraction of democracy is not increased by the mere fact that citizens believe that political leaders are corrupt. On the contrary, corruption is rewarded because it holds out the promise that their own leaders will be magnanimous.[41] Except perhaps in the most egregious or flagrant examples of self-serving greed, the downfall of a politician is not a consequence of a lack of support among their own people or clients.[42] Voters in all regions of the world usually have little trouble forgiving corrupt politicians if they think that those politicians are their one-and-only source of security and social insurance.[43] Africa is no different, and, indeed, the requirement that leaders buy the loyalty of other ethnic representatives helps explain both the sustained unity of complicated and arbitrary states as well as their relative lack of institutionalization. "Resources flow within kin, ethnic groups and webs of clientelism, not from an anonymous, bureaucratic state to citizens who are equal before the law," writes Thomas Hylland Eriksen, who further notes that "Logically, you are unlikely to become a loyal Kenyan citizen if power is held by another ethnic group than yours and various benefits are distributed within the *ethnos* rather than the *demos*."[44] In this way, politics in Africa becomes a kind of positive feedback mechanism: citizens rely on informal networks to get services and other resources, which in turn renders the state less capable of offering these same services to citizens, meaning that citizens have little cause to be loyal to the state. It is no surprise, then, that a *New York Times* correspondent once pointed out that political corruption in Nigeria was "not a flaw in the system. It *is* the system."[45]

Second, Western democracy proponents and peacebuilders tend to understate the diversity that characterizes the contemporary colonial world and to overstate the diversity that historically characterized their own Western states. Consequently, the constitutions that were (and are) normally drawn up to remedy conflict and advance democracy are inappropriate to most colonial states in Africa and elsewhere. Democracy advocates claim that diversity in the developing world is actually served by the checks and balances that are an essential part of Western democracy. But, historically, because of its own policies of ruthless segregation, assimilation, and exclusion, American society, for example, was not as diverse as most African states are today, and the willingness of America's founders to tolerate inclusive policies was not as high as that which is demanded of belligerents in contemporary peace processes.[46] The American view of itself has always been erroneous, writes Robert Packenham. In reality, "American society was only superficially divided and in conflict; more profoundly it was unified and consensual around the inarticulate assumptions of the migrant culture of the Lockean, liberal tradition."[47] To become an American was to subject oneself to an extraordinarily powerful pressure to conform to what was assumed to be an American "national" identity centered around English language, customs, and institutions.[48]

Consequently, the constitutional remedies that are now assumed to address conflict do not easily apply to states that are defined not by conquest, ethnic disaggregation, and borders that reflect territorial control (as was the case in Western states), but by the arbitrary or random encirclement of a territory of diverse peoples. In the United States, checks and balances were meant to secure differences of *opinion* rather than to represent different ethnic groups. Thomas Jefferson did not envision African Americans even holding elected office; nor were African Americans in a position to exercise the *veto* that proponents regard as a central element of contemporary power-sharing arrangements. It is no surprise, then, that when applied to the once-colonized world, liberalization tends to exacerbate differences between competitive groups even while it is rationalized on the promise of pacifying them.

Finally, the effect of the first two factors is to undermine the legitimacy of *office* that is at the heart of rational-legal approaches to the state and that Western democracy advocates have long assumed would evolve over time. A more accurate understanding of political life in Africa may turn Rosberg and Jackson's statement on the absence of a single political tradition on its head.[49] Democracy assumes that there are multiple aspirants to a single office, which all agree is legitimate. In multiethnic states with no single territory-wide political tradition and no state apparatus with the ability to force compromise on the singularity of that office, there are instead multiple aspirants to multiple political offices, the legitimacy of which is linked only to each identity group. Particularly in the aftermath of protracted conflict, a given African leader may hold an "official" government office, but in countries with no means of enforcing that legitimacy across all identity groups, these offices are themselves merely notional in the eyes of political rivals.[50] Moreover, as is the case in the most extreme example of Somalia, rational-legal office must compete with *al Shabaab* insurgents, who, in addition to their formidable coercive powers, can make claims on traditional bases of authority or offers of protection that are deemed more legitimate and persuasive than the secular representatives produced by international peace processes. In that case, the sense of *office* that elections are supposed to confer is really only an expression of wishfulness and intention.[51]

In light of these three factors, we have a better understanding of why African institutional development is regressive, why good governance is so precarious, and why African governments are unresponsive to even sincere efforts on the part of the international community to democratize. Despite its many and nefarious legacies, the most harmful consequence of colonialism is not the deliberate practices of dividing populations against themselves.[52] Rather, it is the retention of colonial borders. The postcolonial state has established a political arena, generated incentives to contestation, and yet failed to provide a sufficiently powerful institutionalized arbiter to mediate group interaction. We also better understand why Rosberg and Jackson viewed personal rule not as a transitional stage but as a *type* of government that is likely to occur whenever the existence of a territorial state is not in question and its borders are arbitrary and permanent. Why would Africans engage in any enthusiastic effort at entrenching the state and democratization when the forces of inertia are so profound and the risks involved in reform are so high? No wonder so many scholars lament the apparent unwillingness to undertake institutional reform in spite of their alleged democratic aspirations and benefits of an institutionalized state.

It should not surprise anyone, then, that political life in much of Africa is characterized by persistent tension between violence and corruption. But while a corrupt government may be lamentable, in a country with no reliable institutions it may also be more desirable than violence—and may be why Kenya's ambassador can celebrate the absence of *interstate*, though not intrastate, conflict in Africa. Indeed, a government that is held together with patronage that is distributed openly and through a process of bargaining may be as close as one gets to decent government. How else does a leader convince individuals bound to their own ethnic, religious, or linguistic leaderships that their authority should prevail? On the other hand, in resource-scarce environments, to the extent that patronage networks are exclusive of other groups, they are bound to create enemies and induce resentment among those outside the circle of patronage. Indeed, as Alex de Waal has argued in the context of Sudan, relations between governments and ethnic communities are characterized by near-constant bargaining through the provision of patronage resources and, when that fails, the use of violence.[53] The persistent instability described by de Waal is a more contemporary rendering of the description offered by Rosberg and Jackson in their initial account of personal rule.

It is important to repeat that while these tendencies have their roots in the nature of the African state, there is nothing about them that is specifically *African* in nature. Rather, they are consequences of colonial state formation and the political development trajectory that results. Efforts to hold leaders to account, as Cheeseman and Klaas, McFaul, Lewis, Zürcher, and others insist, are unlikely to produce the desired results because the underlying structural forces that define the state and give rise to these behaviors remain intact and are beyond the abilities of a single leader to fix. Why do they remain intact? Because a more stable and democratic Africa would require changes to the nature of the state and state borders that local and external interests—the elements of glocalization—understandably regard as too sacred to upend.

Commentators have long lamented the refusal of African leaders to make the reforms necessary or even to acknowledge that their political system is dysfunctional (at least in comparison with the Western rational-legal standard).[54] African rulers regard contemporary borders and juridical sovereignty as the best hedge against subjugation and recolonization, and seek to establish at least the most visible symbols of statehood to legitimize their rule.[55] African leaders have also proven to be finely attuned to the strategies of survival within their own political orbits. They are by nature conservative. As is the case with all political systems, the leadership does not want to jeopardize the delicate balance of power that sustains their rule. African leaders are also disinclined to view political crises in the same terms as outsiders and are highly resistant to efforts of outside powers to correct their behavior. Neither their removal nor efforts to hold them accountable by "closing off avenues to vote rigging" will solve the structural problems associated with statehood or induce more cooperative behavior. Instead, as Fritz Nganje and Kgalalelo Nganje observe, African leaders will "close ranks" with their local and regional allies and find clever ways to evade or manipulate calls to act differently.[56]

This conservatism regarding territory practiced by African leaders is not exclusive to them. The broader international community, too, has an understandable preference for the administrative simplicity of existing political borders, which dovetails with assumptions that domestic political life will eventually evolve into more palatable forms. The fact that personal rule and patrimonialism remain defining features of African politics almost forty years after Jackson and Rosberg began writing about the phenomenon of personal rule and juridical sovereignty, and almost sixty years after independence was granted, is a repudiation of the view that negative sovereignty will eventually contribute to the emergence of nation-states.

Conclusion: The State and Its Glocal Peculiarity

It is worth reflecting on the comments of Ambassador Martin Kimani cited at the beginning of the chapter. Kenya remains a relatively peaceful country and indeed has served as a critical center for foreign diplomatic representation, global tourism, and nongovernmental organizations. Kenya, like most other African countries, has avoided the interstate wars that characterized Europe during its long evolution to statehood.

But neither has Kenya been able to establish sustainable and responsive democratic institutions or manage its internal diversity without resorting to the same practices of instrumentalization of violence, government coercion, and generous patronage practiced in African states as described above. Its first leader, Jomo Kenyatta, was a hero in the anticolonial struggle against the British and benefited from widespread support as a result. Daniel Arap Moi, his successor, resisted democratization, dispensed large quantities of patronage, and warned that democratization would destroy the nation.[57] And the country's subsequent presidents, Mwai Kibaki, Uhuru Kenyatta, and William Ruto, too, have been compelled to manipulate the levers of patronage and coercion with varying degrees of success. Africa's avoidance of interstate conflict has not meant that other illiberal consequences have been avoided.

Kenya may not represent the "powder keg" that commentators have long feared.[58] When the political process, such as it is, has broken down—as it did most notably during elections in 2007 when more than twelve hundred people were killed and hundreds of thousands displaced—the international community imposed itself on the country's leaders, who indeed found ways to avoid even wider violence. But these instances need not manifest themselves as large-scale violent conflagrations to confirm the argument being made here. What they show is that ongoing instability, patronage, coercion, and violence do not represent a transition to a more desirable and stable peace. Rather, they are manifestations of a *type* of government that is likely to persist for the foreseeable future.

In this chapter, I have taken issue with an understanding of glocalization that presents Africa's problems merely in terms of local leaders engaging in bad or corrupt governance matched with foreign power reticence to hold them to account. Instead, glocalization needs to be understood as the confluence of local and external preferences for a political structure that simultaneously secures elites from neocolonial encroachments, politicizes and divides potential rivals, and also frustrates any hope of state integration and institutionalization. The conservative nature of global politics and, specifically, a preference to avoid an even wider upheaval means that the implications of this understanding of glocalization are both insidious and nearly impossible to evade. Africa seems bound to remain as it is.

Recent scholarly defenses of imperialism have been roundly condemned for overplaying the benefits of colonial rule and understating the atrocities committed in its name.[59] The response to this scholarship among both African and non-African scholars is understandable though perhaps somewhat ironic. While most Africans strenuously reject the idea of colonial rule, they continue to embrace the legacy that arguably holds the most subtly troublesome consequences for its political and economic development: its arbitrary colonial borders and juridical statehood that inevitably give rise to personal rule and patrimonialism. Juridical statehood based on colonial borders is the passive and frequently overlooked result of colonial rule. A further irony is that commentators and policymakers insist on holding leaders to account but do not question the nature of the state that gives rise to this behavior. Finally, commentators continue to point to particular challenges that are unique to each country but deflect analysis from the *common* inability of African states to achieve sustainable and peaceful democratic government anywhere on the continent.

Given the uncertainties associated with significant reform, the desire to keep states in their current form is understandable. But there is no escaping the effects of borders, and there is no such thing as natural, bottom-up political development as long as borders are such powerful determinants of political behavior. The African state in its current configuration predisposes groups to seek political power rather than seek common ground with rivals. No group or individual can escape the structural imperative, upheld by glocalization, to seek advantage or deny it to others. In the absence of a dominant force that can overcome these structural tendencies and remake the African state in its image or unravel its territorial boundaries, ongoing clientelism and low-level instability are the best that can be expected. While some African states have enjoyed varying degrees of peace within current borders, they should not be mistaken for democracies or congratulated for their sophisticated institutional design. Instead, they should be understood in terms of the capacity of a dominant leadership or coalition to engage—however temporarily—in patronage and ad hoc suppression of rebellions.

In the end, glocalization provides a lens for examining the African state through the domestic and external drivers of violence and chronic instability. The conclusion reached here is that the African state is fundamentally unable to establish a pathway for making democracy work: a sense of common belonging that can facilitate legitimacy of authority and office holding. To be sure, there have been domestic and external efforts to make and mold African countries into functioning democracies, but they inevitably (and understandably) follow an essential global norm and leave the Western-inspired territorial state as it is. Political instability is the unfortunate outcome of this glocalization: the interaction between global norms and local circumstances.

Notes

1. Chappell, "Kenyan Ambassador Compares Ukraine's Plight."
2. Posner and Young, "The Institutionalization of Political Power in Africa."

3. Cheeseman, "Understanding African Politics: Why We Need to Bring the State Back In."

4. Cheeseman and Klaas, *How to Rig an Election*, 228.

5. Jackson and Rosberg, "Personal Rule: Theory and Practice in Africa"; Chabal and Daloz, *Africa Works*; Bah and Bangura, "Landholding and the Creation of Lumpen Tenants in Freetown."

6. See, for example, Appadurai, *Fear of Small Numbers*.

7. See reports from the Uppsala Conflict Data Program and the Global Terrorism Database that show that conflict in Africa peaked at the end of the Cold War, declined in the mid-2000s, remained relatively stable to 2010, and then increased to 2015.

8. Jackson and Rosberg, "Personal Rule: Theory and Practice in Africa," 430.

9. Diamond, "Facing up to the Democratic Recession," 148.

10. For an early discussion of "glocalization," see Swyngedouw, "Globalisation or 'Glocalisation'?," 25–48.

11. See, for example, Robertson, "Globalisation or Glocalisation," 191–208.

12. See Jackson, *The Global Covenant*.

13. See, for example, Easterly, *The Tyranny of Experts,* chapter 13.

14. The Freedom House report *Freedom in the World, 2024*, considers the following African countries as "free": South Africa, Lesotho, Namibia, Botswana, and Ghana, as are the tiny island nations of Cape Verde, Seychelles, Mauritius, São Tomé, and Principe. See https://freedomhouse.org/report/freedom-world/2024/mounting-damage-flawed-elections-and-armed-conflict.

15. See, for example, Ginifer, *Managing Arms in Peace Processes: Rhodesia/Zimbabwe*, 55.

16. See Onishi, "As Ramaphosa Hails a 'New Dawn,'" and McKaiser, "Don't Get Too Excited About South Africa's New President," O2; York, "South African President Faces Growing Pressure to Resign," and "A Time of Despair on the Birthday of Freedom."

17. See Pringle, "Mali's Unlikely Democracy," 31–39.

18. Leithead, "World's Most Dangerous Peacekeeping Mission." In 2024, Freedom House characterized Mali as "not free."

19. See Chege, "Kenya's Electoral Misfire," 161; Boone, "Africa's New Territorial Politics," 59–81; Bah, "Democracy and Civil War: Citizenship and Peacemaking in Côte d'Ivoire," 597–615. In 2024, Freedom House characterized both countries as "partly free."

20. Ahmed and Goldstein, "Thousands Are Arrested in Ethiopia after Ethnic Violence."

21. Zondi and Nyuykonge in *Peace Agreements and Durable Peace in Africa*, 89, 90.

22. Report of the United Nations Independent Investigation on Burundi (UNIIB), 5, 19.

23. See Walsh, "Sudan Protesters, Devastated but Defiant."

24. O'Connell, "The Inevitability of Instability," 190.

25. World Bank, *Partnership for Capacity Building in Africa*, 5.

26. World Bank, *Partnership for Capacity Building in Africa*, ii.

27. A point noted by Herbst in *States and Power in Africa*, 99.

28. McFaul, "Democracy Promotion as a World Value," 147–63.

29. Lewis, "Aspirations and Realities in Africa," 80–81.

30. Hassan and Kodouda, "Sudan's Uprising: The Fall of a Dictator," 101.

31. Diamond, "Facing Up to the Democratic Recession," 148.

32. Zürcher, "Building Democracy While Building Peace," 87. See also Zürcher, "A Theory of Democratisation Through Peace-Building," 283–99.

33. Zurcher, "Building Democracy While Building Peace," 87.

34. Cited in "Mali Crisis: US Admits Mistakes in Training Local Troops."

35. See Gyimah-Boadi, "Democratic Delivery Falls Short," 86–93.

36. McFaul, "Democracy Promotion as a World Value," 148.

37. Jackson and Rosberg, "Personal Rule: Theory and Practice in Africa," 437–38; and "Sovereignty and Underdevelopment: Juridical Statehood in the African Crisis," 17.

38. Ottaway, "Is Democracy the Answer?," 608.

39. McLean Hilker, "Everyday Ethnicities," 81–100.

40. For two candid statements of this tendency in contrasting contexts, see Holland, *Dinner with Mugabe*, 114–15; and Lemarchand, *Burundi: Ethnic Conflict and Genocide*, 59.

41. See Chabal, *Power in Africa*, chapter 12.

42. Chabal and Daloz, *Africa Works*, 54.

43. See, for example, Kershner, "In Israel's Poorer Periphery, Legal Woes Don't Dent Netanyahu's Appeal," 8; Vaishnav, "Why Voters Sometimes Prefer Criminals as Candidates," 459–61.

44. Hylland Eriksen, "The Problem of African Nationhood," 226.

45. Nossiter, "In Nigeria, Where Graft Is the System." Notably, Nigeria was the starting point for Posner and Young's optimism on Africa's prospects for further institutionalization. Marred by "corruption [that] remains endemic" as well as "military and law enforcement agencies [that] often engage in extrajudicial killings, torture, and other abuses," Freedom House regarded Nigeria as "partly free" in 2024.

46. For two useful sources in this regard, see Claudio Saunt, *Unworthy Republic*, and Amanda Frost, *You Are Not American*.

47. Robert A. Packenham, *Liberal America and the Third World*, 154.

48. Benjamin Schwarz, "The Diversity Myth: America's Leading Export," 62.

49. Jackson and Rosberg, "Sovereignty and Underdevelopment," 17.

50. For a similar argument made in the context of Afghanistan, see Johnson and Mason, "Democracy in Afghanistan Is Wishful Thinking."

51. Nur et al., "Why Mogadishu's Former Mayor Wants to be Somalia's President."

52. See, for example, Mamdani, "Making Sense of Political Violence in Post-Colonial Africa," 132–51.
53. De Waal, "Mission without End?," 99–113.
54. Herbst, "War and the State in Africa," 132; Fukuyama, "The Imperative of State-Building," 30.
55. Englebert, *Africa: Unity, Sovereignty and Sorrow*, especially chapter 7.
56. Nganje and Nganje, "Liberal Internationalism Meets Third Worldism," 522.
57. Africa Watch, *Divide and Rule: State Sponsored Ethnic Violence in Kenya*.
58. See, for example, Berkeley, "An Encore for Chaos."
59. Gilley, "The Case for Colonialism."

References

Africa Watch. *Divide and Rule: State Sponsored Ethnic Violence in Kenya*. New York: Human Rights Watch, 1993.

Appadurai, Arjun. *Fear of Small Numbers: An Essay on the Geography of Anger*. Durham: Duke University Press, 2006.

Ahmed, Hadra, and Joseph Goldstein. "Thousands Are Arrested in Ethiopia after Ethnic Violence." *New York Times*, September 24, 2018.

Bah, Abu Bakarr. "Democracy and Civil War: Citizenship and Peacemaking in Côte d'Ivoire." *African Affairs* 109, no. 437 (2010): 597–615.

———, and Ibrahim Bangura. "Landholding and the Creation of Lumpen Tenants in Freetown: Youth Economic Survival and Patrimonialism in Postwar Sierra Leone." *Critical Sociology* 49, no. 7–8 (2023): 1289–1305.

Berkeley, Bill. "An Encore for Chaos." *The Atlantic*, February 1996.

Boone, Catherine. "Africa's New Territorial Politics: Regionalism and the Open Economy in Côte d'Ivoire." *African Studies Review* 50, no. 1 (2007): 59–81.

British Broadcasting Corporation. "Mali Crisis: US Admits Mistakes in Training Local Troops." *BBC.com*, January 25, 2013.

Chappell, Bill. "Kenyan Ambassador Compares Ukraine's Plight to Colonial Legacy in Africa." *NPR.org*, February 22, 2022, https://www.npr.org/2022/02/22/1082334172/kenya-security-council-russia.

Chabal, Patrick. *Power in Africa: An Essay in Political Interpretation*. New York: St. Martin's Press, 1992.

———, and Jean-Pascal Daloz. *Africa Works: Disorder as a Political Instrument*. Suffolk, UK: James Currey, 1999.

Cheeseman, Nic. "Understanding African Politics: Why We Need to Bring the State Back In." In *Institutions and Democracy in Africa: How the Rules of the Game Shape Political Engagements*, edited by Nic Cheeseman, 1–39. Cambridge: Cambridge University Press, 2018.

———, and Brian Klaas. *How to Rig an Election*. New Haven: Yale University Press, 2018.

Chege, Michael. "Kenya's Electoral Misfire." *Journal of Democracy* 29, no. 2 (2018): 158–72.

De Waal, Alex. "Mission without End? Peacekeeping in the African Political Marketplace." *International Affairs* 85, no. 1 (2009): 99–113.

Diamond, Larry. "Facing Up to the Democratic Recession." *Journal of Democracy* 26, no. 1 (2015): 141–55.

Easterly, William. *The Tyranny of Experts: Economists, Dictators, and the Forgotten Rights of the Poor*. New York: Basic Books, 2013.

Englebert, Pierre. *Africa: Unity, Sovereignty and Sorrow*. Boulder: Lynne Rienner, 2009.

Freedom House. *Freedom in the World, 2022*. Washington, DC.

Frost, Amanda. *You Are Not American: Citizenship Stripping from Dred Scott to the Dreamers*. Boston: Beacon, 2021.

Fukuyama, Francis. "The Imperative of State-Building." *Journal of Democracy* 15, no. 2 (2004): 17–31.

Gilley, Bruce. "The Case for Colonialism." *Third World Quarterly* (2017) (retracted).

Ginifer, Jeremy. *Managing Arms in Peace Processes: Rhodesia/Zimbabwe*. New York: United Nations, 1995.

Gyimah-Boadi, E. "Democratic Delivery Falls Short." *Journal of Democracy* 30, no. 3 (2019): 86–93.

Hassan, Mai, and Ahmed Kodouda. "Sudan's Uprising: The Fall of a Dictator." *Journal of Democracy* 30, no. 4 (2019): 89–103.

Herbst, Jeffrey. "War and the State in Africa." *International Security* 14, no. 4 (1990): 117–39.

Hylland Eriksen, Thomas. "The Problem of African Nationhood." *Nations and Nationalism* 22, no. 2 (2016): 222–31.

Jackson, Robert. *The Global Covenant: Human Conduct in a World of States*. Oxford: Oxford University Press, 2000.

Jackson, Robert H., and Carl G. Rosberg. "Sovereignty and Underdevelopment: Juridical Statehood in the African Crisis." *Journal of Modern African Studies* 24, no. 1 (1986): 1–31.

———, and Carl G. Rosberg. "Personal Rule: Theory and Practice in Africa." *Comparative Politics* 16, no. 4 (1984): 421–42.

Johnson, Thomas H., and M. Chris Mason. "Democracy in Afghanistan Is Wishful Thinking." *Christian Science Monitor*, August 20, 2009.

Kershner, Isabel. "In Israel's Poorer Periphery, Legal Woes Don't Dent Netanyahu's Appeal." *New York Times*, March 18, 2018, 8.

Leithead, Alistair. "World's Most Dangerous Peacekeeping Mission." *BBC.com*, November 20, 2015.

Lewis, Peter. "Aspirations and Realities in Africa: Five Reflections." *Journal of Democracy* 30, no. 3 (2019): 76–85.

Maina, Grace, and Erik Melander, eds. *Peace Agreements and Durable Peace in Africa*. Pietermaritzburg: University of Kwazulu Natal Press, 2016.

Mandani, Mahmood. "Making Sense of Political Violence in Post-Colonial Africa." *Socialist Register* 39 (2003): 132–51.

McFaul, Michael. "Democracy Promotion as a World Value." *Washington Quarterly* 28, no. 1 (2004): 147–63.

McKaiser, Eusebius. "Don't Get Too Excited About South Africa's New President." *Globe and Mail*, February 17, 2018, O2.

McLean Hilker, Lyndsay. "Everyday Ethnicities: Identity and Reconciliation Among Rwandan Youth." *Journal of Genocide Research* 11, no. 1 (2009): 81–100.

Nganje, Fritz, and Kgalalelo Nganje. "Liberal Internationalism Meets Third Worldism: The Politics of International Election Observation in the DRC's Post-War Elections." *Third World Quarterly* 40, no. 3 (2019): 521–41.

Nossiter, Adam. "In Nigeria, Where Graft Is the System." *New York Times*, February 5, 2014.

Nur, Ahmed Mohamud, Yusuf Ahmed Nur, and Andrew Harding. "Why Mogadishu's Former Mayor Wants to Be Somalia's President." CBC. *The Current* (transcript), December 14, 2016.

O'Connell, James. "The Inevitability of Instability." *Journal of Modern African Studies* 5, no. 2 (1967): 181–91.

Onishi, Norimitsu. "As Ramaphosa Hails a 'New Dawn,' South Africans See More of the Same." *New York Times*, February 17, 2018.

Ottaway, Marina. "Is Democracy the Answer?" In *Leashing the Dogs of War*. Washington, DC: United States Institute of Peace, 2007.

Packenham, Robert A. *Liberal America and the Third World: Political Development Ideas in Foreign Aid and Social Science*. Princeton, NJ: Princeton University Press, 1973.

Posner, Daniel N., and Daniel J. Young. "The Institutionalization of Political Power in Africa." *Journal of Democracy* 18, no. 3 (2007): 126–40.

Pringle, Robert. "Mali's Unlikely Democracy." *Wilson Quarterly* (Spring 2006): 31–39.

Robertson, Roland. "Globalisation or Glocalisation." *Journal of International Communication* 18, no. 2 (2012): 191–208.

Saunt, Claudio. *Unworthy Republic: The Dispossession of Native Americans and the Road to Indian Territory*. New York: W.W. Norton, 2021.

Schwarz, Benjamin. "The Diversity Myth: America's Leading Export." *Atlantic Monthly* (May 1995).

Swyngedouw, Erik. "Globalisation or 'Glocalisation'? Networks, Territories and Rescaling." *Cambridge Review of International Affairs* 17, no. 1 (2004): 25–48.

United Nations. Report of the United Nations Independent Investigation on Burundi (UNIIB) established pursuant to Human Rights Council resolution S-24/1 (September 2016).

Uppsala Conflict Data Program and the Global Terrorism Database.

Vaishnav, Milan. "Why Voters Sometimes Prefer Criminals as Candidates." *Governance* 29, no. 4 (October 2016): 459–61.

Walsh, Declan. "Sudan Protesters, Devastated but Defiant, Regroup Underground after Crackdown." *New York Times*, June 9, 2019.

World Bank. *Partnership for Capacity Building in Africa: Strategy and Program of Action.* September 28, 1996.

York, Geoffrey. "A Time of Despair on the Birthday of Freedom." *Globe and Mail*, January 27, 2024.

———. "South African President Faces Growing Pressure to Resign." *Globe and Mail*, July 11, 2022.

Zürcher, Christoph. "Building Democracy While Building Peace." *Journal of Democracy* 22, no. 1 (January 2011): 81–95.

———. "A Theory of Democratisation Through Peace-Building." *Conflict, Security and Development* 18, no. 4 (2018): 283–99.

2

The Anglophone War of Secession in Cameroon

Domestic Problem, Extra-National Challenges, and Shared Responsibility

Walters Tohnji Samah

When the international community ignores government and separatist atrocities of the kind happening in Cameroon, it often pays a massive bill. Sooner or later, we must fund refugee camps and peacekeepers, host negotiations, accommodate thousands of migrants seeking asylum, and help rebuild shattered nations. It makes more sense to use diplomacy to stop the violence at an earlier stage, finding a political solution to a political problem through inclusive peace negotiations.

—Global Campaign for Peace and Justice in Cameroon, 2020

Introduction: The Glocal Dimensions of Secessionism

Secessionism is the demand for a formal separation of a region from an existing state to establish a new state with sovereign status. Buchanan describes secession as the act of defying the rule of the parent state, not through revolution or otherwise trying to change the government of the state, but to exclude the jurisdiction of the parent state from the claimed territory of the secessionists.[1] According to Chiang, secessionism seeks to amputate, either forcibly or nonforcibly, an independent state from part of a territory.[2]

Hechter has framed secessionism under a rational theory comprising two distinct elements. First, the people of a given territory make the collective decision to secede, and second, the leaders of the parent state must make a collective decision that the net cost of ceding the territory in question is negative.[3] Throughout history, secessionism has been the most common practice in state formation. Between 1990 and 2007, it led to the creation of at least twenty-five states that were given international recognition.

Drawing on publicly available data, this chapter examines the Anglophone secessionism in Cameroon, showing how a combination of global and local variables contributed to the making and shaping of the secession problem. Highlighting some implications at the global stage of what is generally perceived and presented as a local issue, the chapter argues that in today's context of globalization, local problems cannot be confined to their localities, and the global stage cannot completely insulate or shield itself from the implications of local issues. In that sense, issues such as the Anglophone effort to secede from Cameroon become glocal issues. This glocality becomes an interesting prism for understanding the state in Africa.

The state-formation process in Africa is often attributed to European colonialism, considered the early phase of globalization.[4] During the decolonization process, the United Nations (UN) leveraged the principle of self-determination to grant colonized territories and peoples the right to secede from the European colonial empires. The outcome was the proclamation of the independence of several new African states recognized by the international community. However, since then, there has been a shift in the meaning of the universal right to self-determination. Today, it is interpreted chiefly as the right of a people to make choices within an existing state and therefore does not allow a pathway to new statehood.[5] This makes it difficult for the international community to facilitate the creation of new states. Brown has examined the stance of the UN on self-determination and secession and concluded that it is contradictory and ambiguous. According to him, "keeping its stance ambiguous allows the organization to act pragmatically without setting a precedent that may undermine the international system of states and to tailor its approach to the specific situation, which more specific and rigid stance on the issue would prevent."[6]

Moreover, in 1964, the Organization of African Unity opted to preserve the preexisting African states by proclaiming that the colonial borders of the new states in Africa were sacrosanct (OAU Res. 16.1). In keeping with this principle, its successor, the African Union, has thus pursued strict policies against any attempted secession on the continent, viewing it as a threat to the security and sovereignty of its Member States.[7]

There is no unanimity among scholars regarding how new states should be formed and recognized. At the core of this disagreement is whether a territory becomes a state by fulfilling specific criteria of statehood or through international recognition. Vladimír Baar distinguishes between two main academic theories regarding the formation of new states: constitutive and declaratory theories.[8] According to constitutive theory, the state formation process starts with the proclamation of independence followed by recognition of that independence by the parent state. A receipt of wide international recognition completes the process. Under this theory, a state becomes an international actor only through its recognition by other countries. However, the limitation of this theory is that it does not provide a clear answer to the question of how many states must recognize the entity for it to become an equal member of the international community.[9]

In contrast, the declaratory theory argues that the existence of a state is independent of its recognition by other states. Accordingly, an entity is not a state because it is recognized, but it is recognized because it is a state.[10] As a result, when such an entity fulfils the legal criteria of statehood, it becomes a de facto state regardless of whether it is recognized. Notwithstanding the above theories, under existing customary international law (Montevideo Convention 1933), becoming a sovereign state through secession requires the fulfilment of four main criteria: territory, a permanent population, government, and sovereignty or capacity to enter into international legal relations.[11]

Significantly, many secessionist movements worldwide end up in violence or civil war, making secessionism a critical issue in international politics. In the late 1990s, almost half of all wars in the world were wars of secession.[12] Secession is also a complicated and highly sensitive issue, as no country is willing to lose sovereignty over any part of its territory. According to Ker-Lindsay, states vigorously contest acts of secession for various reasons, such as economic factors, emotional attachment to the territory, preventing further territorial loss, a sense of injustice, and historical, cultural, and religious significance.

The arbitrary partitioning of Africa by European powers in the late nineteenth century makes postindependence African countries very vulnerable to secessionism. As Banfo aptly puts it, the "haphazard manner in which European powers spliced the continent into colonies makes every country vulnerable to potentially splitting up for a myriad of reasons including a simple disagreement between a region and the central government."[13] Other factors that drive secessionism in Africa include economic and/or political marginalization, identity, historical grievances, bad governance, and unequal distribution of resources. Despite the emergence of several secessionist movements in Africa, there have been very few successful cases, such as Eritrea in 1991 and South Sudan in 2011, which came at a high cost to human life and national and regional stability. As Ekeke and Lubisi rightly put it, "peaceful secession in Africa has become elusive even as there are frequent calls for secession in the African continent."[14] In their edited book *Secessionism in African Politics: Aspiration, Grievance, Performance, Disenchantment*, de Vries, Engelbert, and Schomerus examined fourteen secessionist movements in Africa, placing them into four broad categories. They include secessionism as aspirations or dreams of a solution, secessionism as a grievance or postcolonial metastasis, secessionism as performance and posturing, and secessionism as disenchantment.[15]

Similarly, Ahmed has identified four alternative arguments or claims advanced by secessionist groups.[16] The first, revivalist secession, is an argument for reviving the right to colonial self-determination or claiming a right to reversion for a particular unit. It is applicable where a merger process led to the creation of the state against which a territorial claim is made and where secessionists claim that their action is informed by an altruistic motive to correct a particular historical mistake made during the decolonization process.[17] The second argument recognizes and advocates the constitutional right to self-determination for a region or a subnational group in a multiethnic state. The third, known as remedial secession, involves the contention that in the event of excessive human rights violations, coupled with nonrepresentation in government, the aggrieved people or community is entitled to the right to secede. According to Buchanan, the "remedial right to secede" (RRS) arises from a situation where a people are not having their security protected by their parent state.[18] The theory seems to align with John Locke's right to revolution, which suggests a group has the right to seek a new sovereign state if their rights are abused by the sovereign state. Last, the fourth argument is for national self-determination, which claims that historically, Africa was composed of larger nation-like entities, which make it possible to regroup the current states along the lines of those presumed nations.

Different countries have employed different strategies to deal with secessionism. Seen as a negative phenomenon, many parent states in Africa and beyond have tried to counter secessionism by force (war), with the most illustrative case being the Biafra War (1967–1970) in Nigeria. To avoid war, some countries, such as Tanzania, have offered an alternative to secession by adopting devolutionary approaches such as federalism, thereby transferring significant political power from the central government to the periphery. By so doing, the parent state can accommodate demands for greater autonomy while at the same time retaining majority rule and keeping the state intact as a political entity.[19] Additionally, other parent states have adopted decentralization and other good governance policies to counter or mitigate this rise in secessionist sentiments.[20] As seen in the following section, Anglophone secessionism in Cameroon began with the aggrieved population seeking peaceful or legal means to address their grievances before it evolved into violence and armed conflict due to a lack of adequate action from the national government.

Understanding Anglophone Secessionism

Though considered a domestic problem, the origins of the Anglophone secession are rooted in a historical process intertwined with a complex web of both local and global phenomena including colonialism, involving actors such as Germany, France, Britain, the League of Nations, and the UN. As a former German protectorate, Cameroon was arbitrarily partitioned into two unequal portions by Britain and France during World War I. In 1922, they became Mandated Territories of the League of Nations, and in 1946, they were transformed into Trust Territories of the UN.[21] British Cameroons, significantly smaller than French Cameroun,[22] was further divided into two parts, Southern Cameroons and Northern Cameroons, with no ties between them, and administered as part of Nigeria.

Britain and France followed two very distinct approaches to administrating the respective spheres of Cameroon. The French used direct rule, which required the colonial state to control the people centrally using French laws.[23] According to Mamdani, direct rule, which he likens to centralized despotism, was a system that racially discriminated against Africans considered uncivilized.[24] Anchored on the French policy of assimilation, it disregarded traditional African governance structures and values and sought to transform assimilated Africans into French citizens. Using an indirect rule system, the British enlisted traditional rulers and allowed them some degree of power and autonomy to govern the people using customary laws on their behalf. The distinction between the two systems of colonial administration is an important factor in understanding postcolonial realities in Cameroon, particularly Anglophone grievances and separatism, which is the main thrust of this chapter.

The decolonization process in French Cameroun and its outcome were largely driven and determined by France. On April 10, 1948, French

Cameroun liberation fighters led by Ruben Um Nyobé established the Union des Populations du Cameroun (UPC) to advocate for the unification of British and French Cameroons and independence. This was at odds with France's grand plan for its African colonies. Consequently, on July 13, 1955, the French government banned the UPC, triggering a brutal anticolonial war that claimed tens of thousands of victims.[25] On September 13, 1958, Ruben Um Nyobé was killed by government security forces. On January 1, 1960, French Cameroun gained independence. With the nationalist leaders either killed or silenced, France co-opted and installed Ahmadou Ahidjo as the first president. This ensured that the country's accession to independence was only formal, without full sovereignty. Through the system called Françafrique,[26] real power and influence remained within France, which continued to exercise a systematic hegemonic influence in Cameroun.

In February 1961, the UN organized two independence plebiscites in British Cameroons, the first on February 11, 1961, for Southern Cameroons and the second on February 12, 1961, for Northern Cameroons. The people were asked to choose between integrating with Nigeria or reuniting with former French Cameroun. In essence, the people of British Cameroons were not given the option of having an independent country of their own, even though that is what some of them wanted. While Northern Cameroons voted for reintegration with Nigeria, Southern Cameroons (currently Anglophone Cameroon) voted for reunification with the newly independent La République du Cameroun (Republic of Cameroun). However, this outcome did not accurately reflect the popular political aspirations and preferences of the people of Southern Cameroons.[27] According to Konings and Nyamnjoh, "there is overwhelming evidence to suggest that if a third alternative of either independence or continued trusteeship had been put forward, it would have been considered in a favorable light" by the people of Southern Cameroons.[28] The UN's imposition of two bad options denied the territory the right to self-determination, constituting one of the historical foundations of Anglophone secessionism. Kučera views Anglophone (Southern Cameroons) secessionism as a self-determination conflict.[29] Gitlitz sees it as a "culmination of bad international politics in the 1960s, which amalgamated peoples regardless of their language and culture."[30] Nevertheless, on October 1, 1961, Southern Cameroons officially reunited with the Republic of Cameroun to form a single country, the Federal Republic of Cameroon.

Conscious of the different colonial heritage, the new country adopted a two-state federation that guaranteed equal status for the Francophone and Anglophone parts and sought to protect the rights and interests of the

Anglophone minority. Under the federal constitution, the Anglophone state known as West Cameroon was granted considerable autonomy. However, in May 1972, President Ahmadou Ahidjo abolished the federal system, establishing a centralized unitary system and renaming the country the United Republic of Cameroon. As a result, the Anglophone minority lost its statehood and the autonomy it exercised under the federal system. This was followed by decades of systematic marginalization of Anglophones in the south by the Francophone-dominated state, driven by a deliberate attempt to deconstruct the Anglophone identity and erase the Anglo-Saxon subsystem.[31]

Cameroon is divided into ten administrative regions. Two of those, the Northwest and Southwest regions, comprise Anglophone Cameroon, representing approximately 20 percent of the country's total population. The Southwest region, which is Anglophone, is endowed with rich natural resources, including oil and gas, timber, and fertile lands, contributing a huge proportion of the country's gross domestic product (GDP).[32] It hosts the largest agro-industrial company in the country, known as the Cameroon Development Corporation (CDC), created in 1946 to manage extensive German-era plantations of tropical crops. Anglophone Cameroon also hosts Cameroon's lone oil refinery, the National Refining Company (SONARA). Significantly, the oil-rich peninsular of Bakassi, which lies along the coastline of the Atlantic Ocean, is in the Anglophone Southwest region.[33] According to Pinto, though Anglophone claims for autonomy and independence are rooted in colonial history, the competition for resources also serve as grievance "accelerator," fueling economic self-determination and separatism.[34]

Anglophone Cameroonians have for decades complained of subjugation and have made numerous attempts to address the problem using various political and constitutional means, all of which have been unsuccessful.[35] In 1984, President Paul Biya unilaterally changed the country's name from the United Republic of Cameroon to the Republic of Cameroon or La République du Cameroun, the former name of Francophone Cameroon, before reunification. Anglophone nationalist groups such as the Southern Cameroons National Council (SCNC) argue that by abolishing the federal system and adopting the prior French name, Francophone Cameroon was seceding from the union with Anglophone Cameroon.[36] Anglophone nationalist groups began championing independence for Anglophones and the creation of the Republic of Ambazonia in Anglophone Cameroon. A key figure behind this effort is renowned lawyer and political activist Fon Gorji Dinka.[37]

On April 2–3, 1993, prominent Anglophone leaders convened the All-Anglophone Conference (AAC) of Buea, which adopted a set of resolutions to advance Anglophone interests in Cameroon, including the restoration of the two-state federal system.[38] In a follow-up conference organized in Bamenda the following year, the Anglophone leaders threatened to unilaterally proclaim the "independence and sovereignty of the Anglophone territory if the government did not take all measures to address their demands for a return to the federal system," as stated in paragraph 6 of the statement issued at AAC II. The Cameroon government, which was pursuing a policy of not acknowledging the existence of the Anglophone problem, disregarded the warning. This forced Anglophone pressure groups to begin seeking outright independence.[39] However, in these early years, secession was supported by only a tiny fraction of the English-speaking population, as most Anglophones still believed in the Cameroon nation-building project.[40]

Generally, people often resort to violence to claim their rights when government fails to provide adequate responses to their long-standing unresolved grievances. However, in the case of Cameroon, the immediate cause of the secessionist war was the government's continuous use of disproportionate military force to quash a series of peaceful Anglophone demonstrations in late 2016 and 2017.[41] In response, Anglophone activists symbolically proclaimed the independent Federal Republic of Ambazonia on October 1, 2017. Committed to its "one and indivisible" Cameroon policy, the Cameroon government ordered the militarization of the Anglophone regions to crack down on secessionists.[42] The harsh reprisal by the security forces transformed what had begun as civil unrest into an insurgency and, ultimately, a violent secession conflict.[43]

Since the separatist movement began, numerous separatist groups have been formed cobbled under the umbrella name the Amba-boys to fight the government of Cameroon. The Amba-boys, estimated to be between 2,000 and 4,000, operate mainly in the dense equatorial forests and bushes and along the Cameroon-Nigeria border. Employing guerrilla tactics, the strategy of the secessionist insurgency is to render the Anglophone regions ungovernable for the Cameroon government. The Amba-boys have occupied most rural areas in the English-speaking Northwest and Southwest regions, which have become no-go areas for public administrators appointed by the government of Cameroon. Separatist groups began using rudimentary weapons such as hunting guns to fight against well-trained government forces. They now possess heavy weapons, such as antitank missiles and rocket launchers, believed to have been either seized from the Cameroon military or smuggled from Nigeria.[44] With increased capability, separatists have extended their operations to the French-speaking Littoral and West regions, where they have attacked both military and civilian targets.[45] The Cameroon military attributes the increase in separatists' capability primarily to cooperation with other separatist groups in Nigeria.[46]

Overall, the conflict has had devastating consequences for the civilian population. As of January 2022, more than 6,000 people had been killed and nearly a million displaced (900,000 internally and 60,000 as refugees).[47] According to Chris Fomunyoh, "every time the armed groups attacked the military and someone in uniform was killed, then the military goes into that vicinity or that neighbourhood 'in pursuit of the boys' and mows down civilians."[48] In one of the deadliest attacks on civilians since the start of the conflict, on February 14, 2020, the military killed twenty-one people, including thirteen children and a pregnant mother, during a raid on a remote village in the Northwest Region.[49] Unlike the Biafra War in the late 1960s, which gained extensive international media coverage and drew widespread attention to global humanitarian response, the Anglophone secessionist war has drawn limited international attention, causing it to be classified as the most neglected conflict in the world in 2019 and 2020.[50] The conflict is now at a stalemate, as both sides are reluctant to engage in talks, and there is a lack of sufficient international attention to the conflict.[51]

The Glocalization of the Anglophone War of Secession

Globalization is not a one-way phenomenon or a brakeless train that crushes everything in its path, but a process shaped by the interaction of both global and local realities.[52] The recognition of this reality has led to the concept of glocalization, a term that has resonated and is currently being used in many disciplines. According to Roland Robertson, one of the early users of the term, glocalization involves the "simultaneity and the interpenetration of what are conventionally called the global and the local, or—in more general vein—the universal and the particular."[53] He argues that the need to introduce the concept of glocalization as a theory in social science arose from the fact that much of what is called globalization "tended to assume that it is a process which overrides locality . . . such as exhibited in the various ethnic nationalisms which have seemingly arisen in the various parts of the world."[54] To Shamsuddoha, glocalization refers to the twin process whereby issues shift downward from the global level to the local/national level and upward from the local level to the global level.[55] The Anglophone secessionism in Cameroon has all the hallmarks of glocalization, as it is a conflict rooted in international arrangements, and its dynamics and effects are conditioned by factors within Cameroon and in other countries. It also shows that the glocalized nature of the state in Africa as both its origin and survival are tied to domestic and external conflict drivers. Five core issues emerge that show the glocal nature of the Anglophone secession in Cameroon. These are a) debates about internal and external solutions, b) regional geopolitical implications in the Gulf of Guinea, c) emigration flows and diaspora activism, d) international response to human rights violations and abuses, and e) external mediation efforts.

Internal and External Solutions

Since the outbreak of current crisis in 2017, there has been a protracted debate particularly among Cameroon stakeholders over whether the solution to the conflict should be sought locally or externally. The most prominent proponent for the local option is the Cameroon government. Insisting that the conflict is purely internal, the government has rejected any external offer of assistance to broker a peace deal. Yet the local solutions it has proposed have been inadequate and have failed to address the underlying causes of the conflict. For instance, facing increasing pressure at home and abroad, President Biya organized a national dialogue in 2019 aimed at resolving the Anglophone conflict. However, the dialogue initiative did not meet minimum international standards in terms of credibility, inclusivity and participation, and transparency. Unsurprisingly, despite granting "special status," entailing greater autonomy to the two Anglophone regions, the national dialogue failed to resolve the conflict. On their part, Cameroon civil society groups have undertaken several efforts to try to end the conflict, but they have been undermined by the constrained civil society space. For example, in the early stages of the conflict, the government obstructed an initiative by religious leaders in Anglophone Cameroon, led by the late Cardinal Christian Tumi, to organize an all-Anglophone conference aimed at finding a solution to the conflict.[56] Many civil society groups also suffer threats and attacks from either the Cameroon military or armed separatist groups, which accuse them of colluding with the government.

The conflict parties are divided over whether the solution to the conflict should be sought locally or externally. As shall be seen later, the Cameroon government has rejected all offers of international support to resolve the

Anglophone secessionist conflict, asserting it is purely an internal issue that falls within its jurisdiction. On their part, Anglophone separatists and activists have routinely called for direct outside intervention, insisting the Anglophone problem is a constitutional and international issue that "can only be solved internationally."[57] Many have cited the arbitrary colonial partition of Cameroon in 1916, the UN-organized plebiscites in British Cameroons in 1961, and the colonial-era right to self-determination to argue that the international community, including the UN; the Commonwealth; the African Union; and former colonial powers of the United Kingdom, France, and even Germany, retains responsibility for correcting a historical wrong committed in Cameroon.[58] Anglophone separatist leaders believe that only discussions mediated by a third party can resolve the conflict.

Activism by Cameroonians living abroad has helped draw some international attention to that conflict, including from some members of the US Congress representing constituencies with Cameroonian diaspora communities. According to Anyefru, "by making their plight known to the international community, the Anglophone community believes that the latter might intervene to restore the statehood to the Anglophone community."[59] The willingness of the Anglophone minority to take the case to the international community dates back to colonial times when Britain administered the territory under UN Trusteeship.[60] In the 1950s, the political elites of Southern Cameroons petitioned the UN and paid frequent visits to its headquarters in New York to complain about British neglect of their territory.[61] This resumed again in the early 1990s as more petitions were sent to the UN, the African Court in Banjul, and the Commonwealth to draw the international community's attention to the injustices against the English-speaking minority in Cameroon.[62]

Though the separatist strategy of seeking an outside solution to the Anglophone cause gained some international sympathy in the first two years of the conflict, it failed to mobilize the international community to put adequate pressure on the Cameroon government to address the underlying causes of the Anglophone problem. This failure could be attributed to several factors, notably the government's hostility to foreign involvement and factionalization within the Anglophone separatist movement. In addition, the human rights abuses against the civilian population have undermined separatists' credibility abroad. Some have argued that seeking an outside solution to the Anglophone problem in Cameroon was not the right strategy.

According to Tibor P. Nagy, the former US assistant secretary of state for African Affairs, while the international community has some historical responsibilities for the Anglophone problem dating back to 1961, it is for the "Cameroonian community . . . to come up with a solution."[63] To Christoph Hoffmann, a member of the German Parliament, the Anglophone war of secession is an internal conflict, and it is for the "Cameroon people to decide how they want to live and what constitution they want to have in the future."[64] While this may be a fair argument, the possibility of an inclusive dialogue among the key national stakeholders to resolve the issue is slim, given the deep-seated mistrust among them, particularly between the Francophone-dominated government and the Anglophone community. There is, therefore, a need for the international community's support for a negotiated settlement.

REGIONAL GEOPOLITICAL IMPLICATIONS

The Anglophone secessionist war has diplomatic and geopolitical implications in the Gulf of Guinea, including the heightening insecurity on the 2,100-kilometer Cameroon-Nigeria border. The porous borders between Cameroon's two English-speaking regions (i.e., Northwest and Southwest) with Nigeria, along which separatists from both countries are fighting for independent states, led to a spillover of violence into Nigeria. Cameroon separatist fighters have used Nigeria to smuggle arms and weapons, train for operations, and to hide out, which has prolonged the war, as Cameroon accuses Nigeria of sheltering Anglophone separatists.[65] Furthermore, Cameroon's separatist groups have slipped into Nigeria, from which they can further appeal to Cameroonian refugees to support and join their fight for an independent state.[66] In 2021, the Ambazonia Governing Council, led by Lucas Cho Ayaba, announced it had entered a "strategic and military" alliance with Nigeria's Biafra separatist group, the Indigenous People of Biafra (IPOB), led by Nnamdi Kanu, in which the parties agreed to work together to "secure their common border and ensure an open exchange of arms, intelligence and personnel." As a result of this cooperation, in April 2022, separatists from both countries shut down trade across the Cameroon-Nigeria border, halting about 90 percent of cross-border trade.[67]

Significantly, the Cameroon separatist fighters have since 2017 conducted several raids into Nigeria, creating security challenges in villages close to Cameroon's border and raising questions about the violation of Nigeria's territorial integrity.[68] For instance, in mid-November 2021, suspected Anglophone separatists razed Manga village, a community in Takum Local Government Area, Taraba State, killing several people, including the village head, and displacing others.[69] Again, on May 29, 2022, they crossed the Nigerian border and killed at least twenty people in Boki, a community in Cross River State that hosts many Cameroonians who have fled the violence in the Anglophone regions.[70] According to Senator Emmanuel Bwacha, who represents Taraba South in the Nigerian Senate, the incursion of Anglophone separatists into Nigeria threatens Nigeria's integrity and territorial sovereignty as a country.[71]

Similarly, the Cameroon military has accused separatists of setting up bases and launching attacks from Nigeria and have sometimes crossed the border into Nigeria to conduct raids against Anglophone separatists, raising legal questions relating to violations of Nigerian territorial integrity and sovereignty.[72] The continuation and escalation of the Anglophone secessionist war may reignite tension between Cameroon and Nigeria as the two countries try to normalize relations after decades of diplomatic rows and border skirmishes over the oil-rich Bakassi Peninsula in the Gulf of Guinea. Though Bakassi is a Cameroonian territory, per the 2002 International Court of Justice (ICJ) ruling on the disputed territory, about 90 percent of the peninsula's population (estimated at 200,000 to 300,000) regard themselves and their families as Nigerians.[73] If not resolved, the Anglophone secession war could allow pro-Nigeria separatist groups to mobilize forces against the Cameroon government or join forces with Ambazonia in exchange for recognition. In August 2012, a movement called the Bakassi Self-Determination Front declared independence from Cameroon after hoisting the Nigerian flag and setting up an FM radio station.[74] There are concerns that if the conflict continues to protract, it could increase criminality, extremism, and piracy in the Gulf of Guinea.[75] Notwithstanding this challenge, Cameroon has, over the past decade, forged a viable strategic partnership with Nigeria in the joint fight against Boko Haram terrorists.

Migration and Diaspora Activism

Given their long-standing complaints of exclusion and marginalization and because of political persecution in Cameroon, Anglophone Cameroonians have pursued the international migration pathway since the late 1970s.[76] As a result, there is a significant Cameroon Anglophone diaspora in Nigeria, South Africa, the United States, Canada, the UK, Austria, Belgium, France, Germany, and Switzerland.[77] The presence and activities of secessionist leaders and other Anglophone activists in the diaspora have contributed to exporting the Anglophone secessionist struggle out of Cameroon. In addition to garnering financial and material support for the separatist cause, Anglophones in the diaspora have played a crucial role in bringing some international awareness to the crisis in Cameroon. For instance, they organize demonstrations outside the UN headquarters in New York to pressure the world body to grant the English-speaking regions the right to self-determination as recognized under the UN Charter.[78] In South Africa, hundreds of Anglophone Cameroonians have regularly gathered in front of government buildings in Cape Town, Johannesburg, and Pretoria (including the Embassy of Cameroon) to protest atrocities committed by the government in the Anglophone regions.[79] For example, following the killings in 2022 of seven children at Saint Francisca school in Fiango, Kumba, Southwest region, Anglophone separatists teamed up with Julius Malema, the leader of the South African radical left-wing Economic Freedom Fighters (EFF) party, to condemn the government and call on Cameroonians to rise against the "puppet regime of Paul Biya."[80] On May 25, 2022, Anglophone separatists joined forces with Malema's EFF to stage a peaceful protest in front of the French embassy in Johannesburg, calling on France to "pack out of Africa."[81] Anglophone separatists have long blamed Paris for backing the government of Biya's brutal crackdown in the Anglophone regions.

In Europe, Anglophone secessionists have collaborated with other pro-democracy and anti-Biya groups, such as the Brigade Anti-Sardinard (BAS), to draw international attention to the Anglophone crisis.[82] One of the key demands of BAS is for the government to address the root causes of the Anglophone crisis. Highlighting the atrocities committed by government forces in the two English-speaking regions, BAS has organized several anti-Biya demonstrations in France and Switzerland. In one such demonstration organized on June 26, 2019, in front of the Intercontinental Hotel in Geneva, President Biya's personal security agents attacked Swiss reporter Adrien Krause of Radio-Television Swiss (RTS). They seized the reporter's equipment and mobile phone as he was covering the event.[83] Reporters Without Borders (RSF) condemned the attack and called on the Swiss and Cameroonian authorities to take appropriate action to ensure those responsible were held accountable "despite the legal and diplomatic difficulties that might arise." According to Arnaud Froger, the head of RSF's Africa desk, "If presidential staff can attack journalists with complete impunity, including abroad, this would send a terrible message to those who try to report the news in both Switzerland and Cameroon."[84] On July 2, 2019, five of Biya's security agents were arrested by Geneva Judicial Police. The next day, they were found guilty of coercion, damage to property, and illegal appropriation of an object and slammed with suspended sentences of at least three months.[85]

Some diaspora members have incited violence and engaged in hate speech and misinformation related to the conflict on social media, which have led to calls for their host countries to take action against them. Realizing the diaspora had become a new battleground in its campaign to fight the separatists, the Cameroonian government in November 2017 issued international warrants for the arrest and deportation of separatist leaders in the diaspora.[86] In January 2018, the Nigerian government arrested forty-six Anglophone leaders, including the self-declared president of Ambazonia, Ayuk Tabe. Nigeria extradited them to Cameroon, where they were tried by a military court and convicted on charges related to rebellion and acts of "terrorism."[87] On February 17, 2021, Cameroon's National Assembly wrote to the US Congress to complain about the role of the Anglophone diaspora in the conflict.[88] Since 2021, several US-based Anglophone Cameroonians, including St. Michael Tamufor Nchumuluh, Walters Alambi Muma, Edith Ngang, Wilson Nuyila Tita, Eric Fru Nji, and Wilson Che Fonguh, have been facing federal charges of conspiracy and violation of the US Arms Export Control Act and the Export Reform Control Act.[89] They were accused of illegally shipping or attempting to smuggle weapons and ammunition from the United States to Nigeria to assist Anglophone separatists fighting against the government of Cameroon. According to US Federal investigators, significant quantities of weaponry, including "equipment resembling a full-scale manufacturing operation, capable of inflicting serious damage," was found in Maryland in the basement of one of the suspects, St. Michael Tamufor Nchumuluh.[90] In May 2023, Nchumuluh was sentenced to thirty months in prison followed by two years of supervised release. Eric Fru Nji, Wilson Nuyila Tita, and Wilson Che Fonguh were sentenced to sixty-three months in prison. The three other co-conspirators, Godlove Nche Manchoe, Tse Ernst Bangarie, and Edith Ngang, were each sentenced to forty-six months of imprisonment.[91]

A frequent outcome of secessionist wars is that they generate refugees resulting from forced migration, contributing to the glocalization of the conflict. According to the UNHCR, as of April 2022, an estimated 770,000 Cameroonian refugees were living in the Nigerian border states of Akwa-Ibom, Anambra, Benue, Cross River, Enugu, and Taraba, forcing local authorities to seek assistance.[92] Anglophone migrants also enter the United States through the Mexico-US border.[93] Under Donald Trump, the

US government pursued a hardline policy toward migrants. Between 2017 and 2020, it forcibly deported Cameroon immigrants to Cameroon, where they faced the heightened risk of persecution, detention, torture, and mass displacement by the government, which viewed returnees as secessionists, terrorists, or opposition activists.[94] However, with the election of Joe Biden as US president, the deportation policies of Trump ended, and in April 2022, the US government granted Cameroonian asylum seekers Temporary Protected Status (TPS).[95]

HUMAN RIGHTS

A key feature of the Anglophone secessionist war that has elicited a global response is the systematic human rights violations and abuses committed by government forces and armed secessionist groups. According to Tomás F. Husted, US interest in Cameroon has grown since the outbreak of the Anglophone conflict in 2017. US response has been shaped by Congress and championed mainly by members of Congress representing constituencies with Cameroonian diaspora communities. Reported human rights violations by Cameroonian security personnel have created challenges for bilateral ties, prompting restrictions on some US security assistance and other punitive measures.[96] For example, on February 6, 2019, the United States, a key ally of Cameroon in the fight against Islamist terrorism in Cameroon's Far North region, cut millions of dollars in security and military aid to Cameroon because of human rights violations by the government. According to the US State Department, the military assistance included a C-130 transport aircraft training program, the delivery of four defender patrol boats, nine unidentified armored vehicles, and an upgrade to the Cessna 208 surveillance aircraft to be operated by Cameroon's Rapid Intervention Battalions.[97] Furthermore, an offer for Cameroon to join the State Partnership Program (SPP) was withdrawn. SPP would have included pairing American National Guards with Cameroon armed forces, delivering certain types of equipment, and helicopter pilot training. The US government has also been concerned that US-provided equipment, including vehicles and aircraft intended for use in counterterrorism efforts against Boko Haram, have been diverted and relocated to the Anglophone regions to fight separatists. Furthermore, in 2020, the United States ended Cameroon's preferential trade benefits under the African Growth and Opportunity Act (AGOA) and imposed visa restrictions on individuals believed to be undermining efforts to end the crisis. Similarly, in 2019, the German government terminated its military cooperation with Cameroon to protest the human rights violations and to pressure President Biya to engage in dialogue with the separatists.[98]

External Mediation Efforts

Though the global response to the Anglophone crisis has been inadequate and ineffective, mediation efforts undertaken by two of Cameroon's bilateral partners are worth mentioning. In July 2019, the Swiss government announced that it was leading a mediation effort to broker a peace deal to end the conflict in the English-speaking regions of Cameroon through an inclusive negotiation process.[99] Despite receiving overwhelming backing from the international community, the Swiss-led mediation initiative quickly stalled without making any meaningful progress because of a lack of commitment by the conflicting parties. Similarly, on January 21, 2023, the Canadian government declared that it had been mandated by the Cameroonian authorities and Anglophone separatists to facilitate a peace process to resolve the conflict. However, two days later, the Cameroon government declared that it had "not entrusted any foreign country or external entity with any role of mediator or facilitator to settle the crisis,"[100] dashing any prospects for a peaceful end to the conflict. In rejecting external offers of mediation, the Cameroon government has often called on interested outside stakeholders to instead support the implementation of the resolutions of the 2019 national dialogue.

France is arguably the most important international actor that could facilitate a peaceful resolution to the Anglophone crisis. It is a veto-wielding UN Security Council permanent member and penholder on issues regarding Cameroon. In addition, France has strong historical and cultural ties with Cameroon President Biya. Biya studied in France at the Sorbonne in Paris, which shaped his political ideology. Currently the longest-serving African president, Biya has been able to maintain a tight grip on power largely thanks to the protection and support he enjoys from France. In return, Biya has enabled France to retain influence in Cameroon, allowing it to continue to monopolize Cameroon's rich natural resources such as crude oil, timber, and agricultural products. Confronted by a Cameroonian activist in Paris, on February 22, 2020, over France's silence regarding the situation in Anglophone Cameroon, President Emmanuel Macron promised to apply "maximum pressure" on President Biya to end the "intolerable violence" in the Anglophone regions.[101] More than three years later, the situation has deteriorated. During this period, Paris has strengthened its economic and political ties with Yaoundé.[102] France has also continued to provide military support, including weapons to the Cameroon military, which it uses to sustain its war against Anglophone separatists. Looking at how the Anglophone secessionist conflict has evolved since its outbreak in 2017, there is the potential for continuous escalation with damaging consequences in the country and beyond, unless a conscious effort is made to end it. In one of its letters to the British parliament, Global Campaign for Peace and Justice in Cameroon warned, "When the international community ignores government and separatist atrocities of the kind happening in Cameroon, it often pays a massive bill. Sooner or later, we must fund refugee camps and peacekeepers, host negotiations, accommodate thousands of migrants seeking asylum, and help rebuild shattered nations. It makes more sense to use diplomacy to stop the violence at an earlier stage, finding a political solution to a political problem through inclusive peace negotiations."[103]

Conclusion: The Glocality of the African State

At the core of this chapter is the glocal nature of the African state, in terms of both its roots and its survival. As we see from Cameroon, and even more through the Anglophone crisis, the African state is a colonial creation. In Cameroon, that colonial process of creating states in Africa was complicated by the outcome of European wars in which Germany was defeated and its occupied territories transferred to Britain and France. As such, the problem of the state in Cameroon is tied to global power struggles. This colonial root of the state dovetail with systems of governance that breed marginalization, identity politics, and dictatorship. In Cameroon, the colonial state soon devolved into an authoritarian state that breeds regional political grievances, which eventually resulted in war. The secessionist war in Cameroon not only has external and domestic roots, but it also generated impact beyond Cameroon, especially in Nigeria, where inter- and intrastate conflicts have merged into major forms of violence along the border between Cameroon and Nigeria. Major migrant-receiving countries have also become involved in the human rights and diaspora issues caused by the Anglophone seces-sionist war in Cameroon. Glocalization provides a useful lens to understand the roots and dynamics of the war in Cameroon, which cannot be easily dismissed as a domestic problem, as the government of Cameroon would like to portray it.

Prior to the end of the Cold War, the international community remained largely undisturbed by the armed violent conflicts in Africa, such as the war in Cameroon. Today the dynamics have changed. As the Anglophone conflict in Cameroon demonstrates, local conflicts have the potential to create flows of refugees, jeopardize neighbors, and destabilize entire regions. This chapter examined the Anglophone secessionism in Cameroon, presenting it as a glocal problem that requires a glocalized or dual-level response. Discussing the conflict through the prism of glocalization, the chapter has shown how the constant interaction between global and local phenomena such as European partition and colonization of Cameroon, the UN Trusteeship system, mismanagement of colonial legacies, issues of identity and representation, and marginalization contributed to produce, define, and shape the conflict. While remaining primarily local, the conflict has created significant challenges at the national level, such as threatening Cameroon's territorial integrity, and triggered issues for foreign governments to contend with, including refugee flows, cross-border insecurity, and the activities of Anglophone secessionists in the diaspora.

All of these issues point to glocalization of the separatist insurgency in Cameroon, which validates Robertson's assertion that the "locality is in large degree constructed on a trans- or super-local basis," and "much of the promotion of locality is in fact done from above or outside."[104] It also attests to the fact that in an increasingly globalizing world, what is often considered a local problem can have a global impact. Understanding this complex interplay of impacts is important in crafting an effective and sustainable solution to the conflict. This demands closer cooperation between local and global stakeholders. In this regard, without proffering an external solution, a valid approach is for the international community to broker a peace agreement between the warring parties and then assist national stakeholders to implement the nationally owned and led peace process. The conclusion one draws from examining the case of Anglophone secessionism in Cameroon is that in this fast-globalizing world, the global arena cannot insulate itself from local issues and vice versa. Consequently, local and international actors must work collaboratively to address security challenges regardless of where they occur.

Notes

1. Buchanan, "Toward a Theory of Secession," cited in Brown, "United Nations, Self-Determination, State Failure and Secession," 3.
2. Chiang, *The One-China Policy.*
3. Hechter, "The Dynamics of Secession," 267.

4. Stark, "Theories of Contemporary State Formation in Africa," 335–47; Santos, *Toward an Other Globalization*; Moassab, "Globalization, Neo-Colonization and Urbanization in Africa."

5. Shaw, *Title to Territory in Africa*, 59–91.

6. Brown, "United Nations, Self-Determination, State Failure and Secession," 2–3.

7. Ekeke and Lubisi, "Secession in Africa," 245–60.

8. Baar, "Introduction," 1–2.

9. Baar, "Introduction," 1–2.

10. Baar, "Introduction," 2; Crawford, *The Creation of States in International Law*, 93.

11. Crawford, *The Creation of States in International Law*; Bedjaoui, *International Law*.

12. Spencer and Lalgee, "Conflict Analysis."

13. Bamfo, "The Menace of Secession in Africa," 37–48.

14. Ekeke and Lubisi, "Secession in Africa," 245.

15. de Vries et al., *Secessionism in African Politics*, 11–16.

16. Ahmed, *Boundaries and Secession in Africa and International Law*, 171–214.

17. Ahmed, *Boundaries and Secession in Africa and International Law*, 171–72.

18. Buchanan, "Theories of Secession," *Philosophy and Public Affairs*, 35.

19. Schaeffer, "Secession and Separatism."

20. Mousbaou, "The Rise of Secession Movements in West Africa."

21. Awasom, "The Anglophone Problem in Cameroon Yesterday and Today."

22. Unlike the English spelling of Cameroons, the appellation and spelling of French Cameroun usually refers to France's Mandated and Trust Territory from 1916 to 1945 and 1946 to 1960, respectively.

23. Lee and Schultz, "Comparing British and French Colonial Legacies."

24. Mamdani, *Citizen and Subject*, 18.

25. See, for example, Deltombe, "The Forgotten Cameroon War."

26. Samah, "France and Francophone Africa."

27. Konings and Nyamnjoh, *Negotiating an Anglophone Identity*, 194; Awasom, "The Reunification Question in Cameroon History," 91–119.

28. Konings and Nyamnjoh, *Negotiating an Anglophone Identity*, 194.

29. Kučera, "Mid-Rainy-Season Night's Dream," 110.

30. Gitlitz, "Assessing the Cameroonian Anglophone Crisis."

31. Awasom, "Anglophone Problem in Cameroon"; Konings and Nyamnjoh, "The Anglophone Problem in Cameroon," 207–29; Jua and Konings, "Occupation of Public Space," 609–33; Fochingong, "Exploring the Politics of Identity and Ethnicity," 363–80.

32. International Crisis Group (ICG), *Cameroon's Anglophone Crisis*.

33. Until the 2002 International Court of Justice (ICJ) ruling, Bakassi was subject to a border conflict between Cameroon and Nigeria.

34. Pinto, "In Cameroon, Centralization Leads to Strife."

35. Jua and Konings, "Occupation of Public Space."

36. Jua and Konings, "Occupation of Public Space," 19; ICG, *Cameroon's Anglophone Crisis*; Echitchi, "Legitimacy and Legality," 101–11.

37. The name was derived from Ambas Bay, located on the Gulf of Guinea near the southwest town of Limbe.

38. Orock, "Cameroon's Separatist War."

39. Awasom, "Anglophone Problem in Cameroon."

40. Konings and Nyamnjoh, "Anglophone Secessionist Movements in Cameroon," 70.

41. Willis et al., *Human Rights Abuses in the Cameroon Anglophone Crisis*; Amnesty International, "Cameroon: Arrests and Civil Society"; Cascais, "Separatism in Cameroon."

42. Amnesty International, *Cameroon: Right Cause, Wrong Means*; Gitlitz, "Assessing the Cameroonian Anglophone Crisis."

43. O'Grady, "Divided by Language"; Browne, "Cameroon's Separatist Movement Is Going International"; ICG, *Cameroon's Anglophone Crisis*.

44. Craig, "Caught in the Middle"; Boudombo, "Why Separatists in Cameroon and Nigeria Have United."

45. Reuters, "Five Military Police Killed in Western Cameroon."

46. Boudombo, "Why Separatists in Cameroon and Nigeria Have United."

47. ICG, "Cameroon Needs an African Cup Ceasefire"; Craig, "Violence in Cameroon's Anglophone Crisis"; Bang and Balgah, "The Ramification of Cameroon's Anglophone Crisis."

48. Craig, "Violence in Cameroon's Anglophone Crisis."

49. Office of the Special Representative of the United Nations Secretary-General for Children and Armed Conflict; Craig, "How an 'Execution-Style' Massacre Unfolded in Cameroon."

50. Norwegian Refugee Council (NRC), "Cameroon Tops List of Most Neglected Crises."

51. ICG, "Cameroon Needs an African Cup Ceasefire."

52. Shamsuddoha, "Glocalization: A Theoretical Analysis," 1.

53. Roland, "Glocalization," 25–44.

54. Roland, "Glocalization," 26.

55. Shamsuddoha, "Glocalization: A Theoretical Analysis," 1.

56. Crux, "Cameroon Cardinal Helping Organize Conference to Tackle Anglophone Crisis," August 3, 2018.

57. *Newsday Cameroon*, "Separatists Reject BAS Proposal."

58. Lunn and Brooke-Holland, *The Anglophone Crisis*, 5; Mughe, "Canada Fronts Internationally," 1–3.

59. Anyefru, "Paradoxes of Internationalization of the Anglophone Problem," 85–101.

60. Anyefru, "Paradoxes."

61. Anyefru, "Paradoxes."

62. Anyefru, "Paradoxes"; Kenfo, "Le 'Problème Anglophone' au Cameroun," 8.

63. Chris Anu's interview with Amb. Tibor Nagy, *ABS News*, April 20, 2022.

64. Exclusive Interview with Dr. Christoph Hoffmann, *ABC Amba TV*, March 3, 2021.

65. Carsten and Ross, "Exclusive: Cameroonian Troops Entered Nigeria Without Seeking Authorization."

66. Browne, "Cameroon's Separatist Movement," 1.

67. Kindzeka, "Cameroon: Separatists, Nigerian Militants Paralyze Border."

68. *Guardian*, "Cameroon's Separatist Conflict Spills Across Nigerian Frontier."

69. Umoru, "Cameroonian Separatists Invade Taraba Community"; Shibayan, "Senator Accuses Cameroon Separatist Group."

70. Eyo, "Cameroonian Militants Invade Nigeria."

71. Umoru, "Cameroonian Separatists Invade Taraba Community."

72. Paul and Ross, "Cameroonian Troops Entered Nigeria; Gitlitz, "Assessing the Cameroonian Anglophone Crisis."

73. Reuters, "Nigeria Says Won't Appeal Award of Oil-Rich Bakassi to Cameroon."

74. Reuters, "Nigeria Says Won't Appeal Award of Oil-Rich Bakassi to Cameroon."

75. Gitlitz, "Assessing the Cameroonian Anglophone Crisis."

76. Orock, "Cameroon's Separatist War," 14.

77. Nguonly, "Cameroonians Constitute New Wave of Md. Immigration."

78. Echitchi, "Legitimacy and Legality," 109.

79. Orock, "Cameroon's Separatist War," 11–12.

80. Takambou, "South Africa's Julius Malema."

81. Takambou, "South Africa's Julius Malema"; *Africa Intelligence*, "Malema's Economic Freedom Fighters Take Aim at French African Policy."

82. *Newsday Cameroon*, "Separatists Reject BAS Proposal to Swiss Government Over Separatist Conflict."

83. Reporters Without Borders (RTS), "Cameroonian President's Bodyguards Attack Reporter."

84. Reporters Without Borders (RTS), "Cameroonian President's Bodyguards Attack Reporter."

85. *African Courier*, "Cameroon President's Security Guards Convicted for Assault."

86. Human Rights Watch, "These Killings Can Be Stopped"; *BBC News*, "Cameroon Issues Arrest Warrants for Separatist Leaders."

87. France 24, "Cameroon Anglophone Separatist Leader Handed Life Sentence"; Africa News, "Cameroon Receives Separatist Leader."

88. Orock, "Cameroon's Separatist War."

89. US Department of Justice, "Three Maryland Residents Facing Federal Indictment"; Bagnetto, "Cameroon Anglophone Separatist 'Supporters' in US"; Wu, "From a Basement Near Baltimore."

90. Wu, "From a Basement Near Baltimore."

91. US Department of Justice, "Maryland Resident Sentenced to Over Five Years in Federal Prison for Illegally Transporting Firearms with Obliterated Serial Numbers and Smuggling Firearms to Nigeria," press release, May 26, 2023; "Rosedale Man Sentenced to 30 Months in Federal Prison for a Conspiracy to Smuggle Firearms and Other Military Items from the United States to Assist Separatists Fighting Against the Government of Cameroon," press release, May 17, 2023.

92. UNHCR, *Cameroonian Refugee Operational Update.*

93. Cole and Alvarez, "Blinken Says Immigration Challenges Facing the US."

94. Borger, "US to Send Asylum Seekers Home"; Human Rights Watch, *"How Can You Throw Us Back?";* Cahan, "The United States Has Failed Cameroonian Asylum-Seekers."

95. US Department of Homeland Security, "Secretary Mayorkas Designates Cameroon for Temporary Protected Status."

96. Husted, "Cameroon: Key Issues and U.S. Policy," Congressional Research Center Report, No. 46919, September 22, 2021.

97. Lionel, "US Withdraws Military Assistance to Cameroon."

98. Krippahl, "End of a 'Secret' German Military Mission in Cameroon."

99. *Africa Times,* "Swiss Step In to Mediate Cameroon's Anglophone Crisis." Despite receiving overwhelming backing from the international community, the Swiss-led mediation initiative quickly stalled without making any meaningful progress.

100. Reuters, "Cameroon Denies Seeking Help to Mediate Separatist Conflict after Canada Pledges Aid," January 23, 2023.

101. Foute, "After Weeks of Tensions, Macron Defuses the Situation with Biya."

102. Because of the war in Ukraine, France turned to Cameroon to replace its hydrocarbon imports from Russia, which were on the embargo. In 2022, Cameroon's exports to France increased fourfold compared to 2021, with crude oil alone accounting for 96 percent of the increase. See https://trendsnafrica.com/exponential-growth-in-cameroons-exports-to-france/.

103. Global Campaign for Peace and Justice in Cameroon, "Anglophone Crisis in Cameroon."

104. Robertson, "Glocalization," 26.

References

Africa Intelligence. "Malema's Economic Freedom Fighters Take Aim at French African Policy." May 25, 2022. https://www.africaintelligence.com/southern-africa-and-islands/2022/05/24/malema-s-economic-freedom-fighters-take-aim-at-french-african-policy,109786999-gra.

Africa News. "Cameroon Receives Separatist Leader, 46 Others Deported from Nigeria." January 29, 2018. https://www.africanews.com/2018/01/29/cameroon-receives-ambazonia-leader-46-others-deported-from-nigeria/.

Africa Times. "Swiss Step In to Mediate Cameroon's Anglophone Crisis." June 29, 2019. https://africatimes.com/2019/06/29/swiss-step-in-to-mediate-cameroons-anglophone-crisis.

African Courier. "Cameroon President's Security Guards Convicted for Assault in Switzerland," July 8, 2019. https://www.theafricancourier.de/news/africa/cameroon-presidents-security-guards-convicted-for-assault-in-switzerland/.

Ahmed, Dirdeiry M. *Boundaries and Secession in Africa and International Law.* New York: Cambridge University Press, 2015.

Amnesty International. "Cameroon: Arrests and Civil Society Bans Risk Inflaming Tensions in English-Speaking Regions. January 20, 2017. https://www.amnesty.org/en/latest/news/2017/01/cameroon-arrests-and-civil-society-bans-risk-inflaming-tensions-in-english-speaking-regions/.

Amnesty International. *Cameroon: Right Cause, Wrong Means: Human Rights Violated and Justice Denied in Cameroon's Fight against Boko Haram.* July 14, 2016. https://www.amnesty.org/en/wp-content/uploads/2021/05/AFR1742602016ENGLISH.pdf.

Anyefru, Emmanuel. "Paradoxes of Internationalization of the Anglophone Problem in Cameroon." *Journal of Contemporary African Studies* 28, no. 1 (2010): 85–101.

Awasom, Nicodemus Fru. "The Anglophone Problem in Cameroon Yesterday and Today in Search of a Definition." *Journal of the African Literature Association*, 2020.

———. "The Reunification Question in Cameroon History: Was the Bride an Enthusiastic or a Reluctant One?" *Africa Today* 47, no. 2 (Spring 2000): 91–119.

Baar, Vladimír. "Introduction." In *Perspectives on Secession: Theory and Case Studies,* edited by Martin Riegl and Bohumil Doboš. Cham: Springer, 2020.

Bagnetto, Laura Angela. "Cameroon Anglophone Separatist 'Supporters' in US Charged with Gun Smuggling." RFI, June 18, 2021. https://www.rfi.fr/en/africa/20210618-cameroon-anglophone-separatist-supporters-in-us-charged-with-gun-smuggling.

Bamfo, Napoleon. "The Menace of Secession in Africa and Why Governments Should Care: The Disparate Cases of Katanga, Biafra, South Sudan, and Azawad." *Global Journal of Human-Social Science* 12, no. 10 (2012): 37–48.

Bang, Henry Ngenyam, and Roland Azibo Balgah. "The Ramification of Cameroon's Anglophone Crisis: Conceptual Analysis of a Looming Complex Disaster Emergency." *Journal of International Humanitarian Action* 7, no. 6 (2022). https://jhumanitarianaction.springeropen.com/track/pdf/10.1186/s41018-022-00114-1.pdf.

BBC News. "Cameroon Issues Arrest Warrants for Separatist Leaders." November 9, 2017. https://www.bbc.com/news/world-africa-41928667.

Bedjaoui, Mohammed, ed. *International Law: Achievements and Prospects.* Paris: UNESCO, 1991.

Borger, Julian. "US to Send Asylum Seekers Home to Cameroon Despite 'Death Plane' Warnings." *Guardian*, November 10, 2020. https://www.theguardian.com/

us-news/2020/nov/09/us-to-send-asylum-seekers-home-to-cameroon-despite-death-plane-warnings.

Boudombo, Armand Mouko. "Why Separatists in Cameroon and Nigeria Have United." *BBC News*, October 23, 2021. https://www.bbc.com/news/world-africa-58726231.

Brown, Ed. "The United Nations, Self-Determination, State Failure and Secession." E-International Relations, May 29, 2022, 3.

Browne, Gareth. "Cameroon's Separatist Movement Is Going International." *Foreign Policy*, May 13, 2019. https://foreignpolicy.com/2019/05/13/cameroons-separatist-movement-is-going-international-ambazonia-military-forces-amf-anglophone-crisis/.

Buchanan, Allen. "Theories of Secession." *Philosophy and Public Affairs* 26, no. 1 (1997): 31–61.

Buchanan, Allen. "Toward a Theory of Secession." *Ethics* 101, no. 2 (1991): 322–42.

Cahan, Eli. "The United States Has Failed Cameroonian Asylum-Seekers." *Foreign Policy*, December 13, 2020. https://foreignpolicy.com/2020/12/13/united-states-cameroon-asylum-seekers-ice-deportation/.

Carsten, Paul, and Aaron Ross. "Exclusive: Cameroonian Troops Entered Nigeria Without Seeking Authorization, Sources in Nigeria Say." Reuters, December 20, 2017. https://www.reuters.com/article/us-cameroon-separatists-nigeria-idUSKBN1EE2II.

Cascais, Antonio. "Separatism in Cameroon: 5 Years of Violent Civil War." *Deutsche Welle* (DW). October 2021. https://www.dw.com/en/separatism-in-cameroon-5-years-of-violent-civil-war/a-59369417.

Chiang, Frank. *The One-China Policy: State, Sovereignty, and Taiwan's International Legal Status*. Amsterdam: Elsevier, 2018.

Cole, Devan, and Priscilla Alvarez. "Blinken Says Immigration Challenges Facing the US at the Southern Border Are Beyond Anything That Anyone Has Seen Before." CNN, June 9, 2022. https://edition.cnn.com/2022/06/08/politics/antony-blinken-immigration-challenges-summit-of-americas-cnntv/index.html.

Craig, Jess. "Caught in the Middle: Peace Activists in Cameroon Try to End a Brutal War." *New Humanitarian*, June 1, 2021. https://www.thenewhumanitarian.org/news-feature/2021/6/1/peace-activists-in-cameroon-try-to-end-a-brutal-war.

———. "How an 'Execution-Style' Massacre Unfolded in Cameroon." *New Humanitarian*, March 3, 2020. https://www.thenewhumanitarian.org/analysis/2020/03/03/Cameroon-Ambazonia-Ngarbuh-massacre.

Crawford, James. *The Creation of States in International Law*. 2nd ed. Oxford: Oxford University Press, 2006.

Deltombe, Thomas. "The Forgotten Cameroon War." *Jacobin*, December 10, 2016. https://jacobin.com/2016/12/cameroon-france-colonialism-war-resistance.

de Vries, Lotje, Pierre Engelbert, and Mareike Schomerus, eds. *Secessionism in African Politics*. Freiburg: Palgrave Macmillan, 2019.

Echitchi, Raymond. "Legitimacy and Legality in National Identity Construction—A Study of Southern Cameroons' Secessionist Discourse." *International Journal of Language & Law* 10 (2021): 101–11.

Ekeke, Alex Cyril, and Nombulelo Lubisi. "Secession in Africa: An African Union Dilemma." *African Security Review* 28, no. 3–4 (2019): 245–60.

Eyo, Charles. "Cameroonian Militants Invade Nigeria, Gun Down 20." *Daily Trust,* May 29, 2022.

Fochingong, Charles C. "Exploring the Politics of Identity and Ethnicity in State Reconstruction in Cameroon." *Social Identities* 11, no. 4 (2005): 363–80.

Foute, Franck. "Cameroon: After a Week of Tensions, Macron Defuses the Situation with Biya." March 12, 2020. https://www.theafricareport.com/24498/cameroon-after-a-week-of-tensions-macron-defuses-the-situation-with-biya/.

France 24. "Cameroon Anglophone Separatist Leader Handed Life Sentence." August 20, 2019. https://www.france24.com/en/20190820-cameroon-anglophone-separatist-leader-life-sentence-lawyers.

Gitlitz, Sam. "Assessing the Cameroonian Anglophone Crisis and Potential Impacts of US Inaction." *Real Clear Defense,* March 21, 2022. https://www.realcleardefense.com/articles/2022/03/21/asse.

Global Campaign for Peace and Justice in Cameroon. "Anglophone Crisis in Cameroon: A Submission of Evidence to the International Relations and Defence Committee." UK Parliament, Written evidence (ZAF0028). March 19, 2020. https://committees.parliament.uk/writtenevidence/768/html/.

Guardian. "Cameroon's Separatist Conflict Spills Across Nigerian Frontier." AFP, March 18, 2022. https://guardian.ng/news/cameroons-separatist-conflict-spills-across-nigerian-frontier/.

Hechter, Michael. "The Dynamics of Secession." *Acta Sociologica* 35, no. 4 (1992).

Human Rights Watch. *"How Can You Throw Us Back?" Asylum Seekers Abused in the US and Deported to Harm in Cameroon.* February 10, 2022. https://www.hrw.org/sites/default/files/media_2022/03/us_cameroon0222_web.pdf.

———. "'These Killings Can Be Stopped': Abuses by Government and Separatist Groups in Cameroon's Anglophone Regions." July 19, 2018. https://www.hrw.org/report/2018/07/19/these-killings-can-be-stopped/abuses-government-and-separatist-groups-cameroons.

International Crisis Group. "Cameroon Needs an African Cup Ceasefire." January 7, 2022. https://www.crisisgroup.org/africa/central-africa/cameroon/cameroon-needs-african-cup-ceasefire.

———. *Cameroon's Anglophone Crisis at the Crossroads.* Africa Report No. 250. August 2, 2017.

Jua, Nantang, and Piet Konings. "Occupation of Public Space Anglophone Nationalism in Cameroon." *Cahiers d'études africaines* 44, no. 175 (2004): 609–33.

Kenfo, Joseph Tchinda. "Le 'Problème Anglophone' au Cameroun: La réponse par le processus participatif au Développement Territorial." *Thinking Africa,*

NDR no. 29 (July 1997). https://www.thinkingafrica.org/V2/wp-content/uploads/2017/07/ndr-29-cameroun.pdf.

Kindzeka, Moki Edwin. "Cameroon: Separatists, Nigerian Militants Paralyze Border." *VOA News*, April 25, 2022. https://www.voanews.com/a/cameroon-separatists-nigerian-militants-paralyze-border/6543991.html.

Konings, Piet, and Francis B. Nyamnjoh. "The Anglophone Problem in Cameroon." *Journal of Modern African Studies* 35, no. 2 (1997): 207–29.

———. *Negotiating an Anglophone Identity. A Study of the Politics of Recognition and Representation in Cameroon.* Leiden: Brill, 2003.

Krippahl, Cristina. "End of a 'Secret' German Military Mission in Cameroon." *Deutsche Welle* (DW), July 17, 2019. https://www.dw.com/en/end-of-a-secret-german-military-mission-in-cameroon/a-49610889.

Kučera, Josef. "Mid-Rainy-Season Night's Dream: Cyber-Secessionism in Cameroon, 2016–2018." In *Perspectives on Secession: Theory and Case Studies*, edited by Martin Riegl and Bohumil Doboš, 109–24. Cham: Springer, 2020.

Lawal, Nurudeen. "Cameroonian Militants Invade Nigeria, Gun Down 20 in Cross River." *Legit*, May 30, 2022.

Lee, Alexander, and Kenneth A. Schultz. "Comparing British and French. Colonial Legacies: A Discontinuity Analysis of Cameroon." *Quarterly Journal of Political Science* 7, no. 4 (2012): 365–410.

Lionel, Ekene. "US Withdraws Military Assistance to Cameroon, Citing Allegations of Human Rights Violations." Military Africa, November 3, 2020. https://www.military.africa/2019/02/u-s-withdraws-military-assistance-to-cameroon-citing-allegations-of-human-rights-violations/.

Lunn, Jon, and Louisa Brooke-Holland. *The Anglophone Crisis: April 2019 Update.* Briefing Paper No. 8331. UK House of Commons, April 17, 2019.

Mamdani, Mahmood. *Citizen and Subject: Contemporary Africa and the Legacy of Late Colonialism.* Princeton, NJ: Princeton University Press, 1998.

Moassab, Andréia. "Globalization, Neo-Colonization and Urbanization in Africa." December 11, 2022. https://www.buala.org/en/city/globalization-neo-colonization-and-urbanization-in-africa.

Mousbaou, Atcha Boukari. "The Rise of Secession Movements in West Africa and Its Security Impact on the Region." US Defense Technical Information Center, 2018.

Mutah, Jude. "Global Responses to Cameroon's Anglophone Crisis: The Inadequate International Efforts to End the World's Most Neglected Conflict." *SAIS Review of International Affairs*, November 8, 2022. https://saisreview.sais.jhu.edu/cameroon-anglophone-crisis-global-response.

Newsday Cameroon. "Separatists Reject BAS Proposal to Swiss Government Over Separatist Conflict." July 10, 2019. https://newsdaycameroon.wordpress.com/2019/07/10/separatists-reject-bas-proposal-to-swiss-government-over-separatist-conflict/.

Nguonly, Esther A. "Cameroonians Constitute New Wave of Md. Immigration." Capital News Service (CPS) Maryland, 2007. https://cnsmaryland.org/2007/04/20/cameroonians-constitute-new-wave-of-md-immigration/.

Norwegian Refugee Council (NRC). "Cameroon Tops List of Most Neglected Crises." June 4, 2019. https://www.nrc.no/news/2019/june/cameroon-tops-list-of-most-neglected-crises/.

Office of the Special Representative of the United Nations Secretary-General for Children and Armed Conflict. https://childrenandarmedconflict.un.org/where-we-work/cameroon/.

O'Grady, Siobhán. "Divided by Language: Cameroon's Crackdown on Its English-Speaking Minority Is Fueling Support for a Secessionist Movement." *Washington Post*, February 5, 2019. https://www.washingtonpost.com/graphics/2019/world/cameroon-anglophone-crisis/.

Orock, Rogers. "Cameroon's Separatist War: Anglophone Grievances and Its Diaspora" *Policy Insights*, no. 117 (August 2021).

Pavkovic, Aleksandar, and Peter Radan, eds. *On The Way to Statehood: Secession and Globalization*. Aldershot: Ashgate, 2008.

Pinto, Teresa Nogueira. "In Cameroon, Centralization Leads to Strife. GIS Report, August 14, 2023. https://www.gisreportsonline.com/r/cameroon-anglophone-crisis/.

Reporters Without Borders (RTS). "Cameroonian President's Bodyguards Attack Reporter Outside Geneva Hotel." July 1, 2019. https://rsf.org/en/cameroonian-president-s-bodyguards-attack-reporter-outside-geneva-hotel.

Reuters. "Five Military Police Killed in Western Cameroon, Says Regional Governor." Reuters, June 8, 2022. https://www.reuters.com/news/picture/five-military-police-killed-in-western-c-idUSKBN2NP0Z0.

———. "Nigeria Says Won't Appeal Award of Oil-Rich Bakassi to Cameroon." Reuters, October 9, 2012. https://www.reuters.com/article/ozatp-nigeria-cameroon-bakassi-20121009-idAFJOE89801320121009.

———. "Nigeria Senate Urges Appeal of Cameroon Bakassi Award." Reuters, September 26, 2012. https://www.reuters.com/article/us-nigeria-bakassi-id USBRE88P1JJ20120926.

Robertson, Roland. "Globalisation or Glocalisation?" *Journal of International Communication* 1, no. 1 (1994): 38–39.

———. "Glocalization: Time-Space and Homogeneity-Heterogeneity." In *Global Modernities*, edited by Mike Featherstone, Scott Lash, and Roland Robertson, 25–44. London: Sage, 1995.

Samah, Walters T. "France and Francophone Africa: Can the New Scramble for Africa Put an End to an Enduring Zero-Sum Relationship?" In *Issues of Governance, Security and Development in Contemporary Africa*, edited by M. S. Camara, A. Hailu, and S. O. Abidde, chapter 4. Lanham: Rowman & Littlefield, 2023.

Santos, Milton. *Toward an Other Globalization: From the Single Thought to Universal Conscience*. Cham: Springer, 2017.

Schaeffer, Robert K. "Secession and Separatism." In *Encyclopedia of Violence, Peace, & Conflict*. 2nd ed. 2008. https://www.sciencedirect.com/topics/social-sciences/secession.

Shamsuddoha, Mohammad. "Glocalization: A Theoretical Analysis." Conference of South Asian Management Forum, February 25, 2009.

Shaw, Malcolm. *Title to Territory in Africa: International Legal Issues*. Oxford: Oxford University Press, 1986.

Shibayan, Dyepkazah. "Senator Accuses Cameroon Separatist Group of Attacking Taraba Village." *Cable*, November 17, 2021. https://www.thecable.ng/senator-alleges-cameroon-separatist-group-killed-village-head-in-taraba.

Spencer, Metta, and Rennison Lalgee. "Conflict Analysis." In *Encyclopedia of Violence, Peace, & Conflict*, 3rd ed. 2022. https://www.sciencedirect.com/topics/social-sciences/secession.

Stark, Frank M. "Theories of Contemporary State Formation in Africa: A Reassessment." *Journal of Modern African Studies* 24, no. 2 (June 1986): 335–47.

Swyngedouw, Erik. "Globalisation or 'Glocalisation'? Networks, Territories and Rescaling." *Cambridge Review of International Affairs* 17, no. 1 (2004): 25–48.

Takambou, Mimi Mefo. "South Africa's Julius Malema, Says Cameroonians Should Rise Against France's Puppet, Paul Biya." *Mimi Memo Info*, October 26, 2020. https://mimimefoinfos.com/south-africas-julius-malema-says-cameroonians-should-rise-against-frances-puppet-paul-biya/.

Umoru, Henry. "Cameroonian Separatists Invade Taraba Community, Kill People, Senate Raises the Alarm." *Vanguard*, November 17, 2021. https://www.vanguardngr.com/2021/11/cameroonian-separatists-invade-taraba-community-kill-people-senate-raises-alarm/.

United Nations High Commission for Refugees (UNHCR). *Cameroonian Refugee Operational Update*. April 2022. file:///C:/Users/walte/Downloads/UNHCR%20Nigeria%20Cameroonian%20Refugees%20Operational%20Update%20April%202022.pdf.

US Department of Justice. "Three Maryland Residents Facing Federal Indictment for Attempting to Illegally Export Arms and Ammunitions to Nigeria." Press release. August 27, 2021.

———. "Rosedale Man Sentenced to 30 Months in Federal Prison for a Conspiracy to Smuggle Firearms and Other Military Items from the United States to Assist Separatists Fighting Against the Government of Cameroon." Press release. May 17, 2023.

———. "Maryland Resident Sentenced to Over Five Years in Federal Prison for Illegally Transporting Firearms with Obliterated Serial Numbers and Smuggling Firearms to Nigeria." Press release. May 26, 2023.

US Department of Homeland Security. "Secretary Mayorkas Designates Cameroon for Temporary Protected Status for 18 Months." Press release. April 15, 2022.

Willis, Roxana, Joseph McAulay, Ndjodi Ndeunyema, and James Angove. *Human Rights Abuses in the Cameroon Anglophone Crisis.* Report submitted to UK Parliament. October 30, 2019.

Wu, Daniel. "From a Basement Near Baltimore, He Plotted to Smuggle Guns to Cameroon." *Washington Post*, October 6, 2022. https://www.washingtonpost.com/dc-md-va/2022/10/06/cameroon-gun-smuggling-st-michael/.

3

Domestic and External Militarization under Democratic Governance

The Case of Sierra Leone

Abu Bakarr Bah and Kassandra Gonzalez

Introduction: Democracy, Militarization, and Accountability

As it was amply pointed out and discussed at the workshop on "Security Threats, Militarization and the Democratic Accountability of the Use of Military Force" at the German Institute of Global and Areas Studies (GIGA), democracies are assumed to be peaceful countries where the rule of law is upheld, and all individual and sectional political grievances are resolved through the courts and the electoral process.[1] As such, the use of force to address domestic problems is limited to normal policing. While this is somehow true, there are a whole lot of democracies where there are ongoing or residual violence that continues to threaten the state and the rule of law.[2] Under such conditions, regular policing becomes ineffective in maintaining law and order within the rule of law. In such situations, democratic countries often resort to using the military to restore order and, in some cases, transform a segment of the police into a paramilitary force. In other cases, new democracies may be plagued by authoritarian tendencies, which may lead the elected government to use the military and special police units to pacify opposition groups, especially when the opposition alleges electoral fraud and takes a confrontational position against the government.[3]

All of these lead to what has been viewed as militarization of governance, and in essence militarization of the state not just for external purposes but for domestic reasons as well. These realities have led to a growing scholarly interest in the interrelations between national security threats, militarization of security policy, and democratic accountability. This relationship evokes three critical questions: a) Why and under which circumstances do democratic governments mobilize the military to counter security threats? b) How do democratic governments legitimize the military's deployment against external and/or domestic threats? and c) What are the effects of militarization on the democratic accountability in the use of military force? While there are huge differences among democracies in terms of quality and forms of security threats, these questions are insightful and relevant in both old and new democracies. Even more, there is an interesting intersection of domestic and external factors in the way militarization happens in new democracies, especially in war-torn countries such as Sierra Leone.

Domestically, militarization is the increasing use of military and paramilitary force for governance and the process of increasing the legitimacy of using such force through the frames of national emergency and national security. Too often legitimacy is socially constructed by accentuating social beliefs about the role of force in human affairs, the nature and threat of the adversary, the efficacy of force, and claims to Westphalian state authority.[4] In countries plagued by civil war, especially in Africa, militarization also happens through the application of the doctrine of the Responsibility to Protect (R2P).[5] Militarization is not only contentiously discursive, but it also makes armed forces and combatants essential to the social experience and collective identity of the state and factions within the state.[6] Militarization of the state, and the society at large, rests on material and political interests of the elite that require the mobilization of resources and legitimizing the use of force.[7] In that sense, the military is not necessarily the exclusive bearer of militarization, as domestic political elites, insurgents, and in some cases international actors shape the state and the forms of violence that are used and/or accepted.[8] Militarization dovetails with securitization of the state, which often claims the exclusive authority to use force.[9] Securitization frames acute political, social, and economic issues into national security problems that require the application of major force by the state.[10]

The use of military and/or paramilitary forces are problematic for democracies because of the limited abilities of such forces to operate under a civilian system of rule of law. The continued use of military and/or paramilitary forces to maintain law and order is a form of militarization that not only can undermine the rule of law, but also threaten democracy.[11] This is especially true in new democracies with recent histories of authoritarian rule, and in worst cases civil war. Sierra Leone has been a notable case of the fusion of democracy and militarization because of its brutal civil war on the one hand and the robust international intervention and vibrant civil society on the other hand.[12] Moreover, the massive international intervention in the Sierra Leone civil war brings a critical external element to militarization in Sierra Leone, especially during the wartime democracy. During this period, militarization was glocal in nature, as domestic governance and security norms were fused with external international norms of human security through the doctrine of R2P. Sierra Leone has also had other periods of democracy that are plagued by its authoritarian legacies. Many other African countries have been faced with the challenge of addressing national security threats within a system of democracy. In Nigeria, for example, elected governments have been dealing with insurgencies by minority groups in the Niger Delta fighting for environmental and economic justice and Boko Haram jihadism in the northern part of the country waging an ideological war.[13] In Kenya, too, successive elected governments have been fighting terrorism associated with Al Shabab. Kenyan governments have also been dealing with major political violence associated with disputed election results and ethnic political grievances.[14] Mali has also been plagued by a major insurgency by the Tuareg minority seeking political autonomy, which has now been hijacked by jihadists in the aftermath of the overthrow of Muammar Gaddafi in Libya. The political crisis eventually led to the collapse of democracy in Mali as the military took power. Other governments elected in quasi-free elections, such as in Guinea, Niger, and Burkina Faso, have also been dealing with the terrorism and most recently military coups.

In the case of Sierra Leone, there have been several instances of major security challenges and militarization within the context of democracy. Sierra Leone actually has three periods of democracy. These are a) the governments that emerged out of decolonization (1961–1978), the elected government that emerged during the civil war (1996–2002), and the postwar elected governments, which started in 2002.[15] Each of these has militarized security policies as they respond to varying kinds of security challenges. While these represent distinct periods, there is a clear historical continuity in the ways security threats emerge and the way the governments respond. The historical continuities and specificities in the militarization and the democratization processes in Sierra Leone point to important issues in the way we conceptualize militarization. Notably, militarization in Sierra Leone is shaped by domestic and external factors, which are best captured through the glocalization frame.

The notion of glocalization, which is fairly new, seeks to show how domestic and external factors are fused in a way that produces new dynamics. At its core, glocalization has been used as a critique of the concept of globalization, which has been the primary way of discussing the way countries are connected to the international system, in addition to the world system theory.[16] The concept of glocalization comes out as a critique of the homogenization of Western values and practices under globalization.[17] Though the concept of glocalization has been used in studies of countries, social movements, culture, and globalization generally, it is hardly used in relation to security issues.[18] Most of the studies of the state in international and global terms tend to focus on economic, migration, cultural, and geopolitical issues.[19] However, the state itself as an object of security discourse has not received proper attention from a glocalization perspective. Indeed, Samuel Marfo et al. tried "to make a case for a 'glocalized peace and security architecture,' a comprehensive peace and security design which is both domestically or inward-looking relevant and internationally or outside-looking practicable."[20] Their glocalized peace and security architecture "attempts to suggest an approach which can foster a peaceful co-existence among states without necessarily endangering domestic politics in a seemingly chaotic global environment."[21] This chapter approaches glocalization not so much from an interstate relations angle, but in terms of how the security of African states is shaped by the fusion of domestic and external factors. As this chapter shows, external factors have always shaped the state and its use of force in Sierra Leone. At its core, the state in Sierra Leone is the by-product of colonialism. Its institutional setups, including the military and politics, are rooted in the British colonial system. At the same time, the postcolonial political culture and the application of power are imbued in domestic issues such as poor leadership, corruption, ethnicity, and poverty.[22] As such, the militarization of the state in Sierra Leone is the result of the unique fusion of domestic and external factors that shapes the nature of power and the use of violence.

Security Threats under Elected Governments: Glocal Roots and Continuities

Security threats against the government and state have persisted throughout Sierra Leone's history. Those threats have existed against the one-party regime, military juntas, and the elected governments that have ruled the country since independence from British colonial rule in 1961.[23] The security threats under elected governments are of particular interest because the conventional assumption is that democratic systems of rule would resolve political conflicts through the rule of law and electoral process. In Sierra Leone, this has rarely been the case, as violence is often used to achieve political goals even when there is a system of electoral democracy in place. The major forms of security threats that have occurred in Sierra Leone are military coups, violent demonstrations, periodic election violence, and armed rebellion.[24] Each of these threats are rooted in the failures of the governments to reduce poverty and enhance economic and social well-being and in the propensity of elected governments to engage in ethnic and regional marginalization through nepotism and corruption.[25] These factors are compounded by the colonial roots of the state, which not only perpetuate dependency but also entrench winner-takes-all and authoritarian institutions of power.[26] Sierra Leone has had three periods of democracy. Each of these democracies has been challenged by one or more of the above security threats under conditions that are glocal in nature.

ELECTED GOVERNMENT DURING THE IMMEDIATE POSTCOLONIAL ERA (1961–1978)

Sierra Leone's first democracy emerged out of the end of British colonial rule. When Sierra Leone gained independence in 1961, the country had a parliamentary democracy along the British parliamentary model. The Sierra Leone People's Party (SLPP) formed the majority in parliament with its leader, Milton Margai, serving as prime minister. As a member of the British Commonwealth, the British monarch was the ceremonial head of state represented in Sierra Leone by the governor-general. The SLPP lost power to the opposition All People's Congress (APC) in 1967. The SLPP government was first led by Milton Margai and later succeeded by his brother Albert Margai, who served as prime minister from April 1964 to March 1967. The key problem during this phase of democracy was the deep ethnic and regional divide between the SLPP and the APC. The SLPP was heavily dominated by Mendes in the south, while the APC was mainly dominated by the Limba and Temne in the north. This ethnic-cum-regional divide made elections very violent.[27] During this period, the external problems of the colonial roots of the state fused with domestic systems of patrimonialism to produce a toxic winner-takes-all ethnic political system.[28]

The ethnic and regional divide significantly impacted the military. Increasingly, the military was drawn into politics because of the nepotism in the way military officers were selected and promoted. Moreover, as elections became violent and accusation of election rigging grew, so did the military become tempted to intervene. The political crisis worsened with the March 1967 elections as both SLPP and APC claimed to have won amid allegations of violence and election rigging. APC, which was led by Siaka Stevens, prevailed in the dispute over the election result. Siaka Stevens was sworn in as prime minister by the governor-general but was immediately removed by the military. The coup was led by Brigadier David Lansana, who was force commander of the Sierra Leone military. The coup was directly related to the ethnic politics that had plagued democracy in Sierra Leone.[29]

The 1967 election was fought along ethnic-cum-regional lines. SLPP was supported by southerners, especially the Mende people. Similarly, APC was supported by northerners, especially the Temne and Limba people. Lansana's action was seen as a clear effort to promote the interest of southerners, most notably the Mende. Lansana himself was a Mende and a key member of the southern power elite, which had dominated Sierra Leone under SLPP rule. Lansana argued that a winner should not be declared until the House of Chiefs members had been elected. The expectation was that members of the House of Chiefs would support the SLPP and thereby guarantee an SLPP win. The ethnic feud and involvement of the military intensified. Within a few days, Lansana was overthrown by military officers, and Andrew Juxon-Smith was installed as head of the National Reformation Council (NRC) military regime. Juxon-Smith suspended the constitution and became interested in maintaining a military regime. However, the ethnic political feud continued within the military and between the SLPP and the APC. In April 1968, Juxon-Smith was overthrown in a coup led by John Amadu Bangura. Bangura restored civilian rule and installed Stevens as prime minister.[30] This coup was seen as a direct effort to give power to the APC and northerners. Bangura was a northerner and an ally of Stevens, who was living in exile in Guinea following the Lansana coup. Though democracy was restored, security threats continued to grow as a result of the fusion of ethnic politics and politicization of the military. The net result was growing militarization of security policies and degeneration into one-party dictatorship in 1978.[31] Three key security threats continued to typify Sierra Leone's first democracy, namely political violence, politization of the military, and growing social discontent.

First was the ongoing political violence between APC and SLPP, especially during the 1973 election and use of the military and paramilitary forces to suppress the opposition. Allegations of intimidation and arbitrary arrests continued to create a tense political climate between the APC and SLPP. In fact, the SLPP boycotted the 1973 elections because of political violence. The same problems continued into the 1977 election. The 1977 election was held in the aftermath of mass student riots and political violence between APC and SLPP.[32] All of these forms of violence posed security threats to the government.

The second threat was the politicization of the military and the growing threats of military coups.[33] The threat of coups led the government to further politicize the military through ethnically driven appointments to leadership positions and the co-optation and purging of military leaders by the APC. The military coups that took place in 1967 and 1968 significantly transformed the military. The military leaders were reassigned and removed based on ethnic political consideration. Others were executed for trying to overthrow the government. The most drastic measure by the APC government was the execution of military officers suspected of plotting coups. In 1970, Brigadier John Amadu Bangura was executed for plotting to overthrow Siaka Stevens. The execution of Bangura pointed to a very hard-line securitization policy, especially given the fact that it was Bangura who installed Stevens after he was overthrown by Lansana. Bangura was actually first arrested for political reasons by the SLPP just before the 1967 elections. In 1975, David Lansana was also executed along with several others for plotting to overthrow the government.

The third threat was growing social discontent with the political, economic, and social conditions of the country. Students at Fourah Bay College were exceptionally active in challenging the government through mass demonstrations.[34] The 1977 student demonstration was a major challenge to the government. It not only disrupted daily operations of the state, but also seriously undermined the legitimacy of the government. Also, it fed into the political violence between opposition and government supporters. More importantly, it drew the military further into politics as the military was deployed to suppress the demonstration. In fact, many of the leaders of the Revolutionary United Front (RUF) rebellion during the 1990s were associated with the student demonstrations that took place in the 1970s and 1980s.

Indeed, all of these factors were directly tied to domestic political and social issues. However, the structural condition for ethnic politics came out of colonial rule.[35] In that sense, security threats and militarization were tied to the glocal dynamics of the state. The net result of the security threats and corresponding militarization was the collapse of democracy. Sierra Leone quickly slipped into one-party rule, which ended in a civil war. In 1971, the APC government of Stevens ended the parliamentary democracy. Sierra Leone declared a republic, which removed the office of governor-general. Stevens then became an executive president. While the declaration of a republic was consistent with the decolonization vision of Africa, the establishment of an executive president was seen as a major step toward APC monopolization of power and suppression of political opposition. In 1978, the APC government introduced a new constitution that made Sierra Leone a one-party state under APC rule. The new constitution was rubber-stamped in a dubious referendum opposed by the political opposition. Since then, Sierra Leone has slipped into an authoritarian rule characterized by prebendalism and nepotism.[36] Stevens filled the military with co-ethnic allies and established a paramilitary police forces known as the Special Security Division (SSD). The SSD was loyal to Stevens and led by co-ethnic allies. In 1985 Stevens stepped down at the age of eighty-three and handed power to Major General Joseph Saidu Momoh, who was the head of the military. Momoh was a handpicked co-ethnic successor to ensure that Stevens and the APC one-party regime remained protected. The APC regime led by Momoh was challenged in 1991 by the RUF rebellion and eventually removed from power through a military coup in 1992.

WARTIME DEMOCRACY (1996–2002)

The second democracy era in Sierra Leone occurred in the midst of a civil war (1991–2002). This turbulent democracy started in 1996 with the election of Ahmed Tejan Kabbah as president. However, Kabbah was overthrown in May 1997 by the military in connivance with the RUF rebels. The military junta that took over was led by Johnny Paul Koroma, but the junta failed to get international recognition or widespread domestic support. As such, a concerted international military intervention led to the removal of the military junta in March 1998.[37] Kabbah was immediately restored to power, but the junta and the RUF continued to wage war against the Kabbah government. The war ended in 2002 after the RUF leader was captured and the group pacified by the international military intervention in support of the elected government. The first postwar election was held in 2002.

The massive international military intervention points to the glocalized nature of militarization in Sierra Leone. Domestic militarization occurred through the ethnicization of politics, while international militarization occurred through international military intervention. Domestic militarization dovetailed with state decay, while international militarization was propelled by state collapse.[38] In this sense, militarization in Sierra Leone points to the intersection of domestic and external issues, akin to the way the discourse of glocalization captures the fusion of domestic and global issues.[39]

The Kabbah government was faced with two major national security threats throughout its first term in office, which led to significant international intervention. The first threat was the ongoing civil war, which the RUF started against the APC government in 1991 and continued to wage against the military government that overthrew the APC in 1992 and the elected government of Kabbah that came to power in 1996. The second major threat was the disloyalty of the military and its connivance with the RUF. As such, the Kabbah government was under constant threats from both the RUF and renegade soldiers of the defunct Sierra Leone Army. Throughout this period, the Kabbah government was defended against both the RUF and the Sierra Leone military by the Civil Defense Forces (CDF, also known as Kamajor) and the international intervention forces, notably Economic Community of West African States Monitoring Group (ECOMOG) and later United Nations Mission in Sierra Leone (UNAMSIL).[40] During this period, Sierra Leone's national security became a regional security issue and eventually a grave human security issue of international significance. This led to the application of the R2P doctrine through military humanitarianism, which became another mode of militarization—albeit a largely benevolent one.[41]

The civil war constituted an existential threat to the elected government because RUF refused to participate in the 1996 elections and vowed to overthrow the government and take over power. The RUF rebellion was a direct response to the oppressive and corrupt APC regime, which exploited nepotism and ethnicity to maintain its rule. The RUF had well-founded grievances against the APC one-party regime. However, the RUF itself became a problem rather than a solution to the political, economic, and social problems of Sierra Leone. The RUF refused to participate in multiparty elections until it was militarily pacified and turned into a moribund organization. Right after the RUF launched its armed campaign against the APC regime, the government adopted a new constitution in September 1991, which lifted the ban on opposition political parties. However, this was largely seen as a tactic by the APC to quell the rebellion and other pro-democracy demands. More importantly, the 1992 military coup that ousted the APC stalled any progress toward multiparty democracy. At the same time, RUF rejected the military regime and reaffirmed its commitment to the armed struggle to take power. The National Provisional Ruling Council (NPRC) regime, led by Captain Valentine Strasser, called on the RUF to negotiate a peaceful settlement to the conflict but also vigorously fought the RUF. As the war dragged on, demands for multiparty democracy increased. Pro-democracy activists and civil society organizations along with international pressure forced the military government to allow a multiparty election in 1996.

However, the leadership of the NPRC military regime was actually split as to whether to allow multiparty democracy. One faction of the regime argued against holding multiparty elections until the RUF was defeated or accepted a peaceful resolution of the conflict. In January 1996, the faction opposed to elections actually deposed Strasser in a palace coup and replaced him with Julius Maada Bio.[42] Bio called for more negotiation with RUF and a postponement of the election, which was scheduled for February 1996. However, intense international pressure along with a vibrant civil society movement forced Bio to allow the election. The election was organized under the leadership of James Jonnah, who was a former under-secretary general at the United Nations (UN) and a highly respected Sierra Leonean. The critical issue for the elected government was the context within which it had come to power, namely an unresolved civil war that was increasingly seen as a regional security problem. The government tried to defeat the RUF and negotiate a peaceful agreement, but all of that failed. The threat only ended when Foday Sankoh was finally captured in Freetown and the RUF pacified by international forces, which paved the way for negotiation with a new breed of RUF commanders, notably Issa Sesay.

With respect to the Sierra Leone military, the threat was simultaneously latent and potent. On the one hand, the military was in direct proximity to and interaction with the government, while on the other hand a significant number of soldiers at the battlefront were in direct interaction with the RUF. Most of those soldiers became double agents, who were formally members of the military but covertly collaborating with the RUF in what has been dubbed Sobel (i.e., soldier during the day, but rebel during the night).[43] The disloyalty of the military toward the elected government is rooted in both the military's prior involvement in politics under the military regime that was forced to hand over power and the deplorable conditions at the battlefront.

As already noted, the context in which the Kabbah government came to power created deep mistrust within the military. Kabbah was not really able to assert control over the military. In fact, he relied heavily on the protection of the Kamajor and the international troops in the country. This not only alienated the military, but more importantly hindered the establishment of effective civilian control over the military. As such, the Kabbah government was always vulnerable to the possibility of a military coup, which actually happened in 1997. After international forces ousted the military junta from Freetown and restored Kabbah to power, the renegade military retreated to the countryside and continued to collaborate with the RUF with the goal of taking power. This threat only ended with the pacification of the RUF by international forces.[44]

The Sierra Leone military was not able to defeat the RUF, as it was not well trained or equipped to defend the country against a military attack. As such, Sierra Leone had to rely on external military help. The first help came from neighboring Guinea. Guinean help evolved into Economic Community of West African States (ECOWAS) intervention under Nigerian leadership and eventually into a United Nations military mission. Sierra Leone also hired private military contractors, such as Executive Outcomes, based in South Africa, and received occasional help from the British government. Until 1997, however, external help was limited and intermittent. The Sierra Leone military took the brunt of the initial fighting, even though it was ill prepared. It suffered huge casualties, leading to low morale and disgruntlement about why soldiers were fighting under poor conditions to support a corrupt regime. That disgruntlement resulted in the 1992 military coup that ousted the APC.

When Kabbah came to power in 1996, the RUF had been significantly weakened by private military contractors and ECOWAS forces fighting in support of the government. The RUF signed the Abidjan Peace Agreement, which eased the pressure and gave it room to rebuild. As the Abidjan Peace Accord fell apart, the RUF became stronger while the Sierra Leone military continued to be weak. Members of the Sierra Leone military not only began to question the rationale for fighting on behalf of elitist and corrupt politicians, but also became involved in diamond mining. Soldiers responded to the poor conditions of service by becoming clandestine diamond miners and entrepreneurs in concert with the RUF and Charles Taylor in Liberia. In the end, the renegade military became vested in protecting the interests of its members. Economically, the war had become lucrative as soldiers increasingly controlled diamonds mines. They were also interested in protecting their members from prosecution for war crimes. The Sierra Leone military was notorious for crimes committed under the military regime and at the battlefronts. Gaining power became an existential goal to ensure that its members would be not be prosecuted for treason, war crimes, and other human rights violations.

Overall, the second era of democracy experienced the greatest security threat. In fact, the elected government was under constant threat throughout this period. This reality was directly connected to the context in which the second democracy era emerged, namely an armed rebellion that effectively reduced the country to a failed state. It is also interesting to note that the response to the security threat was largely determined by the international actors who intervened in the conflict, making the Sierra Leone a glocalized security situation. While the wartime era was generally a period of democracy, it was really an odd kind of democracy because the country was in a state of collapse, and the elected government did not have control over a significant part of the country. Sierra Leone virtually depended on international military and humanitarian assistance. Military policies were dictated by the intervening powers under the frames of R2P and global liberal governance.[45] The growing involvement of regional and UN forces shows not only the external influences on the state, but also the glocalized nature of militarization as domestic issues of governance were woven with regional security and international principles on human security.

Postwar Elected Governments

The third era of democracy started in 2002 with the end of the war and the 2002 elections. Since then, elections have been held in 2007, 2012, 2018, and 2023. Security threats were significantly reduced during the early part of the postwar period. However, there have been troubling cases of election violence and a coup plot associated with ethnic and regional divides as well as efforts to infuse nepotism and tribalism into the military. In many ways, Sierra Leone's postwar democracy is looking very much like the democracy of the 1960s. So far, there have been three vivid forms of threats that are eroding the current democracy. These are a) election-related violence, b) violent demonstrations by opposition parties and their violent suppression by the government, and c) prosecution of opposition politicians, including allegations of an attempted coup. Whether the current democracy will mature into a truly consolidated democracy or degenerate into authoritarian rule is an open question. The lack of credibility in the 2023 election and the alleged coup plot point to significant erosion of democracy, if not its actual collapse.

On the surface, the postwar elections in Sierra Leone are a promising manifestation of democracy because each of the two major political parties has been able to gain power through the electoral process. Moreover, each of the first two postwar presidents has handed over power to an elected president after the end of their second consecutive term in office. In 2007, the opposition APC, led by Ernest Bai Koroma, defeated the ruling SLPP. The APC victory also led to a transfer of power from Kabbah to Koroma. Even though the SLPP accepted election defeat, there were major incidents of violence between SLPP and APC supporters, especially in Freetown and Kono.[46] This electoral violence did not last long, as the APC consolidated its control over the security forces and the SLPP accepted defeat in large part because outgoing president Kabbah was willing to accept the result to consolidate his reputation as the person who stood for democracy in Sierra Leone. In addition, the security forces had been undergoing major postwar restructuring with the support of the UK and the UN. As such, the military had no inclinations to interfere in politics at that time. Security significantly increased during the first term of the Koroma presidency.

Security threats reemerged again as Sierra Leone headed into the 2012 election. Violence between the opposition SLPP and ruling APC again erupted. The most significant political violence was an attack on opposition SLPP presidential candidate Julius Maada Bio. The attack on Bio took place in Bo in July 2011 during an election campaign event. The fighting left one person dead, twenty others injured, and several buildings burned, including the local APC party office. There was an attack on APC Minister of Internal Affairs Musa Tarawali by youths in Kono. The attack, which allegedly led Tarawali to order his bodyguards to disperse the crowd with gunfire, is said to have been initiated by APC supporters of Vice President Samuel Sam-Sumana. Tarawali had been suspected of plotting the removal of Sam-Sumana as vice president.[47] However, the security threats decreased after the elections because Koroma and the APC consolidated power while the SLPP was very weak. Also, the postwar economic recovery was still on a positive track. Yet corruption and nepotism were increasingly growing. Virtually all of the progress toward consolidating democracy, rebuilding the economy, and addressing the nepotism and corruption roots of the war evaporated by the end of Koroma's second term as president.

The 2018 elections occurred in a context of intense political animosity, which had significantly escalated. By the time Koroma's second term was ending, corruption and nepotism had increased so much that he had virtually no credibility with the vast majority of people in the country. However, Koroma had amassed so much power and wealth that there were genuine fears that he would alter the constitution to allow himself to stand for a third consecutive term in office. This growing fear of presidential term extension along with ongoing dictatorial actions and corruption significantly increased the confrontation between the opposition SLPP and the APC.

While the SLPP was still struggling to agree on the party's presidential candidate, Koroma had a total grip on the APC.

One of the most troubling signs of a dictatorial tendency was Koroma's decision to remove vice president Sam-Sumana from office through an executive order and replace him with an appointed vice president. The decision was problematic for two key reasons. First, the president does not have a clear authority to remove the vice president with whom he was elected on the same ticket. The normal path would have been to impeach the vice president. Even though the Supreme Court unanimously ruled the action to be constitutional, most people see the court's decision as simply a political decision by a court that is not able to assert its independence.[48] The fact that there was no dissenting opinion in such a very controversial and at best ambiguous constitutional case speaks more to the political nature of the decision rather than the clarity of the legal justifications for removing the vice president. Secondly, it is widely reported that the decision to remove the vice president was based on personal animosity between the two men rather than any grave misconduct by the vice president. Koroma had already sidelined and cut off funding to the office of vice president long before he removed Sam-Sumana.

There were also widespread allegations of corruption against the regime. The mismanagement of the Ebola epidemic and the mudslide in Freetown became the most vivid proof of regime corruption and incompetence. Not only was the government unprepared to manage an appropriate response to the Ebola crisis, but significant amounts of donor funds were embezzled.[49] Koroma even tried to use the Ebola epidemic to prolong his term in office, but the level of outrage over government incompetence and corruption compelled him to abandon any hope of getting a third term in office. Instead, Koroma redirected his strategy toward controlling the APC and installing a loyal successor. While the SLPP held its usual convention to nominate a presidential candidate, Koroma reinforced his grip on the APC. He continued to be party leader and chairman and single-handedly picked the presidential and vice-presidential candidates of the APC. This was highly controversial even within the APC and further intensified fears that Koroma was bent on holding onto power. At the same time, a strong third-party movement emerged to challenge the APC's and SLPP's historic grip on power. The National Grand Coalition (NGC) led by Kandeh Yumkella was composed heavily of disgruntled northerners within the SLPP. Koroma focused on weakening the NGC by invoking controversial dual citizenship laws to undermine and disqualify Yumkella. However, that effort failed. All of these actions further discredited the APC and opened a small window of opportunity for a very narrow opposition electoral victory.

APC lost the 2018 presidential election to the SLPP led by Julius Maada Bio but won the most seats in Parliament. Since Bio's SLPP government came to power, tensions between the APC and SLPP have dramatically increased, which has resulted in violence, a disputed election in 2023, and an alleged failed coup plot in November 2023. This phase of political tension began right before the 2018 election when the APC tried to stifle opposition candidates by prosecuting some opposition politicians for perjury and marital relationship crimes. The SLPP presidential candidate also accused the APC of a plot to assassinate him. Right after the SLPP came to power, it masterminded a dubious process to eliminate APC parliamentarians by nullifying their electoral wins and organizing new elections that favored SLPP candidates. Through that fraudulent process, SLPP ended gaining control of parliament, in addition to the presidency.[50] Also, several military officers along with the former defense minister were investigated by the SLPP government for possession of a cache of weapons allegedly taken from the military.[51] In addition, there was widespread purging of senior civil servants and military officers, most of whom were replaced with SLPP loyalists. For the APC, all of these are merely political witch hunts.

In addition, the SLPP embarked on investigating former APC officials for corruption. Some of the cases were taken to court, while other were settled with fines or simply abandoned by the government. Even more problematic for the APC, the SLPP established a commission of inquiry to investigate crimes committed during the APC regime.[52] APC rejected the legality of the commission by challenging the way the commission was established by the president and the powers given to the commission. APC used both legal and extralegal means to resist the commission, asking the courts to invalidate the commission and simultaneously vowing to not cooperate with the commission. One key tactics that they used was to mobilize a huge crowd of supporters to interrupt and intimidate the police. Huge crowds are used to accompany APC members to police stations and courtrooms. This made it very risky for the SLPP government to detain accused APC members because of the fear of violence erupting between APC supporters and the police. A notable case is that of former President Koroma. The SLPP wanted to interrogate him for corruption but backed off for fear of violence. Despite the serious risk of violence, the SLPP government was determined to continue with the prosecutions, even when the SLPP government itself was engaged in similar forms of corruption.[53] The risk of violence between the APC and the SLPP government significantly grew. The tension between the ruling SLPP and the opposition APC exploded in August 2022 when opposition supporters held demonstrations in Freetown and several other cities. The demonstration intensified into several days of violence in which at least twenty-seven people were killed as military forces were deployed to pacify demonstrators.[54] In the aftermath of the violent demonstration, the security forces arrested opposition supporters as both parties geared up for what was expected to be a violent election in June 2023.

The election ended in total chaos as the APC rejected the results and vowed to not participate in the government because of the SLPP government's refusal to publish accurate results. The stalemate continued as the government declared Bio, the incumbent president, the winner of the election. Bio was sworn as president for a second term amid boycotts by the opposition APC and key Western development partners of Sierra Leone. On November 28, 2023, there was a significant security breach at the armory and main prison in Freetown, which the government later called an attempted coup. Though government forces repelled the attackers and restored order, the security and political situation has been fundamentally shattered. The incident resulted in the arrest and prosecution of members of the APC, including former President Koroma, for treason and related crime. The rapid deterioration of the political order led to high-level mediation efforts by ECOWAS, which led to the relocation of Koroma to Nigeria in what has become an informal exile.[55]

As in the 1960s, politics in Sierra Leone is conditioned by the colonial roots of the state, which created the conditions for ethnic politics. In addition, Sierra Leone's multiparty democracy was shaped by the norms of global liberal governance, which was applied through the international military intervention and postwar reconstruction programs. Sierra Leone's colonial roots and entanglement in global liberal governance have perpetuated a winner-takes-all form of multiparty elections that feeds off ethnicity and degenerates into ethnic and regional political violence. As such, the demise of democracy and the increased militarization of governance and the state are rooted in the intersection of domestic and external factors, which give militarization a glocal character.

Militarization and Democratic Accountability under Elected Governments

While all three democracy eras have been faced with security threats, the second democracy era (i.e., wartime democracy) faced the gravest threats. As such, the reaction of the Kabbah government during his first term has been the most drastic in terms of militarization. Interestingly, the most profound efforts in terms of restoring democratic accountability occurred during Kabbah's second term in office. In many ways, the Kabbah government was a watershed in Sierra Leone in terms of militarization and inculcation of democratic accountability. Kabbah's first term in office coincided with the climax of the civil war, while his second term marked the start of the postwar democracy. The prewar and postwar democracies are very similar in terms of the underlying issues of tribalism and regionalism that create security threats and their response with more nepotism and politicization of the military. Interestingly, they both came about under conditions controlled by external powers, which speaks to the glocal nature of the state and its security, notably under conditions of colonialism and dependency. The only difference between the prewar and the postwar democracy era is that the prewar democracy was interrupted with military coups, while the postwar democracy has not yet experienced a successful coup, but both of them are characterized by state decay and the erosion of democracy.[56]

As already discussed, the second democracy era (i.e., wartime democracy) was plagued by severe security threats against the elected government of Kabbah emanating from the civil war. The RUF armed rebellion sought to depose the Kabbah government and take over the state. RUF came very close to taking over the government when it briefly occupied the capital city of Freetown in 1997 and 1999. The Kabbah government was also deposed by the military in 1997, and renegade soldiers of the Armed Forces Revolutionary Council (AFRC) continued to fight the Kabbah government even after they were removed from Freetown by international intervention forces. The response of the Kabbah government to the security threats was virtually tied to the international support Sierra Leone was receiving. The response can be grouped into three interconnected forms: a) military assistance to defend the government, b) peace mediation to resolve the conflict, and c) restructuring of the security forces. While the former intensified militarization, the latter two sought to promote democratic accountability. A critical issue is whether the postwar democracy will continue to progress toward greater democratic accountability and reduce militarization. The 2023 election and security breach-cum-coup that followed point to erosion of democracy and more securitization of the state. In fact, members of the opposition claim that the incident was staged by the government as a way to further securitize the state.[57]

International Military Assistance and Civil Defense Forces

International military assistance represented significant militarization during the wartime democracy (i.e., second democracy era). Militarization under the elected government of Kabbah was a continuation of extant militarization policies under the NPRC. The most notable fact of militarization under the Kabbah government was the shift toward total reliance on international military and humanitarian support. Right from the start of the war, Sierra Leone sought military help from Guinea and Nigeria through the Manor River Union and ECOWAS mechanisms. As the war intensified, the request for international military help expanded to include the UN and the UK.

International intervention in Sierra Leone started with the deployment of ECOMOG, which was already operating in Liberia. This evolved into a major Nigerian-led ECOWAS support for the government, especially after the 1997 coup. In 1997, the Organisation of African Unity (OAU) called for sanctions against the AFRC junta led by Johnny Paul Koroma and asked ECOWAS to restore the elected government. ECOWAS issued a communiqué urging "that no State recognize the regime installed following the coup of 25 May 1997, and that every effort be made to restore the lawful government by a combination of three measures, i.e.: the use of dialogue; the application of sanctions, including an embargo; and the use of force."[58] Two months later, ECOWAS imposed an embargo against the junta. ECOWAS embarked on dialogue and force to oust the AFRC and its RUF ally. Under the Conakry Accord, ECOWAS presented a six-month peace plan-cum-ultimatum, which the AFRC reluctantly signed in October 1997. It set a timetable for disarmament, resumption of humanitarian assistance, return of refugees, and restoration of the Kabbah government on May 22, 1998. Even before the ECOWAS ultimatum, ECOMOG had clashed with the AFRC and RUF when Nigerian warships shelled Freetown in June 1997. In mid-February, ECOMOG drove the AFRC and RUF out of Freetown. On March 10, 1998, Kabbah returned to Freetown from exile in Guinea.[59]

The UN military intervention began with the establishment of the UN Observer Mission in Sierra Leone (UNOMSIL) in July 1998. UNOMSIL was a modest, unarmed team, charged with monitoring security, disarmament, the conduct of ECOMOG, and human rights.[60] In October 1999, UNOMSIL was replaced with UNAMSIL, which was given a mandate to implement the Lomé Peace Agreement. UNAMSIL's duties were later expanded, and troop levels increased from 6,000 to 11,100. ECOMOG forces were absorbed into UNAMSIL, which became the primary defender of the government along with occasional British military intervention. UNAMSIL had a UN Chapter VII mandate, empowering it to "take the necessary action to ensure the security and freedom of movement of its personnel and, within its capabilities and areas of deployment, afford protection to civilians under imminent threat of physical violence."[61] By March 2001, it had grown to 17,500 troops, and its role had expanded far beyond traditional peacekeeping.[62] Its objectives became "to assist the efforts of the Government of Sierra Leone to extend its authority, restore law and order and stabilize the situation progressively throughout the entire country, and to assist in the promotion of a political process which should lead to a renewed disarmament, demobilization and reintegration program and the holding, in due course, of free and fair elections."[63] When UNAMSIL ended in 2005, the UN Integrated Office for Sierra Leone (UNIOSIL) was established to consolidate peace and democracy, address the causes of the war, promote postwar reconstruction, and meet the millennium development goals.[64]

The government also relied on the CDF (i.e., Kamajor), which began as local efforts in rural areas to self-defend against RUF attacks. Most of the members were hunters and people connected to ethnic secret societies, which have a long history among the peoples of Sierra Leone. The role of the CDF significantly increased when Kabbah was deposed, and the Sierra Leone army started to collaborate with the RUF. However, the CDF was not able to properly defend the government. As international military support increased, the CDF became more of a local knowledge support network for international forces. UN and British forces were finally able to neutralize the RUF and the renegade soldiers of the Sierra Leone military in 2000 to the point that the RUF accepted and implemented the November 2000 Abuja Peace Accord leading to the end of the war.[65] During this period, Sierra Leone was at total war. There were huge numbers of international troops, heavy weapons, and combat under rules that exceeded conventional peacekeeping. Though the government was not in direct control of military policies, it requested and supported the international military intervention. As such, militarization has to be seen largely through the size and activities of international military forces rather than the activities of the Sierra Leone military, which was defunct. Moreover, militarization was largely driven by external regional and international security considerations, which show the glocalized nature of Sierra Leone's securitization.

Peace Mediation and Peace Agreements

The second response of the elected government toward the security threat was peace mediation. The government was under two kinds of pressures to engage in a negotiated settlement of the conflict. First, international actors often called for negotiation in line with UN policies, especially when major

Western powers were not willing to deploy troops. The second pressure was the military resilience of the RUF. The government was never able to defeat the RUF, which controlled significant parts of the country and came very close to capturing Freetown. The lack of a clear path to military victory coupled with international norms on the peaceful resolution of conflict made the peace negotiations and peace agreements key parts of the government response to the security threats. As a career UN diplomat, Kabbah had already been socialized into the UN conflict resolution norms from which he could not easily walk away, especially given his total reliance on international support. As with the militarization, the peace process was also a glocalized issue because Sierra Leone had to navigate both domestic conflict drivers and international norms of democracy and the rule of law under global liberal governance.

The peace mediation efforts mostly engaged the RUF. The first major peace talks between the government and the RUF was mediated by Côte d'Ivoire in collaboration with the UN, the OAU, and the Commonwealth. The Kabbah government followed up on the dialogue started during the NPRC military regime, which led to the 1996 Abidjan Accord. At the time, RUF was under major military pressure. As such, the agreement focused on disarmament and the causes of the war. The RUF tacitly accepted the legitimacy of the elected government but demanded the withdrawal of government mercenaries (i.e., Executive Outcomes) and a strong role in the implementation of the agreement. The accord called for ceasefire, amnesty, disarmament, and political and economic reforms. The reforms were to include transforming the RUF into a political party, establishing a human rights commission and an office of an ombudsman, and restructuring the judiciary, police and electoral system. Article 26 of the accord acknowledged, "there is a socio-economic dimension to the conflict which must also be addressed in order to consolidate the foundation of peace." The Commission for the Consolidation of Peace, composed of the government and the RUF, was to implement the accord with international financial and technical support. The international community, in conjunction with the belligerents, was to supervise the disarmament program. The agreement failed to end the war in large part because the RUF was not committed to the agreement.[66]

The next agreement was the Lomé Peace Accord, which occurred in the context of major RUF military gains, desertion of the renegade Sierra Leone Army, and very gruesome human rights violations including maiming of children. The Kabbah government was compelled to accept the lack of clear military path and share power with the RUF. As such, the Lomé

Peace Agreement was largely about the distribution of power between the government and the RUF. It dealt with ceasefire, disarmament, military restructuring, power sharing, and transformation of the RUF into a political party. The RUF was given four ministerial positions, including one senior position and four deputy ministerial positions in an eighteen-member cabinet. RUF members were to be appointed to various parastatal, diplomatic, and civil-service positions. Sankoh was named chairman of the Commission for Management of Strategic Resources, National Reconstruction and Development and accorded the status of vice president. The agreement gave blanket amnesty to members of the RUF, AFRC, and CDF as well as to ex–Sierra Leone Army members and called for the release of all war prisoners and abductees. The parties agreed to review the constitution, establish a new, impartial National Electoral Commission, and create a human rights commission. Like the Abidjan Accord, the Lomé Peace Accord also failed in large part because of the unwillingness of the RUF to commit to the democratic process. Though RUF members, including Foday Sankoh, came to Freetown and took up government positions, they were covertly working to undermine the power-sharing government. In fact, there were credible speculations that the RUF was planning to forcefully take over the government. The agreement finally collapsed when Sankoh was captured in Freetown. The war intensified as the RUF and the renegade soldiers increased their attacks and captured a huge number of UN forces along with their equipment. At the same time, the international intervention forces increased their offensive against the RUF. With the help of British forces, the rebel forces were significantly degraded, which compelled the RUF to agree to a negotiated settlement of the conflict. In addition, the international community forced RUF to replace Sankoh with new leaders. RUF named its field commander, General Issa Sesay, as interim leader and negotiated the Abuja Ceasefire Agreements.[67]

The November 2000 Abuja Ceasefire Agreement between the government and the RUF was spearheaded by the ECOWAS Committee of Six on Sierra Leone. It was a public endorsement of the new RUF leadership by the international community and a recommitment to implement the Lomé Peace Accord. Fighting declined significantly, but disarmament and transformation of the RUF into a political party did not progress. In May 2001, ECOWAS and the UN brokered the Abuja Ceasefire Review agreement. This agreement, along with the virtual defeat of RUF, led to the end of the civil war. The RUF disarmed and transformed into a political party. It contested the 2002 election but lost very badly. Since then, the RUF has become a moribund organization, as its party has failed to gain significant support. In the 2018 presidential election, the RUF candidate got only about 0.5 percent of the votes.[68]

SECURITY SECTOR REFORMS

Security sector reform, which typically centers on restructuring and retraining the military and police forces, was a major focus of the Kabbah government during his second term in office. Security sector reform can be viewed from two interconnected angles of maintaining state security and ensuring effective law enforcements within the confines of human rights. The state security dimension of security sector reform rests on restructuring and rebuilding the Sierra Leone military. Under security sector reform, the new military not only should be capable of defending the country against external threats, but it also must be trained to be a professional force that respects the principle of civilian control and operates in a manner devoid of sectarianism and human rights violations.[69] State security assumes the existence of a democratic political system that is continuously working toward good governance and enhancement of human development. The law enforcement dimension of security sector reforms rests on rebuilding the police force and related civilian law enforcement apparatuses such as customs and prisons. Rebuilding the police force largely centers on proper recruitment practices, appropriate training (including human rights), gender inclusion, adoption of community policing practices, and providing resources for the police. While military reforms are geared toward state security, police reforms are aimed at effective crime management and delivery of justice within a system that is transparent and effective and ensures human rights. However, given the history of using the police and special security units within the police force to protect the government from civil unrest, police reforms must also be seen as conterminous with state security.

Security sector reform started soon after the disarmament and demobilization process was completed. Most of this occurred right after the Abuja agreement. By the end of 2001, about 75,000 former combatants had been disarmed and demobilized.[70] The most critical task at the end of the war was rebuilding the Sierra Leone military. The restructuring of the military was initiated in 1999 under the International Military Assistance Training Team (IMATT) program. The IMATT program aimed to help develop the Sierra Leone military into a democratically accountable, effective, and sustainable force to fulfill security tasks required by the government.[71] The program was funded by the UK and implemented by the British military in partnership with Sierra Leone's Ministry of Defense. In 2007, the UK allocated 12 million pound starlings to IMATT. IMATT was to build on the Military Reintegration Plan (MRP) envisioned in the Lome Peace Agreement to integrate former RUF and CDF combatants into a new and restructured army. The new force was to reach 9,500 troops by 2007 and eventually attain a full strength of 12,500 troops.[72]

The IMATT program provided assistance to the Armed Forces Training Centre (AFTC) in Benguema with the training of the soldiers recruited under MRP. IMATT's two key components were combat training and professional development. The program trained about 12,500 soldiers (including the air and maritime wings) in basic military skills and provided specialized training for a small group of elite soldiers in logistics, communications, command, and control, and other techniques. In addition to combat training, IMATT aimed to inculcate professionalism within the new RSLA. IMATT was to foster policies and practices aimed at eliminating corruption and enhancing military career paths, salaries, and benefits for soldiers. In addition, IMATT was to promote institutional reforms to inculcate a culture of human rights, loyalty, service, and civilian oversight in the new RSLAF.[73] During the IMATT program period, British military officers assumed executive roles in Sierra Leone's military affairs, which underscores the glocalized nature of securitization in Sierra Leone.[74] IMATT formally ended on March 31, 2013, and was replaced with the British-sponsored International Security Advisory Team (ISAT) program. ISAT was to advise and support the RSLAF in addition to providing advice support to other security agencies, most notably the Sierra Leone Police, the Office of National Security, the National Fire Force, the Prisons Department, the Immigration Office, and the Joint Maritime Committee.

The police reform effort started with the introduction of the Sierra Leone Policing Charter in August 1998 by President Kabbah. The charter essentially committed to community policing practices, human rights, professionalism, and equal opportunity in the police service. As the charter stated, "Our aim is to see a reborn Sierra Leone Police, which will be a 'Force for Good' in our nation."[75] In essence, police reform in Sierra Leone centered on enhancing the management of the police force, providing the necessary equipment to enable the police to do its work, and inculcating community policing practices.

One of the notable police reform efforts in Sierra Leone was the British-sponsored Commonwealth Community Safety and Security Project

(CCSSP). CCSSP was initiated in 1999 when the Sierra Leone Police had been rendered almost obsolete by the rebel RUF and the renegade military that overthrew the elected government. Police officers were killed and amputated, forcing many to abandon their posts and withdraw to the safest areas of Freetown. By the time the war ended, an estimated 900 police officers had been killed by the rebels, while the size of the police force fell from 9,317 to 6,600.[76] The management component of the police reform was led by Keith Biddle, a retired assistant chief constable from Manchester in the UK, who was appointed inspector-general of police in Sierra Leone. A key part of the reform was transforming the senior management team of the police and the introduction of merit, instead of seniority, as the basis for promotion.

Conclusion: The State and Its Glocalized Militarization

African states have been characterized by various challenges that led to militarization. While attention is often directed to the use of force under dictatorial regimes, there are limited efforts to examine militarization under democratic governments and its glocal dimension. Sierra Leone shows an intriguing case of militarization under democratic (and nondemocratic) regimes as well as the fusion of domestic and external factors in the militarization of the state. Since gaining independence, Sierra Leone has been plagued by political conflicts, which often led to the use of the military and paramilitary forces to restore order and protect the state. An important element of this militarization in Sierra Leone is the way domestic and external factors shape militarization. This chapter examines both the domestic and external factors that drove militarization in Sierra Leone after it gained independence. It points to the glocal nature of the state, which generates domestic and external factors that shape its securitization.

Clearly, militarization in Sierra Leone has significant domestic and external forms. This is largely driven by the nature of ethnic politics, which resulted from the colonial roots of the state. Ethnic politics has made democracy very unstable, as political elite fighting for power resort to ethnic manipulation to stay in power. This breeds a system of corruption and nepotism that leads to authoritarianism and military coups. Under such conditions, the government resorts to the military to keep it in power. This problem happens under both democratic and nondemocratic governments. Militarization in this sense revolves mostly around the use of the security forces to maintain power and the involvement of the military in politics.

The diabolical form of politics ultimately led to a catastrophic civil war. The civil war pushed Sierra Leone from state failure to state collapse, which necessitated significant international military intervention.

The international military intervention under regional and UN peacekeeping frameworks represented another form of militarization. As the civil war intensified and the Sierra Leone government, especially the elected government of Kabbah, became totally dependent on international military support, militarization took an external form. Sierra Leone's security became glocalized as its diabolical politics resulted into a war that was tied to regional instability, which attracted the interests of regional and international powers. The deployment of huge international troops to fight the rebel RUF and renegade soldiers of the Sierra Leone military shows how external factors shape the militarization of Sierra Leone. Sierra Leone became a country that was subjected to international state-building, which required fundamental security sector reform. Overall, Sierra Leone is an intriguing case of securitization that gravitated between democracy and dictatorship, order and civil war, and domestic and regional (in)security under varying frames of global liberal governance.

In the end, glocalization provides a lens for examining the militarization of the state through domestic and external securitization regimes, notably state security, regional security, and the R2P doctrine. The state in Sierra Leone posed fundamental problems of governance owing to its colonial roots. Those problem resulted in authoritarian civilian and military regimes that produced violence, including a civil war. In turn, the violence led to more militarization of the state, first through the government's use of the military to suppress dissent and eventually international interventions to restore human security as the state degenerated into failure. All of these point to the glocal dynamics of militarization both in terms of the conflict drivers and the responses of the state and external powers. Sierra Leone's militarization led to state collapse, which in turn necessitated further militarization of the state by external powers. This chapter captures this quagmire of state militarization as it played out in Sierra Leone before and during the civil war. In all of these phases, glocalization captures the domestic and external conflict drivers as well as the domestic and external logics of securitization.

Notes

1. An earlier version of this chapter was presented by Abu Bakarr Bah at the workshop "Security Threats, Militarization and the Democratic Accountability

of the Use of Military Force" supported by the German Institute of Global and Areas Studies (GIGA) in Hamburg, Germany (April 8–10, 2019).

2. Alex Mintz and Nehemia Geva, "Why Don't Democracies Fight Each Other? An Experimental Study," *Journal of Conflict Resolution* 37, no. 3 (1993): 484–503; Scott Gates, Torbjørn L. Knutsen, and Jonathon W. Moses, "Democracy and Peace: A More Skeptical View," *Journal of Peace Research* 33, no. 1 (1996): 1–10; Donald L. Horowitz, *Ethnic Groups in Conflict*, updated edition with a new preface (Berkeley: University of California Press, 1985); Juan J. Linz, Juan J. Linz, and Alfred Stepan, *Problems of Democratic Transition and Consolidation: Southern Europe, South America, and Post-Communist Europe* (Baltimore: Johns Hopkins University Press, 1996; Abu Bakarr Bah, "Democracy and Civil War: Citizenship and Peacemaking in Côte d'Ivoire," *African Affairs* 109, no. 437 (2010): 597–615.

3. Abu Bakarr Bah, "Changing World Order and the Future of Democracy in Sub-Saharan Africa," *Proteus: A Journal of Ideas* 21, no. 1 (Spring 2004): 3–12; Adrienne LeBas, *From Protest to Parties: Party-Building and Democratization in Africa* (Oxford: Oxford University Press, 2011); Adebayo O. Olukoshi, ed., *The Politics of Opposition in Contemporary Africa* (Uppsala, Sweden: Nordic Africa Institute, 1998); Janette Yarwood, "The Struggle over Term Limits in Africa: The Power of Protest," *Journal of Democracy* 27, no. 3 (2016): 51–60.

4. Yagil Levy, "What Is Controlled by Civilian Control of the Military? Control of the Military vs. Control of Militarization," *Armed Forces & Society* 42, no. 1 (2016): 75–98; Max Weber, *Max Weber: Essays in Sociology*, trans. and ed. H. H. Gerth and C. Wright Mills (New York: Routledge, 2009).

5. Abu Bakarr Bah, "The Contours of New Humanitarianism: War and Peacebuilding in Sierra Leone." *Africa Today* 60, no. 1 (2013): 3–26; Abu Bakarr Bah, *International Security and Peacebuilding: Africa, the Middle East, and Europe* (Bloomington: Indiana University Press, 2017).

6. Alexander Wendt, "Anarchy Is What States Make of It: The Social Construction of Power Politics," *International Organization* 46, no. 2 (1992): 391–425; Zubairu Wai, "Rethinking War and Violence in Sierra Leone: The RUF and the Nature and Condition of Insurgency Violence," *African Conflict & Peacebuilding Review* 13, no. 1 (2023): 44–76.

7. Catherine Lutz, "Militarization," in *A Companion to the Anthropology of Politics*, ed. David Nugent and Joan Vincent (Malden, MA: Blackwell, 2004), 318–31.

8. Bah, *International Security and Peacebuilding*.

9. Max Weber, *Max Weber: Essays in Sociology*.

10. Barry Buzan, Ole Waever, and Jaap de Wilde, *Security: A New Framework for Analysis* (Boulder: Lynne Rienner, 1998).

11. Abu Bakarr Bah, "Racial Profiling and the War on Terror: Changing Trends and Perspectives," *Ethnic Studies Review* 29, no. 1 (2006): 76–100; Godfrey Maringira and Diana Gibson, "Maintaining Order in Townships: Gangsterism and Community Resilience in Post-Apartheid South Africa," *African Conflict & Peacebuilding Review*

9, no. 2 (2019): 55–74; Jonny Steinberg, *Thin Blue: The Unwritten Rules of Policing South Africa* (Gauteng, South Africa: Jonathan Ball, 2010); William Pruitt, "The Progress of Democratic Policing in South Africa," *African Journal of Criminology and Justice Studies* 4, no. 1 (2010): 116–40.

12. Ibrahim Bangura, "Democratically Transformed or Business as Usual: The Sierra Leone Police and Democratic Policing in Sierra Leone," *Stability: International Journal of Security and Development* 7, no. 1 (2018); Bruce Baker, "Who Do People Turn to for Policing in Sierra Leone?," *Journal of Contemporary African Studies* 23, no. 3 (2005): 371–90; Bruce Baker, "How Civil War Altered Policing in Sierra Leone and Uganda," *Commonwealth & Comparative Politics* 45, no. 3 (2007): 367–87.

13. Usman Ladan, "Transnational Terrorism Revisited: Is Boko Haram an Al-Qaeda Affiliate?," *African Conflict & Peacebuilding Review* 12, no. 1 (2022): 105–26; Marc-Antoine Pérouse de Montclos, "The Nigerian Military Response to Boko Haram: A Critical Analysis," *African Conflict & Peacebuilding Review* 10, no. 2 (2020): 65–82.

14. David M. Anderson and Jacob McKnight, "Kenya at War: Al-Shabaab and Its Enemies in Eastern Africa," *African Affairs* 114, no. 454 (2015): 1–27; Mutuma Ruteere, "More Than Political Tools: The Police and Post-Election Violence in Kenya," *African Security Review* 20, no. 4 (2011): 11–20; P. A. Opondo, "Ethnic Politics and Post-Election Violence of 2007/8 in Kenya," *African Journal of History and Culture* 6, no. 4 (2014): 59–67.

15. The 2023 election results have been rejected by the opposition, which is boycotting the government and demanding a rerun of the election. See "APC Party Continues Rejection of Election Results and Demand for a Rerun of the Vote," *SwitSalone*, July 3, 2023, https://www.switsalone.com/45888_apc-party-continues-rejection-of-election-results-and-demand-for-a-rerun-of-the-vote.

16. Ulrich Beck, *What Is Globalization?* (Cambridge: Polity Press, 2000); Ulrich Beck, Natan Sznaider, and Rainer Winter, eds., *Global America? The Cultural Consequences of Globalization*, vol. 8 (Liverpool: Liverpool University Press, 2003); Ali A. Mazrui, *Africa's International Relations: The Diplomacy of Dependency and Change* (London: Routledge, 2019); Immanuel Wallerstein, *The Capitalist World-Economy* (Cambridge: Cambridge University Press, 1979); Abu Bakarr Bah, ed. *Glocalized Security: Domestic and External Issues in International Security* (Bloomington, IN: Indiana University Press, 2025).

17. Roland Robertson, "Globality and Modernity," *Theory, Culture & Society* 9, no. 2 (1992): 153–61; Roland Robertson, "Globalisation or Glocalisation?," *Journal of International Communication* 1, no. 1 (1994): 33–52; Roland Robertson, "Glocalization: Time-Space and Homogeneity-Heterogeneity," *Global Modernities* 2, no. 1 (1995): 25–44; Richard Giulianotti and Roland Robertson, "The Globalization of Football: A Study in the Glocalization of the 'Serious Life,'" *British Journal of Sociology* 55, no. 4 (2004): 545–68; Richard Giulianotti and Roland Robertson, "Glocalization, Globalization and Migration: The Case of Scottish Football Supporters

in North America," *International Sociology* 21, no. 2 (2006): 171–198; Roland Robertson and Kathleen E. White, "What Is Globalization?," in *The Blackwell Companion to Globalization* (2007), 54–66.

18. Bettina Köhler and Markus Wissen, "Glocalizing Protest: Urban Conflicts and the Global Social Movements," *International Journal of Urban and Regional Research* 27, no. 4 (2003): 942–51; Dannie Kjeldgaard and Søren Askegaard, "The Glocalization of Youth Culture: The Global Youth Segment as Structures of Common Difference," *Journal of Consumer Research* 33, no. 2 (2006): 231–47; Giulianotti and Robertson, "The Globalization of Football," 545–68; Ulrich Beck, *What Is Globalization?*

19. Mazrui, *Africa's International Relations: The Diplomacy of Dependency and Change*; Wallerstein, *The Capitalist World-Economy*; Abu Bakarr Bah and Nikolas Emmanuel, "Migration Cooperation Between Africa and Europe: Understanding the Role of International Incentives," in *The Oxford Research Encyclopedia of International Studies* (Oxford: Oxford University Press, 2022).

20. Samuel Marfo, Halidu Musah, and Dominic DeGraft Arthur, "Beyond Classical Peace Paradigm: A Theoretical Argument for a Glocalized Peace and Security," *African Journal of Political Science and International Relations* 10, no. 4 (2016): 47–55, 48.

21. Marfo et al., "Beyond Classical Peace Paradigm," 47–55, 48.

22. Abu Bakarr Bah, "State Decay: A Conceptual Frame for Failing and Failed States in West Africa," *International Journal of Politics, Culture, and Society* 25, no. 1–3 (2012): 71–89; Abu Bakarr Bah, "State Decay and Civil War: A Discourse on Power in Sierra Leone," *Critical Sociology* 37, no. 2 (2011): 199–216; Abu Bakarr Bah and Nikolas Emmanuel, *International Statebuilding in West Africa: Civil Wars and New Humanitarianism in Sierra Leone, Liberia, and Côte d'Ivoire* (Bloomington: Indiana University Press, 2024).

23. David John Harris, *Sierra Leone: A Political History* (Oxford: Oxford University Press, 2014); Jimmy D. Kandeh, "What Does the 'Militariat' Do When It Rules? Military Regimes: The Gambia, Sierra Leone and Liberia," *Review of African Political Economy* 23, no. 69 (1996): 387–404.

24. Robert M. Press, "Sierra Leone's Peaceful Resistance to Authoritarian Rule," *African Conflict & Peacebuilding Review* 2, no. 1 (2012): 31–57; Ibrahim Abdullah, "Bush Path to Destruction: The Origin and Character of the Revolutionary United Front/Sierra Leone," *Journal of Modern African Studies* 36, no. 2 (1998): 203–35; Lansana Gberie, *A Dirty War in West Africa: The RUF and the Destruction of Sierra Leone* (Bloomington: Indiana University Press, 2005).

25. Bah, "State Decay and Civil War."

26. Bah and Emmanuel, *International Statebuilding in West Africa*.

27. John R. Cartwright, *Politics in Sierra Leone 1947–1967* (Toronto: University of Toronto Press, 1970); Jimmy D. Kandeh, "Politicization of Ethnic Identities in

Sierra Leone," *African Studies Review* 35, no. 1 (1992): 81–99; Bah, "State Decay and Civil War."

28. Abu Bakarr Bah and Ibrahim Bangura, "Landholding and the Creation of Lumpen Tenants in Freetown: Youth Economic Survival and Patrimonialism in Postwar Sierra Leone," *Critical Sociology* 49, no. 7–8 (2023): 1289–1303; Bah and Emmanuel, *International Statebuilding in West Africa*.

29. Humphrey J. Fisher, "Elections and Coups in Sierra Leone, 1967," *Journal of Modern African Studies* 7, no. 4 (1969): 611–36; Christopher Allen, "Sierra Leone Politics Since Independence," *African Affairs* 67, no. 269 (1968): 305–29.

30. Jimmy D. Kandeh, "Sierra Leone: Military Coups and Dictatorships," *Oxford Research Encyclopedia of Politics*, 2021.

31. Bankole Kamara Taylor, *Sierra Leone: The Land, Its People and History* (Dar es Salaam, Tanzania: New Africa Press, 2014); David Fasholé Luke, "Continuity in Sierra Leone: From Stevens to Momoh," *Third World Quarterly* 10, no. 1 (1988): 67–78; Gerald H. Smith, "The Dichotomy of Politics and Corruption in a Neopatrimonial State: Evidence from Sierra Leone, 1968–1993," *African Issues* 25, no. 1 (1997): 58–62.

32. Luke, "Continuity in Sierra Leone: From Stevens to Momoh"; Press, "Sierra Leone's Peaceful Resistance to Authoritarian Rule"; Augustine Kposowa, "Erosion of the Rule of Law as a Contributing Factor in Civil Conflict: The Case of Sierra Leone," *Police Practice and Research* 7, no. 1 (2006): 35–48.

33. Kandeh, "Sierra Leone: Military Coups and Dictatorships"; Fisher, "Elections and Coups in Sierra Leone, 1967"; Allen, "Sierra Leone Politics since Independence."

34. Press, "Sierra Leone's Peaceful Resistance to Authoritarian Rule"; Abdullah, "Bush Path to Destruction"; Lansana Gberie, *A Dirty War in West Africa: The RUF and the Destruction of Sierra Leone* (Bloomington: Indiana University Press, 2005).

35. Mahmood Mamdani, *Citizen and Subject: Contemporary Africa and the Legacy of Late Colonialism* (Princeton, NJ: Princeton University Press, 1996).

36. Luke, "Continuity in Sierra Leone: From Stevens to Momoh"; Smith, "The Dichotomy of Politics and Corruption in a Neopatrimonial State"; Bah, "State Decay and Civil War."

37. Bah, "The Contours of New Humanitarianism."

38. Bah and Emmanuel, *International Statebuilding in West Africa*.

39. Marfo et al., "Beyond Classical Peace Paradigm," 4; Bettina Köhler and Markus Wissen, "Glocalizing Protest: Urban Conflicts and the Global Social Movements," *International Journal of Urban and Regional Research* 27, no. 4 (2003): 942–51; Dannie Kjeldgaard and Søren Askegaard, "The Glocalization of Youth Culture: The Global Youth Segment as Structures of Common Difference," *Journal of Consumer Research* 33, no. 2 (2006): 231–47; Beck, *What Is Globalization?*

40. Gberie, *A Dirty War in West Africa*; Bah, "The Contours of New Humanitarianism."

41. Bah and Emmanuel, *International Statebuilding in West Africa*; Bah, *International Security and Peacebuilding*.

42. David J. Francis, "Torturous Path to Peace: The Lomé Accord and Postwar Peacebuilding in Sierra Leone," *Security Dialogue* 31, no. 3 (2000): 357–73; Manoj Kumar Sinha, "The Creation of Another Court: A Case Study of Special Court for Sierra Leone," *ISIL Year Book of International Humanitarian and Refugee Law* 4 (2004): 89.

43. Mats Utas and Magnus Jörgel, "The West Side Boys: Military Navigation in the Sierra Leone Civil War," *Journal of Modern African Studies* 46, no. 3 (2008): 487–511; Jimmy D. Kandeh, "Sierra Leone: 'Sobels' and 'Foot of State,'" in *Coups from Below* (New York: Palgrave Macmillan, 2004), 143–78.

44. Bah, "The Contours of New Humanitarianism."

45. Bah, "The Contours of New Humanitarianism"; Mark Duffield, *Global Governance and the New Wars: The Merging of Development and Security* (London: Zed Books, 2014).

46. Katrina Manson, "Elections Violence Grips Sierra Leone," Reuters, September 1, 2007, https://www.reuters.com/article/us-leone-elections/elections-violence-grips-sierra-leone-idUSL0121450220070901.

47. "Ahead of Elections, Sierra Leone Focuses on Mitigating Political Violence Election Security, All Electoral Integrity and Transparency," IFES, January 17, 2012, http://www.ifes.org/Content/Publications/News-in-Brief/2012/Jan/Ahead-of-Elections-Sierra-Leone-Focuses-on-Mitigating-Political-Violence.aspx.

48. "Breaking News: President Koroma Had Powers to Remove Sam Sumana, Supreme Court Rules," Cocorioko, September 9, 2015, https://cocorioko.net/breaking-news-president-koroma-had-powers-to-remove-sam-sumana-supreme-court-rules-3/.

49. IRIN, "Sierra Leone's Missing Ebola Millions," Refworld, March 30, 2015, https://www.refworld.org/docid/552394c54.html.

50. Abdul Rashid Thomas, "Rioting at Sierra Leone's Opposition APC Office as Party Loses Election Petitions," *Sierra Leone Telegraph*, May 31, 2019, https://www.thesierraleonetelegraph.com/rioting-at-sierra-leones-opposition-apc-office-as-party-loses-election-petitions.

51. Foday Moriba Conteh, "Free from Treason Charge . . . Palo Conteh Sentenced to 2 Years Imprisonment," *Calabash Newspaper*, July 3, 2020, https://thecalabashnewspaper.com/free-from-treason-charge-palo-conteh-sentenced-to-2-years-imprisonment/.

52. Abdul Rashid Thomas, "Properties of Former APC Ministers Impounded by Anti-Corruption Commission," *Sierra Leone Telegraph*, August 1, 2019, https://www.thesierraleonetelegraph.com/properties-of-former-apc-ministers-impounded-by-anti-corruption-commission/.

53. Daniel Finnan, "Sierra Leone: First Lady at Centre of Graft Allegations Rocking the Presidency," AllAfrica, March 11, 2021, https://allafrica.com/stories/202103110414.html.

54. "Explosion of Violence: Sierra Leone Picks up the Pieces After Protests," *The Guardian*, August 21, 2022, https://www.theguardian.com/global-development/2022/aug/21/sierra-leone-protests-inflation-cost-of-living.

55. "Indicted Sierra Leone Ex-President Koroma Flies to Nigeria," Reuters, January 19, 2024, https://www.reuters.com/world/africa/indicted-sierra-leone-ex-president-koroma-flies-nigeria-2024-01-19/.

56. Bah, "State Decay: A Conceptual Frame for Failing and Failed States in West Africa"; Bah, "State Decay and Civil War: A Discourse on Power in Sierra Leone."

57. Abdul Rashid Thomas, ""Staged Coup Attempt by President Bio as a Pretext to Go After Opposition APC?," *Sierra Leone Telegraph*. November 27, 2023, https://www.thesierraleonetelegraph.com/staged-coup-attempt-by-president-bio-as-a-pretext-to-go-after-opposition-apc/#google_vignette.

58. ECOWAS, "Final Communiqué: The Ministers of Foreign Affairs," June 26, 1997, Conakry, Guinea: ECOWAS.

59. Bah, "The Contours of New Humanitarianism."

60. United Nations, "Resolution 1181 (1998) Adopted by the Security Council at Its 3902nd Meeting," New York: United Nations, 1998.

61. United Nations, "Fourth Report of the Secretary-General on the United Nations Mission in Sierra Leone (S/2000/455)," New York: United Nations, 2000.

62. United Nations, "Report of the Secretary-General on the Establishment of a Special Court for Sierra Leone (S/2000/915)," New York: United Nations, 2000.

63. United Nations, "Ninth Report of the Secretary-General on the United Nations Mission in Sierra Leone (S/2001/228)," New York: United Nations, 2001, 9.

64. Bah, "The Contours of New Humanitarianism."

65. Bah, "The Contours of New Humanitarianism."

66. Bah, "The Contours of New Humanitarianism."

67. Bah, "The Contours of New Humanitarianism."

68. Bah, "The Contours of New Humanitarianism."

69. Kenneth W. Kemp and Charles Hudlin, "Civil Supremacy Over the Military: Its Nature and Limits," *Armed Forces and Society* 19, no. 1 (1992): 7–26.

70. UNAMSIL, "UNAMSIL: A Success Story in Peacekeeping," New York: UN Department of Peacekeeping Operations, March 2, 2005, http://www.un.org/en/peacekeeping/missions/past/unamsil/Overview.pdf.

71. Abu Bakarr Bah, "People-Centered Liberalism: An Alternative Approach to International State-Building in Sierra Leone and Liberia," *Critical Sociology* 43, no. 7–8 (2017): 989–1007; Mark Malan, "Sierra Leone: Building the Road to Recovery," in *Security and Military Reform* (Institute for Security Studies, 2003), http://

www.iss.co.za/pubs/monographs/No80/Chap5.html; Al-Hassan Kharamoh Kondeh, "Security System Transformation in Sierra Leone: 1997–2007," *Formulating Sierra Leone's Defence White Paper*, Paper No. 6, October 2008, http://www.ssrnetwork.net/documents/Publications/SierraLeoneWPs/working%20paper%206.pdf.

72. UNDG, "Guidance Note to United Nations Country Teams on the PRSP (Poverty Reduction Strategy Papers)," http://www.undg.org/index.cfm?P=16; Republic of Sierra Leone, *An Agenda for Change: Second Poverty Reduction Strategy (PRSP II) 2008–2012* (Freetown: Government of Sierra Leone (2008).

73. Malan, "Sierra Leone: Building the Road to Recovery."

74. Bah, "People-Centered Liberalism"; Kondeh, "Security System Tranformation in Sierra Leone: 1997–2007."

75. Joseph P. Chris Charley and Freida Ibiduni M'Cormack, *Becoming and Remaining a "Force for Good"—Reforming the Police in Post-Conflict Sierra Leone*, Institute of Development Studies Research Report, Vol. 2011, No. 70, September 2011, Appendix I, http://www.ids.ac.uk/files/dmfile/rr70.pdf.

76. Bruce Baker, "Sierra Leone Police Reform: The Role of the UK Government," Discussion Paper 10-06 presented at the GRIPS Policy Research Center State-Building Workshop "Organizing Police Forces in Post-Conflict Peace-Support Operations," Tokyo, January 27–28, 2010.

References

Abdullah, Ibrahim. "Bush Path to Destruction: The Origin and Character of the Revolutionary United Front/Sierra Leone." *Journal of Modern African Studies* 36, no. 2 (1998): 203–35.

"Ahead of Elections, Sierra Leone Focuses on Mitigating Political Violence Election Security, All Electoral Integrity and Transparency." IFES, January 17, 2012. http://www.ifes.org/Content/Publications/News-in-Brief/2012/Jan/Ahead-of-Elections-Sierra-Leone-Focuses-on-Mitigating-Political-Violence.aspx.

Allen, Christopher. "Sierra Leone Politics Since Independence." *African Affairs* 67, no. 269 (1968): 305–29.

Anderson, David M., and Jacob McKnight. "Kenya at War: Al-Shabaab and Its Enemies in Eastern Africa." *African Affairs* 114, no. 454 (2015): 1–27.

Bah, Abu Bakarr. "Changing World Order and the Future of Democracy in Sub-Saharan Africa." *Proteus: A Journal of Ideas* 21, no. 1 (Spring 2004): 3–12.

———. "The Contours of New Humanitarianism: War and Peacebuilding in Sierra Leone." *Africa Today* 60, no. 1 (2013): 3–26.

———. "Democracy and Civil War: Citizenship and Peacemaking in Côte d'Ivoire." *African Affairs* 109, no. 437 (2010): 597–615.

———, ed. *Glocalized Security: Domestic and External Issues in International Security*. Bloomington, IN: Indiana University Press, 2025.

———, ed. *International Security and Peacebuilding: Africa, the Middle East, and Europe.* Bloomington, IN: Indiana University Press, 2017.

———. "People-Centered Liberalism: An Alternative Approach to International State-Building in Sierra Leone and Liberia." *Critical Sociology* 43, no. 7–8 (2017): 989–1007.

———. "Racial Profiling and the War on Terror: Changing Trends and Perspectives." *Ethnic Studies Review* 29, no. 1 (2006): 76–100.

———. "State Decay: A Conceptual Frame for Failing and Failed States in West Africa." *International Journal of Politics, Culture, and Society* 25, no. 1–3 (2012): 71–89.

———. "State Decay and Civil War: A Discourse on Power in Sierra Leone." *Critical Sociology* 37, no. 2 (2011): 199–216.

———, and Nikolas Emmanuel. "Migration Cooperation Between Africa and Europe: Understanding the Role of International Incentives." In *The Oxford Research Encyclopedia of International Studies.* Oxford: Oxford University Press, 2022. doi:10.1093/acrefore/9780190846626.013.735.

———, and Nikolas Emmanuel. *International Statebuilding in West Africa: Civil Wars and New Humanitarianism in Sierra Leone, Liberia, and Côte d'Ivoire.* Bloomington: Indiana University Press, 2024.

———, and Ibrahim Bangura. "Landholding and the Creation of Lumpen Tenants in Freetown: Youth Economic Survival and Patrimonialism in Postwar Sierra Leone." *Critical Sociology* 49, no. 7–8 (2023): 1289–1303.

Buzan, Barry, Ole Waever, and Jaap de Wilde. *Security: A New Framework for Analysis.* Boulder: Lynne Rienner, 1998.

Beck, Ulrich. *What Is Globalization?* Cambridge: Polity Press, 2000.

———, Natan Sznaider, and Rainer Winter, eds. *Global America? The Cultural Consequences of Globalization.* Liverpool: Liverpool University Press, 2003.

Baker, Bruce. "How Civil War Altered Policing in Sierra Leone and Uganda." *Commonwealth & Comparative Politics* 45, no. 3 (2007): 367–87.

———. "Sierra Leone Police Reform: The Role of the UK Government." Discussion Paper 10-06 presented at the GRIPS Policy Research Center State-Building Workshop "Organizing Police Forces in Post-Conflict Peace-Support Operations," Tokyo, January 27–28, 2010.

———. "Who Do People Turn to for Policing in Sierra Leone?" *Journal of Contemporary African Studies* 23, no. 3 (2005): 371–90.

Bangura, Ibrahim. "Democratically Transformed or Business as Usual: The Sierra Leone Police and Democratic Policing in Sierra Leone." *Stability: International Journal of Security and Development* 7, no. 1 (2018).

"BREAKING NEWS: President Koroma Had Powers To Remove Sam Sumana, Supreme Court Rules." Cocorioko. September 9, 2015. https://cocorioko.net/breaking-news-president-koroma-had-powers-to-remove-sam-sumana-supreme-court-rules-3.

Cartwright, John R. *Politics in Sierra Leone 1947–1967*. Toronto: University of Toronto Press, 1970.

Charley, Joseph P. Chris, and Freida Ibiduni M'Cormack. *Becoming and Remaining a "Force for Good"—Reforming the Police in Post-Conflict Sierra Leone*. Institute of Development Studies Research Report, Vol. 2011, No. 70, September 2011. Appendix I. http://www.ids.ac.uk/files/dmfile/rr70.pdf.

Conteh, Foday Moriba. "Free from Treason Charge . . . Palo Conteh Sentenced to 2 Years Imprisonment." July 3, 2020. https://thecalabashnewspaper.com/free-from-treason-charge-palo-conteh-sentenced-to-2-years-imprisonment.

Fasholé, David. "Continuity in Sierra Leone: From Stevens to Momoh." *Third World Quarterly* 10, no. 1 (1988): 67–78.

de Montclos, Marc-Antoine Pérouse. "The Nigerian Military Response to Boko Haram: A Critical Analysis." *African Conflict & Peacebuilding Review* 10, no. 2 (2020): 65–82.

Duffield, Mark. *Global Governance and the New Wars: The Merging of Development and Security*. London: Zed Books, 2014.

ECOWAS. "Final Communiqué: The Ministers of Foreign Affairs." June 26, 1997. Conakry, Guinea: ECOWAS.

"'Explosion of Violence': Sierra Leone Picks Up the Pieces After Protests." *The Guardian*. August 21, 2022. https://www.theguardian.com/global-development/2022/aug/21/sierra-leone-protests-inflation-cost-of-living.

Finnan, Daniel. "Sierra Leone: First Lady at Centre of Graft Allegations Rocking the Presidency." March 11, 2021. https://allafrica.com/stories/202103110414.html.

Fisher, Humphrey J. "Elections and Coups in Sierra Leone, 1967." *Journal of Modern African Studies* 7, no. 4 (1969): 611–36.

Francis, David J. "Torturous Path to Peace: The Lomé Accord and Postwar Peacebuilding in Sierra Leone." *Security Dialogue* 31, no. 3 (2000): 357–73.

Gates, Scott, Torbjørn L. Knutsen, and Jonathon W. Moses. "Democracy and Peace: A More Skeptical View." *Journal of Peace Research* 33, no. 1 (1996): 1–10.

Gberie, Lansana. *A Dirty War in West Africa: The RUF and the Destruction of Sierra Leone*. Bloomington: Indiana University Press, 2005.

Giulianotti, Richard, and Roland Robertson. "The Globalization of Football: A Study in the Glocalization of the 'Serious Life.'" *British Journal of Sociology* 55, no. 4 (2004): 545–68.

———, and Roland Robertson. "Glocalization, Globalization and Migration: The Case of Scottish Football Supporters in North America." *International Sociology* 21, no. 2 (2006): 171–98.

Harris, David John. *Sierra Leone: A Political History*. Oxford: Oxford University Press, 2014.

Horowitz, Donald L. *Ethnic Groups in Conflict*. Updated edition with a new preface. Berkeley: University of California Press, 1985.

"Indicted Sierra Leone Ex-president Koroma Flies to Nigeria." Reuters, January 19, 2024. https://www.reuters.com/world/africa/indicted-sierra-leone-ex-president-koroma-flies-nigeria-2024-01-19/.

IRIN. "Sierra Leone's Missing Ebola Millions." Refworld, March 30, 2015. https://www.refworld.org/docid/552394c54.html.

Kandeh, Jimmy D. "Politicization of Ethnic Identities in Sierra Leone." *African Studies Review* 35, no. 1 (1992): 81–99.

———. "Sierra Leone: Military Coups and Dictatorships." *Oxford Research Encyclopedia of Politics*, 2021.

———. "Sierra Leone: 'Sobels' and 'Foot of State.'" In *Coups from Below*, edited by Jimmy D. Kandeh, 143–78. New York: Palgrave Macmillan, 2004.

———. "What Does the 'Militariat' Do When It Rules? Military Regimes: The Gambia, Sierra Leone and Liberia." *Review of African Political Economy* 23, no. 69 (1996): 387–404.

Kemp, Kenneth W., and Charles Hudlin. "Civil Supremacy Over the Military: Its Nature and Limits." *Armed Forces and Society* 19, no. 1 (1992): 7–26.

Kjeldgaard, Dannie, and Søren Askegaard. "The Glocalization of Youth Culture: The Global Youth Segment as Structures of Common Difference." *Journal of Consumer Research* 33, no. 2 (2006): 231–47.

Köhler, Bettina, and Markus Wissen. "Glocalizing Protest: Urban Conflicts and the Global Social Movements." *International Journal of Urban and Regional Research* 27, no. 4 (2003): 942–51.

Kondeh, Al-Hassan Kharamoh. "Security System Transformation in Sierra Leone: 1997–2007." *Formulating Sierra Leone's Defence White Paper*. Paper No. 6, October 2008. http://www.ssrnetwork.net/documents/Publications/Sierra LeoneWPs/working%20paper%206.pdf.

Kposowa, Augustine. "Erosion of the Rule of Law as a Contributing Factor in Civil Conflict: The Case of Sierra Leone." *Police Practice and Research* 7, no. 1 (2006): 35–48.

Ladan, Usman. "Transnational Terrorism Revisited: Is Boko Haram an al-Qaeda Affiliate?" *African Conflict & Peacebuilding Review* 12, no. 1 (2022): 105–26.

LeBas, Adrienne. *From Protest to Parties: Party-Building and Democratization in Africa*. Oxford: Oxford University Press, 2011.

Levy, Yagil. "What Is Controlled by Civilian Control of the Military? Control of the Military vs. Control of Militarization." *Armed Forces & Society* 42, no. 1 (2016): 75–98.

Linz, Juan J., and Alfred Stepan. *Problems of Democratic Transition and Consolidation: Southern Europe, South America, and Post-communist Europe*. Baltimore: Johns Hopkins University Press, 1996.

Luke, David Fasholé. "Continuity in Sierra Leone: From Stevens to Momoh." *Third World Quarterly* 10, no. 1 (1988): 67–78.

Lutz, Catherine. "Militarization." In *A Companion to the Anthropology of Politics*, edited by David Nugent and Joan Vincent, 318–31. Malden, MA: Blackwell, 2004.

Malan, Mark. "Sierra Leone: Building the Road to Recovery." *Security and Military Reform*. Chapter 5. Institute for Security Studies, Monograph No. 80, March 2003. http://www.iss.co.za/pubs/monographs/No80/Chap5.html.

Mamdani, Mahmood. *Citizen and Subject: Contemporary Africa and the Legacy of Late Colonialism*. Princeton, NJ: Princeton University Press, 1996.

Manson, Katrina. "Elections Violence Grips Sierra Leone." Reuters, September 1, 2007. https://www.reuters.com/article/us-leone-elections/elections-violence-grips-sierra-leone-idusl0121450220070901.

Marfo, Samuel, Halidu Musah, and Dominic DeGraft Arthur. "Beyond Classical Peace Paradigm: A Theoretical Argument for a Glocalized Peace and Security." *African Journal of Political Science and International Relations* 10, no. 4 (2016): 47–55.

Maringira, Godfrey, and Diana Gibson. "Maintaining Order in Townships: Gangsterism and Community Resilience in Post-Apartheid South Africa." *African Conflict & Peacebuilding Review* 9, no. 2 (2019): 55–74.

Mazrui, Ali A. *Africa's International Relations: The Diplomacy of Dependency and Change*. London: Routledge, 2019.

Mintz, Alex, and Nehemia Geva. "Why Don't Democracies Fight Each Other? An Experimental Study." *Journal of Conflict Resolution* 37, no. 3 (1993): 484–503.

Olukoshi, Adebayo O., ed. *The Politics of Opposition in Contemporary Africa*. Uppsala, Sweden: Nordic Africa Institute, 1998.

Opondo, P. A. "Ethnic Politics and Post-election Violence of 2007/8 in Kenya." *African Journal of History and Culture* 6, no. 4 (2014): 59–67.

Press, Robert M. "Sierra Leone's Peaceful Resistance to Authoritarian Rule." *African Conflict & Peacebuilding Review* 2, no. 1 (2012): 31–57.

Pruitt, William. "The Progress of Democratic Policing in South Africa." *African Journal of Criminology and Justice Studies* 4, no. 1 (2010): 116–40.

Republic of Sierra Leone. *An Agenda for Change: Second Poverty Reduction Strategy (PRSP II) 2008–2012*. Freetown: Government of Sierra Leone, 2008.

Robertson, Roland. "Globalisation or Glocalisation?" *Journal of International Communication* 1, no. 1 (1994): 33–52.

———. "Globality and Modernity." *Theory, Culture & Society* 9, no. 2 (1992): 153–61.

———. "Glocalization: Time-Space and Homogeneity-Heterogeneity." *Global Modernities* 2, no. 1 (1995): 25–44.

Robertson, Roland, and Kathleen E. White. "What Is Globalization?" In *The Blackwell Companion to Globalization*, edited by George Ritzer, 54–66. Malden, MA: Blackwell, 2007.

Ruteere, Mutuma. "More Than Political Tools: The Police and Post-Election Violence in Kenya." *African Security Review* 20, no. 4 (2011): 11–20.

Sinha, Manoj Kumar. "The Creation of Another Court: A Case Study of Special Court for Sierra Leone." *ISIL Year Book of International Humanitarian and Refugee Law* 4 (2004): 89–108.

Smith, Gerald H. "The Dichotomy of Politics and Corruption in a Neopatrimonial State: Evidence from Sierra Leone, 1968–1993." *African Issues* 25, no. 1 (1997): 58–62.

Steinberg, Jonny. *Thin Blue: The Unwritten Rules of Policing South Africa.* Gauteng, South Africa: Jonathan Ball, 2010.

Taylor, Bankole Kamara. *Sierra Leone: The Land, Its People and History.* Dar es Salaam, Tanzania: New Africa Press, 2014.

Thomas, Abdul Rashid. "Properties of Former APC Ministers Impounded by Anti-Corruption Commission." *Sierra Leone Telegraph*, August 1, 2019. https://www.thesierraleonetelegraph.com/properties-of-former-apc-ministers-impounded-by-anti-corruption-commission.

———. "Rioting at Sierra Leone's Opposition APC Office as Party Loses Election Petitions." *Sierra Leone Telegraph*, May 31, 2019. https://www.thesierraleonetelegraph.com/rioting-at-sierra-leones-opposition-apc-office-as-party-loses-election-petitions.

UN. "Fourth Report of the Secretary-General on the United Nations Mission in Sierra Leone (S/2000/455)." New York: United Nations, 2000.

———. "Ninth Report of the Secretary-General on the United Nations Mission in Sierra Leone (S/2001/228)." New York: United Nations, 2001.

———. "Report of the Secretary-General on the Establishment of a Special Court for Sierra Leone (S/2000/915)." New York: United Nations, 2000.

———. "Resolution 1181 (1998) Adopted by the Security Council at its 3902nd Meeting." New York: United Nations, 1998.

UNAMSIL. *UNAMSIL: A Success Story in Peacekeeping.* New York: UN Department of Peace Keeping Operations, 2005. http://www.un.org/en/peacekeeping/missions/past/unamsil/Overview.pdf.

UNDG. "Guidance Note to United Nations Country Teams on the PRSP (Poverty Reduction Strategy Papers)," 2001. http://www.undg.org/index.cfm?P=16.

Utas, Mats, and Magnus Jörgel. "The West Side Boys: Military Navigation in the Sierra Leone Civil War." *Journal of Modern African Studies* 46, no. 3 (2008): 487–511.

Wai, Zubairu. "Rethinking War and Violence in Sierra Leone: The RUF and the Nature and Condition of Insurgency Violence." *African Conflict & Peacebuilding Review* 13, no. 1 (2023): 44–76.

Wallerstein, Immanuel. *The Capitalist World-Economy.* Cambridge: Cambridge University Press, 1979.

Weber, Max. *Max Weber: Essays in Sociology.* Translated and edited by H. H. Gerth and C. Wright Mills. New York: Routledge, 2009.

Wendt, Alexander. "Anarchy Is What States Make of It: The Social Construction of Power Politics." *International Organization* 46, no. 2 (1992): 391–425.

Yarwood, Janette. "The Struggle Over Term Limits in Africa: The Power of Protest." *Journal of Democracy* 27, no. 3 (2016): 51–60.

4

Boko Haram and Glocalization of Child Soldier Recruitment in Nigeria

Mary-Jane Fox

The academic study of child soldiers has been active for several decades now, perhaps beginning in the early 1990s with the appearance of Ilene Cohn and Guy Goodwin-Gill's substantive book *Child Soldiers: The Role of Children in Armed Conflict*.[1] Before that, if there was any one violent non-state actor that grabbed the international media's attention, it was likely the Lord's Resistance Army (LRA), originally based in northern Uganda, for its atrocities. From there, it was not long before the abduction of young people—mostly males—to be armed and coerced to kill began appearing elsewhere, from Liberia and Sierra Leone to Sri Lanka, the Philippines, and most other locations where armed conflict was taking place. Although it is true that then and now some states have enlisted youth under the age of eighteen into their armed forces, how this can be addressed and reduced is quite different than dealing with armed, violent non-state actors, especially minors. At one point it was estimated that there were approximately 300,000 child soldiers globally, but that number has been challenged.[2] Although these possibly related instances of child soldier recruitment were not and have not been recognized and discussed as examples of glocalization, child soldier recruitment has begun to shift and change in recent years, and some of this might well be seen as glocalization. The danger of child soldier recruitment of any kind is that it perniciously breaks down and erodes society and social norms and does nothing to enhance it. And the longer it persists, the more damaging it becomes. Nigeria has a problem in this regard, and it appears to be a security intelligence failure, if not state failure.

Since 2002, there have been two main armed groups in Nigeria collectively known as Boko Haram: *Jama'atu Ahlis-Sunna Lidda'Awati Wal-Jihad* (JASDJ) and Islamic State West Africa Province (ISWAP).[3] Both have been recruiting young boys into their ranks, often through force or persuasion and sometimes desperation on the part of families and their children. At the same time, they were also attempting to gain the approval and support of the Islamic State in Iraq and Syria (ISIS), which was in the process of losing ground in Syria and Iraq but slowly establishing itself in other regions. One particular ISIS approach to child recruitment in Syria was to indoctrinate entire families to become part of their vision, with a role for every member of the family.[4] For forced or family-level recruitment to function, however, three previously overlooked variables need to exist: youth bulge, low primary school attendance, and access to weapons (discussed later in this chapter). This chapter examines how Boko Haram picked up on the ISIS family-level recruitment model and attempted to replicate it, but of course in its own way. It is an example of the downside of glocalization at work in the context of state failure.

Indeed, it was ISIS that began this deliberately different approach to recruitment. It was the very beginning of a shift in recruitment practices; it involved long-term strategizing, early indoctrination, and young people's detachment from extreme acts of violence. This was achieved by ISIS through recruiting families, couples, and single mothers with children, the latter paired off with available active combatants to serve as husbands and father figures. The women would contribute by bearing sons and rearing future combatants or having daughters to raise as future mothers. This chapter argues that Boko Haram in Nigeria had been replicating the ISIS recruitment approach to different degrees, and they continue to do so, seeking approval and gaining support from ISIS.[5] Evidence is presented in the form of primary sources as known instances of video and photographic material that included children and were often produced by media-trained cadres from both ISWAP and JASDJ. Some of this evidence was recorded by technology-trained child soldiers.[6] Consisting of thirty instances dating from May 2014 to January 2022, which were initially made available on various social media such as Telegram and YouTube, the more violent ones were eventually banned.[7] The method used for evaluating these thirty instances was visual ethnography, a novel approach that is discussed subsequently.[8] What is interesting is that training youth for recording their group's activities was not attempted by ISIS, which is one way that Boko Haram's variation was more local than global. With this in mind, it is important to state that this evidence does not and in fact cannot represent all aspects of children living under ISWAP or JASDJ, but it is important to consider since it represents what the two groups want the outside world (including other armed groups) to know about their activities. It is important to stress that neither faction posted any denials of the images and videos.

From this perspective, the thirty instances mentioned above can be understood as ISWAP and JASDJ preliminary examples of replicating the ISIS objective for family-level recruitment toward a global caliphate through its transformation into a glocalized undertaking. Although other ISIS global objectives have been followed in other places, Boko Haram is the first group attempting to create and supply its own future combatants through family-level recruitment.

The Glocal Dimension of the Child Soldier Phenomenon

Although the literature on glocalization rarely includes discussions on its link with conflict, there is far less available on the even more compelling link of glocalization and child soldiers. The recruitment of children younger than eighteen as armed combatants or in support roles is hardly new, but some significant changes in how child soldiers are currently recruited and trained could be perceived as linked to glocalization. In the 1980s and 1990s there were widespread but seemingly discrete instances of forced and unforced child soldier recruitment, as in Uganda (Lord's Resistance Army), Sierra Leone,[9] Liberia, and several other conflicts, some of which might be argued as preliminary instances of glocalization that are also linked to the diffusion of conflict.

Simply put, the concept of global and local matters simultaneously taking place and influencing each other (i.e., glocalization) has been a growing part of scholarly discussions since the 1980s. It is a response to the simplistic concept of globalization, which does not take the role of local influences and adaptations into account. Before a fuller discussion on this, just what is and is not meant by glocalization is discussed first. As understood and applied in this chapter, the work of Roudometof is used here. By avoiding the monism and shortcomings of Robertson and White as well as Ritzer's problem with ideal types and a dualism that falls short of reality,[10] Roudometof's glocalization offers a solution with more "analytical autonomy" that happens to be more applicable to a wider range of instances—beyond what globalization theory offers. His understanding of glocalization is expressed as "a process possessing analytical autonomy vis-à-vis other related concepts (local, global). This requires the specification of the process or mechanism that offers an explication of this autonomy."[11] Importantly, he stresses the word *process*, indicating the ebb and flow of glocalization's capacity for movement, where shifts and changes either toward or away from the global or local are to be expected. Understood in this way, glocalization is not necessarily a static or motionless notion, but it captures experiences that shift and change as internal and external events also shift and change. Originally a concept applied within agriculture, the term has now been stretched and widened to have been included in sociology, economics, politics, international conflict and security, the media, community organization, human rights, climate change, and more.

Glocalization's link to conflict has been discussed at length by Marret in 2008 and then Pham in 2011, both in regard to Al Qaeda in the Islamic Maghreb (AQIM), which was formed in 2006.[12] Neither brings up the topic of child recruitment because it was quite limited at that time in terms of unusual recruitment practices that did not begin in Syria until shortly after the conflict with ISIS started in 2013. Glocalization has not yet been linked to child soldiers perhaps partly because of the haphazard way in which children were recruited prior to the 1990s and into the early 2000s, which primarily consisted of the forcible recruitment of kidnapped young people, convincing homeless children they would be looked after, and a campaign to attract recruits from abroad. It was not until June 2014 that ISIS initiated a new approach to recruitment for their envisioned global "caliphate" by creating or using extant families and promoting their active involvement with ISIS through family-level recruitment.

The ISIS presence and ambitions in Syria and eventually northern Iraq have been well documented. Since the spring of 2011 there have been several groups opposing the Syrian government, the largest and most dominant being ISIS, which began indoctrinating children from an early age expressly for the purpose of creating second-generation mujahedeen for its own future. Indeed, reports by those such as Almohammad, Bloom, Horgan, Nyamutata, Pearson, Vale, Warner, and others have comprehensively described the ISIS process of grooming and training young males for fighting.[13] Almohammad, however, observed recruitment as being of two types: predatory and structural, with the structural integrated into ISIS bureaucracy through these family-level programs. How children were indoctrinated and weaponized has led to a "transgenerational capability" consisting of "committed, trained, and aggressive future soldiers" who have endured the demise of ISIS in Syria and Iraq and most likely are presently dispersed throughout Africa, Asia, and the Middle East, contributing to the long-term ISIS global caliphate vision.[14] Even back in 2006, Peter W. Singer released *Children at War*, wherein he described at length the tendency for child soldiering to perpetuate itself, providing examples as well as analysis. As he notes, "the past use of children in war breeds the conditions for future war. . . . Each round of fighting creates a new cohort, traumatized by the war and bereft of hope and skills, who then become a potential pool and catalyst for the next spate of violence."[15]

In a 2018 wider discussion of child soldiers, Bloom notes that "ISIS's priority is ensuring the continuity and longevity of the group," which it addresses in their own schools by fostering "a unique form of resilience by combining intense physical and military training with deep levels of ideological and psychological indoctrination." This family level form of ISIS recruitment Bloom further notes is "a systematic process that produces competent militants who embrace every aspect of its teachings" that has proven to be highly adaptable and transportable as ISIS has been expanding into Africa and Southeast Asia.[16] Despite the 2018–2019 gains made in undermining ISIS in Iraq and Syria, ISIS was not dismantled completely.[17]

Although ISIS in Syria engaged in kidnapping and forcing youth to fight with them or blackmailing some parents to hand over their boys (and sometimes girls), the family-level approach was intended to become a cornerstone of recruitment: why rely on exogenous reluctant recruits when endogenous ambitious ones could be available indefinitely?[18] Of course, considering how widespread and culturally diverse Islam was and still is, it would be impossible for the family-level recruitment to be identical everywhere. Here we can observe the link between glocalization and the aim of an armed group to establish an Islamist territory under Islamist-interpreted law. To expand the group's global aspirations and reputation, allowances would have to be made for some degree of local and regional practices and customs to avoid infighting as much as possible. With this in mind, ISIS intentions and glocalization fit into each other almost perfectly, "hand in glove."

ISIS recruitment of children somehow connects with the social disintegration and plight of children, especially in the education sector. The effort by ISIS to create its own Islamist schools in Syria was not only to avoid Western-style teaching and any liberal notions associated with it, but also to ensure that its armed youth would have some level of Islamist-based education and indoctrination. With more than 7,000 schools damaged or completely destroyed and about 2.4 million children out of school, the necessity to offer education was an imperative.[19] Thus did ISIS set itself up as shelter from a storm that was its own doing. In the process, the combination of low school attendance, youth bulge, and access to weapons created a new approach to recruiting child soldiers that was deeply local but very potent in the global expansion of jihadist ideology and played well into state failure.

Essential Recruitment Factors and Nature of the State

In terms of the drivers of those conflicts using child soldiers in general, and all the more so for those using the ISIS family-level recruitment approach, there are generally three crucial factors that must be present to a high degree: low school attendance, youth bulge, and access to weapons. These factors are not only critical in themselves, but are also related to the problematic nature of the state. Problems of low school attendance, abnormal population structure, and the proliferation of light weapons are among the various ways in which the state fails to meet the core needs of its citizens. Nigeria and many other countries in Africa have all been plagued by states that fail to deliver core elements of social and human development. In addition, they exhibit traits of poor governance and dictatorship that make the state problematic as citizens demand political rights and economic and social justice. Varying forms of insurgencies, including Boko Haram, have capitalized on these problems to take up arms against the Nigerian state. As already noted, low school attendance, youth bulge, and access to weapons are common factors that facilitate armed insurgencies against the state.

Regarding school attendance, it is important to stress here that the concept of school attendance is not interchangeable with unequal access to education or school enrollment: neither access nor enrollment guarantees attendance, and it is actual presence in the classroom that is paramount here.[20] The reasons for low school attendance are many, so no matter whether it is lack of proximate schools, lack of security, high cost of schooling, poor education system, discrimination of a particular group, being orphaned, or any combination of the above, low attendance for any reason means a significant sector of young people are not present in school and thus are more accessible for and susceptible to both urban and rural recruitment of the more conventional kind.[21] School attendance is important not only for keeping children off the streets, but also for the fact that a literate child is less vulnerable than a child who is not literate. Importantly, this underscores why the ISIS approach to family recruitment was so appealing in spite of the military training that inured them to commit extreme violence.

The second factor is the demographic condition referred to as "youth bulge." Broadly understood as a disproportionately large percentage of youth within the overall population, youth bulge originally was based on lower infant mortality rates and high fertility rates.[22] When youth bulge is combined with the presence of armed conflict interfering with school attendance,[23] even regionally, it creates a weighty concoction that an armed group like ISIS or JASDJ/ISWAP was only too willing, efficient, and adaptive to almost seamlessly integrate with its own short- and long-term caliphate strategies.[24] Offering to provide young people with education in the name of militant Islam—along with, of course, military and communications technology training—would appeal to many parents who were devoted to Islam and valued education for their sons. Such a lure was attractive for families or guardians to be part of ISIS or ISWAP.

There is a known link between youth bulge and armed conflict, and it has generally correlated with poverty, lack of education and/or employment, marginalization, urbanization, and political factors.[25] For youth bulge to be effective for family-level recruitment, an armed conflict has to have been going on for several years so that a young adult combatant has time to marry and produce children: a nineteen-year-old combatant whose wife had a son in 2014 would be twenty-seven years old in 2022 with a son soon ready for military training.

The third factor to consider would be access to weapons and the increasing availability of small arms and light weapons (SALW) globally, through smuggling, the black and gray markets, and capture or raid of state military arsenals. In fact, in very recent years, "craft production" has also been on the rise.[26] With the legal small arms trade alone having increased by 95 percent from 2001 to 2011, and trade in ammunition having increased by 205 percent during the same period, the role of SALW in legal and illegal trade has been indisputable.[27] Of course, using terms like *weapons* and *arms* can be misleading because they could mean anything, from a handgun to a missile launcher to all-terrain tanks. When comparing how well armed two parties to a conflict are, such variables as power asymmetries are based on both large and small weapons; this would have limited relevance where the terrain precludes the use of tanks or where non-state combatants are young, well trained, and particularly well armed with modern light weapons.

Non-military types of power or weakness can also be pivotal, such as a state army's poor morale or a non-state group that is orientated toward communications and media technology and knows how to make good use of it.

With small arms and their ammunition understood as a key enabler of conflict, there is an argument to be made for how the continuous recruitment of child soldiers is at least partly explained by the rising manufacture and distribution of second- and third-generation weapons over the years.[28] Because they are deliberately designed to be small and lightweight, have significantly reduced recoil, and are easy to assemble and operate, they are ideal for children and youths.[29] Indeed, there are even several models of machine guns on the market weighing less than four and a half kilograms.[30] This is not to claim that all child combatants are armed with new, state-of-the-art weapons, but even lightweight weapons that were manufactured twenty-five years ago would make a difference.

Without these three factors, the role of youth less than fifteen years old in armed conflict would likely be restricted to support positions. These three factors stand in contrast to more complex and fluctuating variables derived from quantitative studies and then reapplied within quantitative research on child soldiers. Such factors include cost-benefit calculations, conventional power asymmetries, rebel group strength, and leadership and command issues often found in quantitative studies.[31] Although quantitative research commonly uses such derived variables, repeated reductive adaptations of variables from previously developed data sets can compromise validity.[32]

Geographical and temporal factors are also used in studying the child soldiers phenomenon. In terms of the former, and especially in cases where violent non-state actors can be difficult to pin down geographically, periods of seeming inactivity have been found to have more to do with regrouping than folding. Thus, an unidentifiable, constantly changing and elusive core can be difficult to detect *while* and *because* it evades detection. Considering the constant ebb and flow of that core and determining such standardized variables as territorial control, leadership, troop strength, and troop capacity, the shortcomings of annually aggregated variables become apparent.[33] After all, shifts and changes within most violent non-state groups occur in much shorter time frames: troop strength in March might be profoundly different by November, and an annual average would fail to convey the strategic significance of this in understanding a group's movements and operations. Regarding annual child recruitment numbers, an annual value is not revealed if that value reflects a single abduction incident of many children or youth in a single location, or several recruitment incidents taking place throughout the year, or at certain locations or times of the year. All of these are crucial in terms of assessing, predicting, preventing, and indeed reducing abductions. Thus, quantitative measurements certainly have relevance, but their limitations also need to be considered, especially when estimating the recruitment of families.

Considering the deliberate efforts JASDJ/ISWAP made with family-level recruitment, a new category has been added to the child soldier subculture in general. This in turn becomes a tautological trap since child soldiers are already perceived as a tangible threat because of their magnified image, yet child soldiers have a magnified image because they are perceived as a tangible threat; it is all the more so when they have parents or guardians standing behind them and supporting them.

Observing through Visual Ethnography

The visual ethnography applied here is limited to thirty videos and photographic images from 2014 to 2021, all of which include children and were recorded by either JASDJ or ISWAP. They are part of an extensive publicly available online archive belonging to a specialist of Nigerian terrorist groups.[34] Limiting the observation to those under fifteen years of age makes it easier to identify children than, for example, someone fifteen, sixteen, or seventeen years old who has reached near-adult height and is filled out in terms of musculature and has an adult voice and facial hair. It must be stressed that most social media images produced during this period did not include children, but there did appear to be a pattern of them, some seemingly innocent enough, yet others sufficiently disturbing to not be ignored. They clearly represent a preliminary look at the expanded role of children.[35]

Among the advantages of visual ethnography are the additional perspectives it brings, especially those not possible because of Boko Haram's covert nature and the impossibility of an academic field study. According to Pink, visual ethnography simply indicates any visual source that represents ethnographic interest or knowledge, and this can entail video clips and photographs.[36] Pink also identifies and discusses two distinct modes within visual ethnography, the first related to more traditional sociological research. The second is more phenomenological than reliant on empiricist data collection and relates more to how knowledge is produced and comes to be known.[37]

It almost goes without saying that some of the materials have been used by JASDJ and ISWAP for the purposes of propaganda and some have not. As such, it is important to distinguish "staged media" that is produced for propaganda from "non-staged media" created for internal or local recruitment purposes. Both of these may incidentally include children and/or child soldiers. Such a distinction might offer a better context of how children are used in videos and photos. Although visual ethnography is still relatively new,[38] one advantage is how it creates an opportunity for researchers to review each image for unlimited observations, something not possible in conventional fieldwork. It allows for repeated viewings and deeper analysis.[39] For example, researchers might take unlimited notes, pause, rewind, and play a video clip several times.[40] Although some subjects might find being recorded on film or video unwelcome, this is likely to be less so when the camera operator is someone they know and is part of their group.[41]

For at least two decades, northeastern Nigeria has had child soldiers as well as varying degrees of each of the three factors of low school attendance, youth bulge, and access to weapons. For example, while there were some under-eighteens early on in Boko Haram's existence, it seemed to expand exponentially just after the Chibok kidnapping incident in May 2014. Since then, it appears to have evolved into family-level recruitment strategies along with more conventional recruitment.

It was Boko Haram's founder, Muhammed Yusuf, who, before his death in 2009, initially tried to link Boko Haram with Al-Qaeda, insisting his followers—and in fact all of Nigeria—follow Al-Qaeda as well as the Taliban model for living according to sharia law. After Yusuf's death, Abubakr Shekau replaced him, but almost immediately after that problems developed between Shekau and his commanders, who had written letters of complaint to AQIM leadership regarding Shekau's at times outlandish actions and harsh methods. Shekau eventually lost the support of AQIM and began to seek support from ISIS. It did not take long for Shekau to catch on to the novel ISIS approach to family recruitment and attempt his own version of it. From the time of the kidnapping of the Chibok girls in May 2014, the international response was perhaps much greater than anyone anticipated. By December 2014, Shekau produced his first in a series of videos and photos on the internet for ISIS showing a range of practices, from boys in blue uniforms learning how to handle simulated practice rifles, to others executing Nigerian soldiers as well as attending family-style religious gatherings and studying the Quran. The first video included a narrated letter to ISIS indicating that children were being militarily trained as well as provided with Islamist teaching. It was the beginning of a series of videos and photographs made available for ISIS.[42]

Shekau's pledge of allegiance to ISIS was finally accepted by ISIS leader Al-Baghdadi in March 2015—perhaps because of the kidnapping of the Chibok girls and the military and Islamist training he was providing for boys—and he was also awarded the role of leader (Waly) of ISWAP. At the time of this acceptance, he changed the name of JASDJ to ISWAP, even though ISIS leader Al-Baghdadi was never convinced of Shekau's reliability. He also began to promote his group as part of the ISIS global "caliphate" as JASDJ became inactive. Negative reports about Shekau's actions continued to be received by Al-Baghdadi. Despite receiving orders to curtail his behavior, he did not, and in just under a year and half after his allegiance was accepted, a new leader of ISWAP was assigned by ISIS. Shekau immediately revived JASDJ and continued as he had been, though often referring publicly to his link with ISIS. Ironically, in May 2021, Shekau was killed during an ISWAP attempt to seize him, and since then, JASDJ seems to have dwindled. ISWAP is still active, having been reported in July 2022 to have arranged a major prison break of at least 800 prisoners.[43] Shortly after that, it took control of more Nigerian territory near Marte in the northeast as well as further afield in the Sahel.[44]

Returning to the three factors of primary school attendance, youth bulge and access to weapons, the only change was that these factors gradually increased over time. This needs to be understood in light of the overall Nigerian population, which is 211 million,[45] with 43.31 percent in the zero to fourteen age group in 2021.[46] Nigeria has been awash with weapons for a fairly long time, as studies on SALW in Nigeria show.[47] A report from 2013 estimated that 80 percent of the weapons in the country are illegally acquired.[48] More recent reporting describes a country that is overstocked with black and gray market weapons,[49] so access to weapons should be considered quite high. As for primary school attendance, Onapajo notes that "given Boko Haram's ideological opposition to Western civilization . . . schools have specifically been targeted for attacks . . . making the region unsafe for the acquisition of Western education."[50] Since the armed conflict in the northeast started in 2013, more than 1,400 schools have been destroyed, 2,295 teachers killed, and 19,000 teachers displaced.[51] UNICEF also reports that in the north, the school attendance rate is only 53 percent,[52] which can be compared to the national attendance rate of 66.7 percent.[53] Onapajo further reports that most of the destroyed schools were "converted to military bases where the group launched attacks and stocked weapons."[54]

He continues with more alarming statistics showing that in the three most affected states (Adamawa, Borno, and Yobe States), the attacks on schools have caused 2.8 million children to require urgent educational support. Clearly, this development has greatly contributed to the rising numbers of out-of-school children in Nigeria, as 10.5 million children between the ages of five and fourteen are not attending any school. With this statistic, it is estimated that "one in every five of the world's out-of-school children is in Nigeria."[55]

Such statistics on education indicate something about young people not only absent from schooling and vulnerable to recruitment, but also how they are part of a larger constellation of issues and factors that contribute to state failure. Youth bulge and access to weapons almost seem to be auxiliary add-ons rather than equal contributors, especially since not every location with youth bulge has a problem with child soldier recruitment and not every location with gun availability is at war and recruiting minors for it. With low school attendance added, however, it becomes a potent concoction. Some might even think of them as precursors to state failure.

In fact, this very well could be what Nigeria is headed for when taking into account the other factors, such as the national economy, poverty, healthcare, government corruption, and of course inter- and intrareligious strife. The most serious aspect of this is that it has been taking place for years and is not the same problem now that it was ten years ago and from there, twenty years ago. It has mushroomed into a threat that has seen little to no improvement and has only been steadily growing. It is too soon to make predictions about the capabilities and strategies of the new president and vice president, Bola Tinubu and Kashim Shettima. Both are wealthy and moderate Muslims, with Shettima hailing from Borno State, which has seen enormous Boko Haram activity over the years when compared with other states. Borno tops the list of Boko Haram fatalities (May 2011 to July 2023) with more than 38,000 deaths; Zamfara State is second on the list, with 6,800 deaths, about a fifth of Borno's number.[56] With both Boko Haram groups slowly making inroads toward and to Lagos, it is difficult to speculate regarding Nigeria ten years or even only five years from now. Notwithstanding the regional variations, all of this reaffirms the precarious nature of the Nigerian state in terms of meeting the core needs of its citizens. In that sense, Boko Haram, which is notorious for violating human rights, becomes not only an ideological and terrorist organization, but also one that challenges the democratic objectives of the Nigerian state.

Visual Ethnography: Boko Haram's Glocal Projection

Overall, the kind of glocalization we have seen in Nigeria with JASDJ/ISWAP is unlikely to take place in other seemingly similar cases. Most are lacking some element of the three crucial factors discussed in the previous section. What is most important to keep in mind here is that in most other cases, digitally produced visual ethnography is unlikely to be as available and consistent as it has been with Boko Haram groups.

A non-state armed group can recruit both individuals and families if they have the means and ability to orchestrate it. This was especially the case with JASDJ/ISWAP in terms of internet access as well as the dark web, where the skills of technology-minded young recruits seem to have well exceeded similarly skilled personnel within ISIS and other groups. These young JASDJ/ISWAP recruits are unique in that they became so able to recognize the power of the lens, so to speak, that they exceeded the visual work of others, and are on their way to becoming a model for other groups to follow, having learned there are few limits to what they can project onto followers, enemies, the region, and the international community. This might lead to concerns about how what is glocal might fuse with what is global, but in terms of family-level recruitment, it is far too early to speculate on this. That would require several ISIS subgroups to have family-level recruitment programs well underway, and JASDJ/ISWAP, for now, appears to be the only group attempting it outside of Syria. It is important to bear in mind that family-level recruitment requires extensive planning and preparation, something that many, if not most, non-state armed groups are not accustomed to, tending to be more reactive than reflective.[57]

Seven examples from the thirty photos and video clips have been selected to demonstrate the advantages and insights derived from visual ethnography (see figures 4.1 to 4.7). Collectively, they show the glocal projection of Boko Haram. They are not only examples of family recruitment, but also serve as examples of how the children are used more generally. It is important to bear in mind that it is known that some orphaned children are adopted into a family that is a member of a Boko Haram community, but it is not possible to determine which children are adopted and which one are not.

Figure 4.1 (February 14, 2015) is a photo with several children wearing blue and some black uniforms and having drill practice with real firearms.[58]

Figure 4.1 might seem to be an excellent example of the availability of small and light weapons and the young ages of the children. However,

Figure 4.1. Photo of Children Drill Practice. *Source:* Jacob Zenn archive on Boko Haram in Nigeria. Used with permission.

looking carefully, it seems that at least two in the back are holding wooden firearms painted black, and on the right side of the photo, in the center, is a boy who seems to be holding nothing and is not caught up in it all.

Figure 4.2 (September 2015) is composed of two screenshots (screenshots A [front view] and B [side view]) from a videos of an outdoor Eid al Fitr (marking the end of Ramadan) event with hundreds of attendees, including dozens of children.[59] In the front row, there are two small children on the left and a youth to their right (4.2A). In the 4.2B screenshot, at the center, just in front of the small child, there are four children seated.

There are literally dozens of such videos with small children in them. This is indoctrination at a young age: being part of the community, taking part in songs, hearing readings, and otherwise showing parents how their children will become part of the community. For any single parent or couple who has been impoverished, this has great appeal.

Figure 4.3 (May 2017) is a screenshot of a video showing four Chibok schoolgirls, wearing black, full-body chadors, one of them armed, and their parents being invited by the girls to join them and convert to Islam.[60] Clearly an effort that is staged and made to appeal to parents, believing they are demonstrating how their daughters are so very cared for. It is also meant for the approval of ISIS, to show how diligent Boko Haram was in

Figure 4.2A. Screenshot of Outdoor Eid al Fitr (front view). *Source*: Jacob Zenn archive on Boko Haram in Nigeria. Used with permission.

Figure 4.2B. Screenshot of Outdoor Eid al Fitr (side view). *Source*: Jacob Zenn archive on Boko Haram in Nigeria. Used with permission.

Figure 4.3. Screenshot of Chibok Schoolgirls. *Source*: Jacob Zenn archive on Boko Haram in Nigeria. Used with permission.

managing the girls' cooperation. However, three are looking down or away, and the eyes of the girl on the left can hardly be seen.

Figure 4.4 (January 17, 2020) is a screenshot of a video similar in style to ISIS videos from Syria, with an armed and uniformed child seconds before he executed a Christian student from the University of Maiduguri as a response to Christians killing Muslims in Plateau State.[61] The screenshot in figure 4.4 was taken just seconds before the young man was shot and killed. Certainly it was designed for ISIS, the Nigerian military and government, and anyone in the international audience to prove how serious Boko Haram is and how they train and support young people to do the killing.

Figure 4.5 (February 25, 2021) is composed of two screenshots (screenshots A and B) of a raid footage on split screen with Aubakar Shekau on the right claiming the attack and then raid footage showing children firing weapons in combat.[62] In the screenshots in figure 4.5, Shekau is on the right and delivering a speech. The viewers are offered footage of two young men taking part in either a battle or more likely training for a battle. This would likely be shown to ISIS to prove how diligent Shekau was in making sure the youth were well trained.

Figure 4.6 (February 28, 2021) is composed of two screenshots (screenshots A and B) of a video with approximately twenty-five children in military uniform engaged in practicing punching, push-ups, sit-ups, and shooting drills as well as studying and reading the Quran in a makeshift

Figure 4.4. Screenshot of Armed and Uniformed Child Executing. *Source*: Jacob Zenn archive on Boko Haram in Nigeria. Used with permission.

Figure 4.5A. Screenshot of a Raid Footage with Shekau (boy center). *Source*: Jacob Zenn archive on Boko Haram in Nigeria. Used with permission.

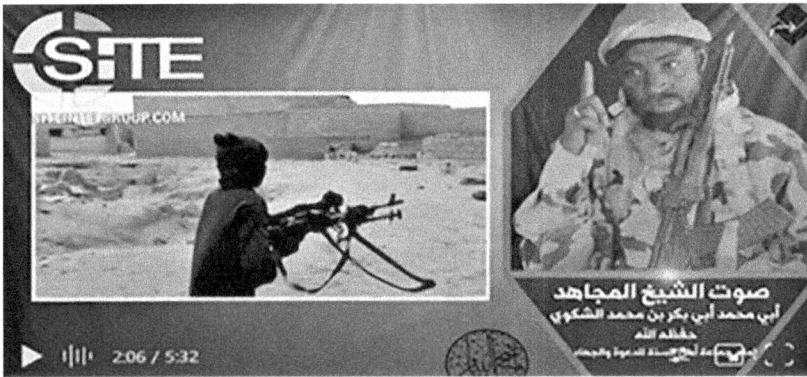

Figure 4.5B. Screenshot of Raid Footage with Shekau (boy on far side).

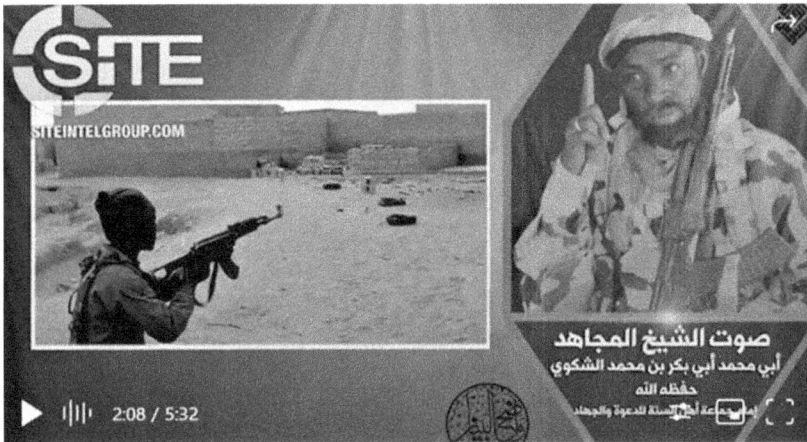

Islamic school.[63] Figures 4.6A and B show an interesting pair of stills from the same video, as those who are younger and yellow-uniformed are in the back in screenshot A yet are front and center in screenshot B. This is clearly made for potential family recruitment as well as ISIS approval.

Figure 4.7 (October 31, 2021) is a screenshot of video with a series of ISWAP battles and a child soldier making a threatening speech to the Nigerian Army and then immediately executing two soldiers.[64] The screen-

Figure 4.6A. Screenshot of Children in Military Uniform Practicing. *Source*: Jacob Zenn archive on Boko Haram in Nigeria. Used with permission.

Figure 4.6B. Screenshot of Children in Military Uniform in a Makeshift Islamic School. *Source*: Jacob Zenn archive on Boko Haram in Nigeria. Used with permission.

shot in figure 4.7 was also intended for ISIS, the Nigerian military, the Nigerian government, and anyone in the international audience to see just how serious they are, especially in terms of using children.

THE STATE, GLOCALIZATION, AND VISUAL ETHNOGRAPHY

Collectively, the visuals all point to three intriguing lines of analysis, two of them about the core concepts and issues of the African state and glocalization

Figure 4.7. Screenshot of Child Soldier Threatening Nigerian Army and Executing Two Soldiers. *Source*: Jacob Zenn archive on Boko Haram in Nigeria. Used with permission.

and the third about visual ethnography. While on one hand the visuals show a certain level of brutality, which together constitute a direct challenge to the authority of the Nigerian state, on the other hand they are quick to provide evidence of the sense of educational responsibility Boko Haram has toward children who are growing up uneducated in Islam. This in turn challenges the Nigerian state, which is further buttressed in the messages that express the grievances and demands of Boko Haram. All of these point to the precarious nature of the Nigerian state, both in terms of its failures to meet the core needs of its citizens and its inability to exert authority and protect its citizens. The fact that this has been taking place for so long suggests that there has not been sufficiently consistent and stalwart support for the people of the northeast, where Boko Haram has been more or less allowed to proliferate.

There is also the matter of the family recruitment model becoming glocalized with its deployment in Nigeria. The visuals show not just children but also community members, some of whom may even be parents. These visuals are for both local and external audiences. They deploy children and families in a way that draws upon both local and global jihadist "moralities" and shows the involvement of domestic and external actors. In fact, Boko Haram appears to be glaringly aware of the global and the local as well as how to combine them as needed in what is a glocal presentation of Boko Haram. Considering they do not have a central command or headquarters, this glocality is notable.

Visual ethnography allows us to see Boko Haram's horrors, challenge to the state, and glocal form of terrorism. What Boko Haram is showing to the world is clear to everyone and deliberately intentional. Through their trained cadres of video experts, they have been well able to convey fear, concern, toughness, and even the importance of religion. Even their range of visuals clearly portrays the ubiquitousness of children. The timing of their appearance—after the Chibok kidnappings—is hardly coincidence. Suddenly children had more value than Boko Haram realized, and it was not just Christian children as helpless quarry, but their own children were more than just happenstance soldiers. To continue family-level child recruitment, the three factors mentioned earlier represent the perfect storm. In fact, child soldier and family-level recruitments' muted place in security studies and conflict literature more specifically represents a kind of intelligence failure. This is especially so with the Nigerian state, which is increasingly failing in its core duties.

More recent research has begun to shift toward how armed conflict in general is affected by child soldier recruitment, but primarily through the broad lens of quantitative studies. While the benefits of quantitative research are acknowledged, there is equal value in systematic individual case studies, which allow policy-relevant subtleties to be laid out coherently and concretely. Several general observations follow, based on the understanding that ISIS is the globalizing influence (aiming for a global caliphate), and JASDJ/ISWAP is a glocalized version.

Earlier ad hoc recruitment of child soldiers within Boko Haram has been transforming into more deliberate and calculated long-term strategies. Moreover, within ISIS, part of that strategy has included family-level recruitment, something Boko-Haram has been attempting to replicate to solicit continued ISIS support. JASDJ/ISWAP's child and family-level recruitment has been taking place for almost ten years now, and it is sufficiently self-generated and developed so that it can continue to build from it. This combination of low primary school attendance, youth bulge, and access to SALW are important enabling factors for both child and family-level recruitment, but especially the latter.

A visual ethnographic approach creates an overall representation that helps outsiders to understand the place of children in these groups, at least what Boko Haram has wanted outsiders to know. Outsiders are not only White, Western-educated scholars or workers from NGOs or other states, but also other violent non-state groups who might be zealous rivals. Whatever they post on any social media site is fair game for us all.

It is too soon to predict how lasting and robust Boko Haram's own glocalized version of ISIS family-level recruitment will be. Once it is more widely up and running, it may well begin to self-perpetuate, at which point it will be far more difficult to shut it down or even interfere with it. Of course, the ISIS family-level recruitment is not as smooth running or robust as ISIS might like to project, as shown in an eye-opening 2020 research article by Speckhard and Ellenberg.[65] However, the reported family-level recruitment problems ISIS has had in Syria in recent years, as observed by Speckhard and Ellenberg, are not likely to be the same problems JASDJ/ISWAP might have today. Assumptions that treat apparently similar problems and their solutions as being between a localized issue and a globalized one would be misguided, no doubt overlooking aspects of one or the other that are not sufficiently shared or similar. If a solution for a glocal issue was indiscriminately applied as a globalized one, this would likely undermine the security of the state. This could be one explanation for why so many conflicts have not been resolved: applying methods or approaches that helped in one conflict, but perhaps were too specialized to function anywhere else. Conflating solutions for conventional child soldier recruitment with the family-level recruitment as practiced by ISIS, and now ISWAP, for example, are unlikely to be successful.

Conclusion: The Nigerian State and Boko Haram Family-Level Recruitment

This chapter examines the application of the family recruitment model by Boko Haram to Nigeria in its fight against the Nigerian state and its connection to global jihadism, notably ISIS. It shows the increased presence and involvement of children in the violent conflict between Boko Haram and government forces in Nigeria, particularly in the northeast. Boko Haram's own social media portrayals of young boys with real or wooden replica rifles being trained to hold and use them, their subsequent participation in military actions against government troops, and then idyllic instances of them reading the Quran and attending large outdoor feasts and prayer meetings with family and friends all seemed familiar. And it was: the visuals appeared oddly congruent with descriptions in recent years of ISIS and how entire families were indoctrinated to work toward the vision of a global caliphate. With each family member having a duty to work toward that vision, it was a way to begin to populate its fighting ranks without resorting to force or persuasion. Boko Haram was quick to begin to develop a localized version of this model shortly after it appeared. Boko Haram's efforts appeared to be the first instance of glocalization of ISIS family-level child soldier recruitment. The three possible factors selected, which rarely gained much attention in child soldier studies (youth bulge, low primary school attendance, and access to weapons), all have had their roles to play in the attempted establishment of family-level recruitment. At the same time, these three factors are good indicators of the failure of the Nigerian state to ensure the well-being of its citizens. It is precisely this intersection of state failure and global jihadism that found a Nigerian variant in the form of Boko Haram. Boko Haram has adopted and localized a savvy and very crude form of family recruitment that will continue to breed child soldiers.

Realizing that family-level child recruitment does not simply or easily end, we can begin to alleviate some of its effects through its gradual erosion, similar to how child and family-level recruitment has managed to erode humanitarian norms. Perhaps ultimately the "intangible power" of ISIS will be found with armed groups that successfully follow their lead.[66] Bearing in mind how those who carry out child and family-level recruitment are persistent, highly resourceful, and adaptable to changing circumstances, responses to it must, at the very least, be equally persistent, resourceful, and adaptable. The answer to the problem of child soldiers will not be found in a singular dose of a singular remedy: conflicts recruiting children and families will require well-strategized responses. The practice of children coercively recruited and trained for combat and desensitized to extreme violence is already a growing scourge; having the support of their parents or guardians is a wildfire that will be difficult to extinguish. Even more, the problem of child soldiers is easily tied to state failure, which breeds violent conflicts that are glocalized through terrorism warfare. If Nigeria is to function properly as a state, it needs to reclaim the northeast and be responsible for all of its citizens. It might even benefit from its own understanding and practice of glocalization.

Notes

1. Ilene Cohn and Guy Goodwin-Gill, *Child Soldiers: The Role of Children in Armed Conflict*. The International Committee of the Red Cross was also actively involved.

2. Mike Wessells, for example, elaborates on the estimated population figures in his *Child Soldiers: From Violence to Protection*, 9–10. For a 2006 estimate of

250,000, see United Nations General Assembly, "Report of the Special Representative of the Secretary-General for Children and Armed Conflict," A/61/275, 4.

3. For the purposes of this chapter, the term Boko Haram refers to both JASDJ and ISWAP; in some cases, one group might have been more engaged than the other, but the extent to which one group or another participated in that engagement is not always simple to determine.

4. Marion Deslandes-Martineau et al., "The Programming Curriculum within ISIS."

5. To avoid confusion, here I refer to Islamic State as IS and generally avoid the ISIS/ISIL forms.

6. For more on applied visual ethnography, see Zacharias Pieri et al., "Boko Haram's Child Soldiers: Media Mujahids, Martyrs, and Militants," 3.

7. These videos and photographs were found on the two factions' own accounts and are archived as part of a Boko Haram collection by specialist Jacob Zenn, https://unmaskingbokoharam.com/archived-sources-2/.

8. Pieri et al., "Boko Haram's Child Soldiers," 12.

9. Macartan Humphreys and Jeremy M. Weinstein, *What the Fighters Say: A Survey of Ex-Combatants in Sierra Leone*; "Sierra Leone 2019 Crime & Safety Report," *US Department of State*.

10. Victor Roudometof, "Theorizing Glocalization: Three Interpretations," 393–95 and 397–98.

11. Ibid., 398.

12. Jean-Luc Marret, "Al-Qaeda in the Islamic Maghreb: A 'Glocal' Organization"; J. Peter Pham, "Foreign Influences and Shifting Horizons: The Ongoing Evolution of al Qaeda in the Islamic Maghreb."

13. See Asaad Almohammad, "ISIS Child Soldiers."

14. Mia Bloom has claimed that "many, if not most children, are killed in battle and few survive to progress through the ranks to become leaders" without evidence; see Mia Bloom, "Child Soldiers in Armed Conflict," 12. A more recent work has modified this to "Many children are killed in battle and few progress up the ranks to become adult leaders . . ." but still without supporting evidence; see Mia Bloom," Weaponizing the Weak: the Role of Children in Terrorist Groups," 213.

15. Peter W. Singer, *Children at War*, 109.

16. Bloom, "Child Soldiers in Armed Conflict"; see also James S. Morris and Tristan Dunning, "Islamic State Schooled Children."

17. Ahmed Aboulenein, "Iraq Holds Victory Parade"; see also *New York Times* Editorial Board, "Islamic State: Landless but Still Dangerous."

18. National Coordinator for Security and Counterterrorism (NCTV) and the General Intelligence and Security Service (AIVD), "The Children of ISIS, the Indoctrination of Minors in ISIS-Held Territory," 5.

19. UNICEF, "Every Day Counts: An Outlook on Education for the Most Vulnerable Children in Syria."

20. The Norwegian Afghanistan Committee also noted this, stating, "The numbers for registration are much higher, but give a false picture of real attendance."

21. The kidnapping and otherwise forced recruitment that have often taken place through or in boarding schools in rural and remote areas have a somewhat different dynamic and need to be examined separately.

22. The UN, World Bank, CIA, and others generally accept that *youth* consist of people between the ages of fifteen and twenty-four, although the age range can sometimes vary according to the nature of a particular project. The World Bank and United Nations, for example, keep track of children in the zero to fourteen age group. For varied definitions of youth, see for example CIA, "The Youth Bulge," xiii; Justin Yifu Lin, "Youth Bulge: A Demographic Dividend"; Isabel Ortiz and Matthew Cummins, "When the Global Crisis and Youth Bulge Collide," 6; UNDESA, "World Youth Report," providing a definition with no age range, 14.

23. School attendance refers to presence in the classroom rather than being registered for school. In times of armed conflict in any context, school attendance is often impossible, and in locations where more extreme forms of Islam are active, Western-style learning and subjects are forbidden.

24. Marc Sommers, "Governance, Security and Culture: Assessing Africa's Youth Bulge."

25. Henrik Urdal, "A Clash of Generations? Youth Bulges and Political Violence." It is present in almost all contemporary armed conflicts, but also present in some non-armed conflict circumstances as well.

26. Nigeria's "deeply embedded" role in this is thoroughly covered by Joly and Shaban, "Between Tradition and the Law: Artisanal Firearm Production in West Africa."

27. Paul Holtom et al., "Trade Update: Transfers, Tetransfers," 114. For more on Nigeria's involvement, see, for example, Nicolas Florquin et al., "Perceptions, Vulnerabilities, and Prevention: Violent Extremism Threat Assessment in Selected Regions of the Southern Libyan Borderlands and North-Western Nigeria."

28. United Nations General Assembly, *The Illicit Trade in Small Arms and Light Weapons in All Its Aspects: Report of the Secretary-General*; Charlene Rodrigues and Mohammed Al-Qalisi, "Yemen Crisis: Meet the Child Soldiers Who Have Forsaken Books for Kalashnikovs."

29. Christopher Steinmetz, *Small Arms in the Hands of Children*; Ben Knight and Ben Quinn, "Guns Assembled in the UK May Be Arming Child Soldiers, Says Report"; see also the following Small Arms Survey documents at www.smallarmssurvey.org: *Documenting Weapons in Situations of Armed Conflict: Methods and Trends*.

30. A table of more than twenty models of light machine guns is even provided by Wikipedia, https://en.wikipedia.org/wiki/Light_machine_gun.

31. This highlights an important chapter by Ames on research and methodological problems in child soldiers research, wherein he makes a distinction between the importance of "recognizing the gap between the data one has and the data

one wants." Ames, "Methodological Problems in the Study of Child Soldiers," 14.

32. In cautioning about "statistical studies that rely on existing data sets," George and Bennett note that in case study methods, determining "which independent variables are relevant . . . remains open to revision as research proceeds . . ." and that "the researcher may inductively discover independent variables that previous theories may have overlooked"; Alexander George and Andrew Bennett, *Case Studies and Theory*, 18, fn. 32.

33. Territorial control can vary according to population density, location, size, and natural resources: i.e., controlling a large isolated rural area might not be as crucial as controlling a well-populated area. Likewise, leadership is not necessarily unidimensional and can be divided up among different areas with different leadership. As such, it might not be as important as troop morale. Also, troop strength or capacity cannot be determined purely through an estimated head count. Studies that heavily rely on such variables can be misleadingly ambiguous and not adequately capture current conditions.

34. Boko Haram collection by specialist Jacob Zenn, https://unmaskingboko haram.com/archived-sources-2.

35. The original article in which my co-authors and I applied visual ethnography to the thirty images explains the rigorous analysis and assessment these images went through to be methodologically acceptable. See Pieri et al., "Boko Haram's Child Soldiers," 11–13.

36. Sarah Pink, *Doing Visual Ethnography*, 169.

37. Pink, *Doing Visual Ethnography*, 35.

38. Visual ethnography applied to conflict is relatively new, though it has been used sociologically in the past. Among the earlier applications to conflict, there is Pierre Bourdieu's outstanding collection of essays, *Algeria 1960*.

39. Robert R. Emerson et al., *Writing Ethnographic Fieldnotes*, 143.

40. Giampietro Gobo, *Doing Ethnography*.

41. Some videos from 2013 to 2015 were discovered by the Nigerian Army and handed to Voice of America and promoted in a documentary titled "Boko Haram: Journey From Evil." These were largely internal videos filmed by media-trained children regarding their everyday lives. For discussion and assessment, see Zacharias Pieri and Jacob Zenn, "Under the Black Flag in Borno: Experiences of Foot Soldiers and Civilians in Boko Haram's 'Caliphate,'" 645–72.

42. Pieri et al., "Boko Haram's Child Soldiers."

43. Caleb Weiss, "Islamic State Claims Prison Break Outside of Nigeria's Capital."

44. Abdulkareem Haruna, *Humangle Media*; and "Violent Extremism in the Sahel," *Council on Foreign Relations Center for Preventive Action*, August 10, 2023.

45. https://statisticstimes.com/demographics/country/nigeria-population.php #:~:text=The%20population%20of%20Nigeria%20is,people%20for%20the%20 year%202020.

46. https://www.statista.com/statistics/382296/age-structure-in-nigeria/#:~:text=
Age%20structure%20in%20Nigeria%202021&text=In%202021%2C%20about%20
43.31%20percent,aged%200%20to%2014%20years.

47. See, for example, John Ime et al., "Gun Violence in Nigeria: A Focus on Ethno-Religious Conflict in Kano."

48. National Working Group on Armed Violence & Action on Armed Violence, "The Violent Road."

49. https://www.gunpolicy.org/firearms/topic/firearms_in_nigeriahttps.

50. Onapajo, "Children in Boko Haram Conflict: The Neglected Facet of a Decade of Terror in Nigeria," 202.

51. Ibid., 203.

52. UNICEF, "Nigeria, Education."

53. For 2018; no statistics available since then: https://data.unicef.org/resources/
data_explorer/unicef_f/?ag=UNICEF&df=GLOBAL_DATAFLOW&ver=1.0&dq=
NGA.ED_ANAR_L1.&startPeriod=1970&endPeriod=2020.

54. Onapajo, 203.

55. Ibid., 203 from https://www.unicef.org/nigeria/education.

56. https://www.statista.com/statistics/1197570/deaths-caused-by-boko-haram-in-nigeria/.

57. To see the tenets the four authors of the article in *Terrorism and Political Violence* established, see Pieri et al., 12.

58. Photo: https://unmaskingbokoharam.files.wordpress.com/2019/09/alurwhaal
wutqhatweetsjan2015tomar.ch2015-1.pdf.

59. Screenshots from a video: https://unmaskingbokoharam.com/2019/04/11/
boko-haram-and-iswap-eid-videos-2015-iswap-2016-bh-2017-bh-2018-bh.

60. Screenshot from a video: https://unmaskingbokoharam.com/2019/03/30/
boko-haram-video-of-chibok-girls-thanking-out-father-abubakar-shekau-january-2018/.

61. Screenshot from a video: https://unmaskingbokoharam.com/2019/04/11/
iswap-amaq-video-of-liquidation-of-supporters-of-nigeria-april-2-2019.

62. Screenshots from a video: https://unmaskingbokoharam.com/2021/02/27/
boko-haram-abubakar-shekau-claiming-maiduguri-raid-video-february-25-2021.

63. Screenshots from a video: https://unmaskingbokoharam.com/2021/02/28/
boko-haram-cubs-of-monotheism-video-february-28-2021/.

64. Screenshot from a video: https://unmaskingbokoharam.com/2021/11/15/
iswap-creators-of-epic-battles-video-october-31-2021.

65. Speckhard and Ellenberg, "ISIS in Their Own Words: Recruitment History, Motivations for Joining, Travel, Experiences in ISIS, and Disillusionment over Time—Analysis of 220 In-depth Interviews of ISIS Returnees, Defectors and Prisoners."

66. Smith, "Fitna, a Failed Coup and a Squandered Opportunity to Undermine the Islamic State's 'Intangible Power.'"

References

Aboulenein, Ahmed. "Iraq Holds Victory Parade after Defeating Islamic State." Reuters, December 10, 2017. https://www.reuters.com/article/us-mideast-crisis-iraq-parade/iraq-holds-victory-parade-after-defeating-islamic-state-id USKBN1E407Z.

Africa, Sandy. "South Africa's Deadly July 2021 Riots May Recur if There's No Change." *The Conversation*. July 9, 2022. https://theconversation.com/south-africas-deadly-july-2021-riots-may-recur-if-theres-no-change-186397; https://qz.com/africa/1312257/south-africas-child-soldiers-trauma-and-township-violence-in-children-of-war-movie/.

Almohammad, Asaad. "ISIS Child Soldiers in Syria: The Structural and Predatory Recruitment, Enlistment, Pre-Training Indoctrination, Training, and Deployment." *International Centre for Counter-Terrorism—The Hague* 8, no. 14 (2018).

Ames, Barry. "Methodological Problems in the Study of Child Soldiers." In *Child Soldiers in the Age of Fractured States*, edited by Scott Gates and Simon Reich, 14–24. Pittsburgh: University of Pittsburgh Press, 2010.

Becker, Jo. "This Is Our Opportunity to End the Taliban's Use of Child Soldiers." *The Hill* (Opinion), September 18, 2021. https://www.hrw.org/news/2021/09/20/our-opportunity-end-talibans-use-child-soldiers.

Bloom, Mia. "Child Soldiers in Armed Conflict." In *Armed Conflict Survey 2018*. International Institute for Strategic Studies, 2018. https://www.iiss.org/publications/armed-conflict-survey/2018/armed-conflict-survey-2018/acs2018-03-essay-3.

———. "Weaponizing the Weak: The Role of Children in Terrorist Groups." In *Research Handbook on Child Soldiers*, edited by Mark A. Drumbl and Jastin C. Barrett, 195–216. Cheltenham, UK: Edward Elgar Publishing, 2019.

Bloom, Mia, John Horgan, and Charlie Winter. "Depictions of Children and Youth in the Islamic State's Martyrdom Propaganda, 2015–2016." *CTC Sentinel* 9, no. 2 (2016): 29–32.

Bourdieu, Pierre. *Algeria 1960*. English translation: Maison des Sciences de l'Homme. Cambridge: Cambridge University Press, 1979.

Central Intelligence Agency (CIA). *World Factbook*. https://www.cia.gov/library/publications/the-world-factbook.

Central Intelligence Agency (CIA). "The Youth Bulge: A Link between Demography and Instability." 1986. https://www.cia.gov/library/readingroom/docs/CIA-RDP97R00694R000500680001-1.pdf.

Coalition to Stop the Use of Child Soldiers (2008), 306–7.

Deslandes-Martineau, Marion, Patrick Charland, Hugo G. Lapierre, Olivier Arvisais, Chirine Chamsine, Vivek Venkatesh, and Mathieu Guidère. "The Programming Curriculum within ISIS." *PLoS One* 17, no. 4 (2022): e0265721. https://doi.org/10.1371/journal.pone.0265721.

Doxsee, Catrina, Jared Thompson, and Grace Hwang. "Examining Extremism: Islamic State Khorasan Province (ISKP) Islamic State Khorasan (IS-K)." Center for Strategic and International Studies. Washington DC, September 8, 2021. https://www.csis.org/blogs/examining-extremism/examining-extremism-islamic-state-khorasan-province-iskp.

Drumbl, Mark. *Reimagining Child Soldiers in International Law and Policy.* Oxford: Oxford University Press, 2012.

Robert R. Emerson, Rachel I. Fretz, and Linda L. Shaw. *Writing Ethnographic Fieldnotes.* Chicago, IL: University of Chicago Press, 1995.

Florquin, Nicolas, Hafez S. AbuAdwan, Gergely Hideg, and Alaa Tartir, "Perceptions, Vulnerabilities, and Prevention: Violent Extremism Threat Assessment in Selected Regions of the Southern Libyan Borderlands and North-Western Nigeria." Small Arms Survey Report, November 2022. https://www.smallarmssurvey.org/resource/perceptions-vulnerabilities-and-prevention-violent-extremism-threat-assessment-selected.

Friedersdorf, Conor. "How U.S. Weapons Fall into the Hands of Terrorists." *Atlantic,* November 24, 2014. https://www.theatlantic.com/international/archive/2014/11/how-us-weapons-fall-into-the-hands-of-terrorists/383095.

George, Alexander L., and Andrew Bennett. *Case Studies and Theory Development in the Social Sciences.* Cambridge, MA: MIT Press, 2005.

George, Susannah, and Sayed Salahuddin. "Afghan Presidential Election Outcome Remains in Limbo as Results Are Delayed." *Washington Post,* October 19, 2019. https://www.washingtonpost.com/world/asia_pacific/afghan-presidential-election-remains-in-limbo-as-results-delayed/2019/10/19/559f4b44-f12b-11e9-bb7e-d2026ee0c199_story.html.

Haruna, Abdulkareem. *Humangle Media,* July 10, 2023. https://humanglemedia.com/iswap-restricts-farming-activities-in-remote-areas-amid-military-strikes/.

Holtom, Paul, Irene Pavesi, and Christelle Rigual. "Trade Update: Transfers, Retransfers and the ATT." In *Small Arms Survey 2014: Women and Guns.* Cambridge: Cambridge University Press, 2014.

Horgan, John G., Max Taylor, Mia Bloom, and Charlie Winter. "From Cubs to Lions: A Six Stage Model of Child Socialization into the Islamic State." *Studies in Conflict and Terrorism* 40, no. 7 (2017); 645–64.

Humphreys, Macartan, and Jeremy M. Weinstein. *What the Fighters Say: A Survey of Ex-Combatants in Sierra Leone.* Columbia University Earth Institute and the Post-Conflict Reintegration Initiative for Development and Empowerment (PRIDE, Sierra Leone), June/August 2003. https://au.int/en/documents/20200901/what-fighters-say-survey-ex-combatants-sierra-leone.

Inayatullah, Sohail. "YOUTH BULGE: Demographic Dividend, Time Bomb, and other Futures." *Journal of Future Studies* 21 no. 2 (December 2016): 21–34.

Ime, John A., Aminu Z. Mohammed, Andrew D. Pinto, and Celestine A. Nkanta. "Gun Violence in Nigeria: A Focus on Ethno-Religious Conflict in Kano." *Journal of Public Health Policy* 28, no. 4 (2007): 420–31.

Joly, Julien, and Aline Shaban. "Between Tradition and the Law: Artisanal Firearm Production in West Africa." November 2023. https://www.smallarmssurvey. org/sites/default/files/resources/Craft%20Production_BP_Web.pdf.

Knight, Ben, and Ben Quinn. "Guns Assembled in the UK May Be Arming Child Soldiers, Says Report." *Guardian*, March 1, 2017. https://www.theguardian.com/ global-development/2017/mar/01/guns-assembled-uk-may-be-arming-child-soldiers-says-report-berlin-information-center-for-transatlantic-security.

Lin, Justin Yifu. "Youth Bulge: A Demographic Dividend or a Demographic Bomb in Developing Countries?" *World Bank Blogs*, January 5, 2012. http://blogs. worldbank.org/developmenttalk/youth-bulge-a-demographic-dividend-or-a-demographic-bomb-in-developing-countries.

Marret, Jean-Luc. "Al-Qaeda in the Islamic Maghreb: A 'Glocal' Organization." *Studies in Conflict and Terrorism* 31 (June 2008): 541–52.

McCue, Colleen, Joseph T. Massengill, Dorothy Milbrandt, John Gaughan, and Meghan Cumpston. "The Islamic State Long Game: A Tripartite Analysis of Youth Radicalization and Indoctrination." *CTC Sentinel* 10, no. 8 (2017): 21–26.

Morris, James S., and Tristan Dunning. "Islamic State Schooled Children as Soldiers—How Can Their 'Education' Be Undone?" *The Conversation*. March 28, 2018. http://theconversation.com/islamic-state-schooled-children-as-soldiers-how-can-their-education-be-undone-93266.

National Coordinator for Security and Counterterrorism (NCTV) and the General Intelligence and Security Service (AIVD). "The Children of ISIS, the Indoctrination of Minors in ISIS-Held Territory." *The Hague*, 2017. https://english.aivd.nl/publications/publications/2017/04/26/ the-children-of-isis.-the-indoctrination-of-minors-in-isis-held-territory.

National Working Group on Armed Violence & Action on Armed Violence. "The Violent Road." 2013. https://aoav.org.uk/wp-content/uploads/2013/12/ The-Violent-Road.pdf.

New York Times Editorial Board. "Islamic State: Landless but Still Dangerous." *New York Times*, May 1, 2019. https://www.nytimes.com/2019/05/01/opinion/baghdadi-islamic-state.html?action=click&module=Opinion&pgtype=Homepage.

Norwegian Afghanistan Committee. "Education." 2013. http://www.afghanistan.no/ English/Sectors/Education/index.html.

Onapajo, Hakeem. "Children in Boko Haram Conflict: The Neglected Facet of a Decade of Terror in Nigeria." *African Security* 13, no. 2 (2020): 195–211.

Ortiz, Isabel, and Cummins, Matthew. "When the Global Crisis and Youth Bulge Collide: Double the Jobs Trouble for Youth." UNICEF, February 2012. https:// www.unicef.org/socialpolicy/files/Global_Crisis_and_Youth_Bulge_-_FINAL. pdf.

Overseas Security Advisory Council. "Sierra Leone 2019 Crime & Safety Report." *US Department of State*, April 10, 2019. https://www.osac.gov/Content/Report/ fee7f77e-7389-45ed-81a5-15f4aec723c8.

Pham, J. Peter. "Foreign Influences and Shifting Horizons: The Ongoing Evolution of al Qaeda in the Islamic Maghreb." *Orbis* 45, no. 2 (2011): 240–54.

"Recruitment of Child Soldiers on the Increase." Integrated Regional Information Networks (IRIN). *The New Humanitarian*, March 21, 2011. http://www.irinnews.org/feature/2011/03/21/recruitment-child-soldiers-increase.

Pieri, Zacharias, Mary-Jane Fox, Lily Lousada, and Jacob Zenn. "Boko Haram's Child Soldiers: Media Mujahids, Martyrs, and Militants." *Terrorism and Political Violence*, May 22, 2023. https://doi.org/10.1080/09546553.2023.2199873.

———, and Jacob Zenn. "Under the Black Flag in Borno: Experiences of Foot Soldiers and Civilians in Boko Haram's 'Caliphate.'" *Journal of Modern African Studies* 56, no. 4 (2018): 645–72.

Pink, Sarah. *Doing Visual Ethnography*. London: Sage Publications Limited, 2021.

Rodrigues, Charlene, and Mohammed Al-Qalisi. "Yemen Crisis: Meet the Child Soldiers Who Have Forsaken Books for Kalashnikovs." *Independent*, April 19, 2015. http://www.independent.co.uk/news/world/middle-east/yemen-crisis-meet-the-child-soldiers-who-have-forsaken-books-for-kalashnikovs-10187235.html.

Roudometof, Victor. "Theorizing Glocalization: Three Interpretations." *European Journal of Social Theory* 19, no. 3 (2015): 391–408.

Salah, Hana. "Al-Qassam Youth Training Camps Open Again." *Al-Monitor*, January 29, 2015. https://www.al-monitor.com/pulse/originals/2015/01/gaza-al-qassam-training-military-camps.html.

Singer, Peter W. *Children at War*. Berkeley: University of California Press, 2006.

Small Arms Survey. https://www.smallarmssurvey.org/databases.

Small Arms Survey Briefing Paper: "Nigeria: National Small Arms and Light Weapons Survey." Small Arms Survey Briefing Paper, August 2021. https://www.smallarmssurvey.org/resource/nigeria-national-small-arms-and-light-weapons-survey.

Smith, Michael S. II. "Fitna, a Failed Coup and a Squandered Opportunity to Undermine the Islamic State's 'Intangible Power.'" *Lawfare*, March 29, 2019. https://www.lawfareblog.com/fitna-failed-coup-and-squandered-opportunity-undermine-islamic-states-intangible-power.

Speckhard, Anne, and Molly D. Ellenberg. "ISIS in Their Own Words: Recruitment History, Motivations for Joining, Travel, Experiences in ISIS, and Disillusionment over Time—Analysis of 220 In-depth Interviews of ISIS Returnees, Defectors and Prisoners." *Journal of Strategic Security* 13, no. 1 (2020): 82–127.

Sommers, Marc. "Governance, Security and Culture: Assessing Africa's Youth Bulge." *International Journal of Conflict and Violence* 5, no. 2 (2011): 292–303.

Special Representative to the Secretary-General for Children and Armed Conflict. "Report of the Special Representative to the Secretary-General for Children and Armed Conflict." UN Doc. A/61/275, August 16, 2006. https://www.un.org/ga/search/view_doc.asp?symbol=S/2006/497&Lang=E&Area=UNDOC.

Steinmetz, Christopher. *Small Arms in the Hands of Children*. Brot für die Welt, Kindernothilfe, Terre des Hommes, *World Vision Deutschland*, 2017. https://

www.ohchr.org/Documents/Issues/RuleOfLaw/ArmsTransfers/TerreHommes-Kindernothilfe.pdf.

UN News. "Yemen: UN Verifies Nearly 1,500 Boys Recruited for Use in Armed Conflict." February 28, 2017. http://www.un.org/apps/news/story.asp?NewsID=56255#.WRnUI_krIdU.

UNICEF. "Every Day Counts: An Outlook on Education for the Most Vulnerable Children in Syria." *UNICEF*, Syria; Education Challenges, May 1, 2022. https://www.unicef.org/syria/education.

———. https://www.unicef.org/media/132331/file/Paris%20Principles%20.pdf.

———. "Nigeria, Education." https://www.unicef.org/nigeria/education.

United Nations Department of Economic and Social Affairs (UNDESA). "World Youth Report: Youth and the 2030 Agenda for Sustainable Development." 2018. https://www.un.org/development/desa/youth/wp-content/uploads/sites/21/2018/12/WorldYouthReport-2030Agenda.pdf.

United Nations General Assembly. *The Illicit Trade in Small Arms and Light Weapons in All Its Aspects: Report of the Secretary-General.* Part II, §4, October 2016. A/71/438–A/CONF.192/BMS/2016/1. https://www.un.org/disarmament/wp-content/uploads/2016/10/english.pdf.

———. Human Rights Council. *Written Statement Submitted by United Nations Watch, a Non-Governmental Organization in Special Consultative Status.* A/HRC/46/NGO/42. March 5, 2021.

———. "Report of the Special Representative of the Secretary-General for Children and Armed Conflict." A/61/275.

United Nations Security Council. Report of the Secretary-General. *Small Arms and Light Weapons.* S/2015/289, April 27, 2015. http://www.security councilreport.org/atf/cf/%7B65BFCF9B-6D27-4E9C-8CD3-CF6E4FF96FF9%7D/s_2015_289.pdf.

Urdal, Henrik. "A Clash of Generations? Youth Bulges and Political Violence." *United Nations Expert Group Meeting on Adolescents, Youth and Development*, July 22, 2011, UN/POP/EGM-AYD/2011/10.

Warner, Jason, and Hilary Matfess. "Exploding Stereotypes: The Unexpected Operational and Demographic Characteristics of Boko Haram's Suicide Bombers." *Combating Terrorism Center at West Point*, August 2017. https://ctc.usma.edu/posts/new-ctc-report-examines-boko-harams-use-of-suicide-bombers.

Wasike, Andrew. "Rights Group: Al Shabab Forcibly Recruits Children." *Deutsche Welle*, January 15, 2018. https://www.dw.com/en/rights-group-al-shabab-forcibly-recruits-children/a-42155456.

Weiss, Caleb. "Islamic State Claims Prison Break Outside of Nigeria's Capital." *Long War Journal*, July 7, 2022. https://www.longwarjournal.org/archives/2022/07/islamic-state-claims-prison-break-outside-of-nigerias-capital.php.

Yom, Sean, and Katrina Sammour. "Counterterrorism and Youth Radicalization in Jordan: Social and Political Dimensions." *CTC Sentinel* 10, no. 4 (2017): 25–30.

5

International Responses to the Glocalized Conflict in Mali

Matthew Pflaum

Despite nearly a decade of significant international military interventions in Mali to address ongoing and deteriorating insecurity, the situation continues to worsen in terms of fatalities, security, and stability.[1] Achieving and maintaining security in the region has been complicated by local, regional, and international factors.[2] While the French and their partner military forces successfully halted the insurgent and extremist expansion southward in 2013, much of the country remains embroiled in overlapping conflicts of political violence involving communal violence, insurgencies, extremism, and armed or self-defense militias. Furthermore, citizens' faith in both foreign interventions, such as United Nations (UN) and France, and their own government remains increasingly skeptical, recently exemplified by a series of coups and expulsion of foreign military powers.

Lack of coordination between organizations, accusations of corruption and incompetence, and persistent neglect of underlying factors of insecurity reveal the increasing complexity of resolving the Malian conflict. These complexities are illustrated by the recent expulsion of several foreign forces (particularly the French, who had the largest force) and replacement by a Russian private military contractor (Wagner Group).[3] The political and security dynamics in Mali raise a critical question about the roots and remedies to African conflicts and the precarious security situation of the state.

In the case of Mali, the critical question in this chapter is why substantial international efforts at peacekeeping and intervention have failed and what international and regional implications of the conflict emerge. Moreover, what are the implications for state security and sovereignty?

This chapter seeks to clarify the dynamics and limitations of regional and international causes and implications of the Malian conflict. It examines Malian insecurity and conflict apropos of the involvement of diverse regional and international actors within the frameworks of glocalization and globalization to clarify the distinct roles of these diverse actors, address their successes and failures, and articulate how intranational and transnational conflicts like Mali are both influenced by wider processes of regional and international implications as well as the nature of the state itself. The chapter examines the successes and failures of both regional and international interventions as well as the implications of the recent involvement of Russian security firm in Mali.

Within the Central Sahel (consisting of Niger, Burkina Faso, and Mali, along with their borderlands), Mopti, a region and major city in Central Mali, has become one of the epicenters of violence and insecurity. In Central Mali around Mopti, there are complex and overlapping forms of violence involving armed militias, communal/ethnic militias, self-defense groups, pro-government militias, political violence and grievances, and extremism. The outcomes of this insecurity have been described as a hybridization of violence in which armed militias and extremist groups produce cycles of violence, retaliation, and ethnic targeting.[4] Many of these outcomes resulted from the long-term processes of militarism and militarization, in which American and other Western powers identified much of the Sahel as security vacuums with weak governance that could potentially generate insecurity, while others stem from more local factors related to historical grievances, power, and resources. In all these issues, the role and capacity of the state becomes a critical issue. Insecurity in Mali has attracted a complex coterie and reaction of interventions involving multinational forces (G5 Sahel), peacekeeping by the UN Multidimensional Integrated Stabilization in Mali (MINUSMA), regional partnerships and militaries and foreign militaries (United States, France), all of which have had various levels of success in ameliorating insecurity and maintaining human rights.[5] These diverse international, national, and regional actors particularly demonstrate the glocalized processes at play in what ostensibly appears to be a local context of Mopti,[6] but which involves streams of global and glocal influences.[7]

The chapter shows that international interventions have had several accomplishments yet failed to sufficiently address the complex local and regional factors contributing to insecurity, both state security and human security. One potential failure of the complex and robust international response to the Malian conflict is the mistake of treating the local conflict in Mali as commensurate to every other global conflict in a homogenizing globalized and modernized vision of global politics and conflicts. Indeed, while France, G5 Sahel, and other military and multinational responses had limited success in Mali, the most acute failure was that of failing to tackle very critical local grievances within the country related to poverty, insecurity, and politics—all of which raise questions about the nature of the state and its capacity. Beyond the real-world failures of interventions, there is a related problem of lack of trust in state authorities and international actors. Ultimately, it has become clear that the blind faith in international and Western institutions and powers to resolve local and regional African crises is misguided and dangerous, given their lack of attention to under-lying social, economic, and institutional issues and grievances, while local and regional interventions have been hamstrung by insufficient power or resources, lack of will, or ideological and policy fears of replicating Western colonial-style liberal governance and democratization missions.

This chapter leverages the Armed Conflict and Location Event Database (ACLED) data alongside analyses of recent dynamics and trends in the region in the scholarship and policy literature. It analyzes the complex conflict in Mali's Mopti region from a glocalization framework, proposing that the seemingly localized conflict has both international and regional causes and implications. The dynamic and shifting nature of conflict—proliferation of violent non-state actors, transnational dispersion, extremism, and global ideologies like Jihadism—both complicates the resolution to the conflict and integrates diverse regional, national, and international actors. While a concerted and significant international response aimed at stabilization and maintaining security quickly became involved in the conflict, frustrations emerged over its failures to curtail violence and insecurity, resolve underlying factors of the conflict, address political grievances, and tackle widespread and increasing political violence.[8] Implicit is all of these is the state, especially in terms of its colonial roots, authoritarian nature, and poor capacity to prioritize the core needs of its citizens.

Background and Overview of the Conflict

The Malian conflict, despite significant regional causes and outcomes (like dispersion of violence, transnational violence, and extremist groups), is often perceived as a national or local conflict. The incipient and triggering event of the conflict—a 2012 civil war staged by the Tuareg rebel group National Movement for the Liberation of Azawad (MNLA; in French *le Mouvement national de libération de l'Azawad*)—was itself the fourth iteration of a Tuareg rebellion in Mali and has foundations in complex and geographically widespread insecurity processes in North and West Africa and beyond.[9] This chapter positions the Malian conflict not as an isolated conflict emerging in a vacuum, but rather as inherently related to regional (and international) processes and crises, like those in Nigeria and Libya, such as refugee crises, poverty, ethnic grievances, and others. The expulsion of France and its military early in 2022 following a decade of operations amid tensions and ambivalent support, and the subsequent replacement by Russian security firm Wagner, demonstrates that the conflict has far-reaching implications for global political and international relations, trade, security, migration, and peace.[10] Although pro-Russian rhetoric has increased in West Africa and Sahel, Russia's involvement raises concerns over political and ethical issues over human rights, sovereignty, geopolitics, accountability, and wider political processes.

The Malian conflict has proved to be a recalcitrant one, persisting despite significant investment, personnel, and programs to curtail violence and insecurity. While there has been some regional involvement—Chadian military forces, G5 Sahel, African Union, Economic Community of West African States (ECOWAS), and others—the wider region is embroiled in its own crises—political instability and conflicts in Burkina Faso, two consecutive coups in Mali, military coups in Chad and Guinea, civil war in Libya, various Nigerian conflicts, and political instability in Niger (including the July 2023 coup). Most critically, the underlying factors contributing to insecurity have been neglected or insufficiently addressed.[11] Furthermore, there have been several notable failures of international securitization and stabilization missions: two successive coups within twelve months and intensifying and expanding violence from extremism and communal violence.[12] Claims of human rights abuses, corruption, and ineffectiveness have also plagued international and regional responses. This dilemma has clear implications related to globalization and glocalization theories: extensive national, regional, and international actors and funding both have failed to assuage, and instead have complicated, a local conflict in Central Mali, largely by entirely failing to account for local factors and issues such as culture, ethnicity, grievances, and politics.

The Malian conflict is often perceived as a highly localized conflict—stemming from ethnic and sovereignty grievances of Tuaregs, jihadist ideologies, and general political instability[13]—yet it has significant regional and international causes and implications, suggesting a prototypical model of simultaneous glocalized and globalized processes interacting. Distant and global events, such as the Ukrainian crisis, for example, have provoked severe shortages of wheat and other goods in West Africa (particularly Senegal, the world's most wheat-dependent nation),[14] while the Malian crisis involves multinational partners and forces like UN's MINUSMA, G5 Sahel, or ECOWAS that will have direct impacts on regional stability but also foreign investment, migration, security, and relations with the country.

The Malian crisis is also provoking out-migration, refugees, and displacement, which further intensify Europe's attempts at border security through Frontex and other programs.[15] Security and stability in Mali have also been inevitably threatened by regional wars and conflicts in Libya, Burkina Faso, Niger, Chad, Algeria, and Nigeria.[16] One example is the strong international pressure on Mali following its two coups to immediately reimplement democratic elections, despite widespread internal and regional support for delaying elections with hopes of better candidates and political stability, or the regional ECOWAS and UEMOA pressure on Mali that included diplomatic and financial sanctions. The punitive sanctions imposed by ECOWAS and UEMOA (economic community)—including border closures, economic, and diplomatic sanctions—imposed on Mali in late 2021 and 2022 show the significance of the Malian conflict and insecurity to regional stability.[17] Another example in recent years was the introduction of suicide bombing and other techniques and strategies into Malian and Sahelian conflicts via jihadists trained and serving in international conflicts in Iraq, Syria, and Afghanistan, or the transport of arms into Mali via Malian (especially Tuareg) soldiers who had served in militias and armies during the Libyan conflict.[18] Connections between conflicts in Mali and wider regional and international criminal trafficking networks also generate criminality, weapons, drugs, and profits for criminal activities.[19] These few examples show the diverse international and regional linkages the Malian conflict has with the rest of the world.

Regional conflicts have economic and political implications that inevitably impact neighboring countries through migration, insecurity, grievances, refugees, and borders. The many civil wars in West Africa in the 1990s strongly illustrated the risk of conflict dispersion and regional instability, particularly those of Sierra Leone, Liberia, and Côte d'Ivoire. Meanwhile, it is not inevitable that conflict or insecurity spreads—the Casamance conflict in Senegal, for example, has been constrained to southern Senegal and has remained at very low levels of fatalities and violence.[20] The conflict in Central African Republic has resulted in more than one million internally displaced and refugees in neighboring countries like Cameroon and Gabon, with inevitable consequences in security, stability, ethnic tensions, and regional politics.[21]

Increasingly, global powers treat the Sahel opportunistically as a chance to rival other powers for international prestige, resources, and power—with Turkey, UAE, Russia, China, the United States, France, Germany, and others all staking claims. While not a direct substitution—considering the differences in troop size, scales, accountability, and strategies—Russia's Wagner Group supplanted France in Mali and was almost immediately accused of various human rights violations.[22] While France's missions and activities during its term in Mali may have been justifiably accused of failing to curtail the growing extremist threat and was controversial for its power dynamics and perhaps colonial relations and even an occasional transgression—France's presence was mostly internationally and domestically sanctioned (including serving at Mali's request) and therefore under the purview of international law.[23] In fact, France's various Malian missions (Serval, Barkhane) were often in conjunction with other multinational efforts like G5 Sahel and MINUSMA (UN's stabilization program) and worked alongside regional militaries like those of Chad and Nigeria. In Russia's case, it is currently perpetrating similar war crimes both in the neighboring nation of Ukraine, a near neighbor, and in the distant country of Mali, a far neighbor. Mali is also the fifth country where Wagner Group will have a presence in Africa, and likely will not be the last.[24]

Globalization, Glocalization, and Security

The concept of globalization and its application to the examination of various complex processes has developed over several decades with diverse and critical attention to states, institutions, inequality, and other global processes. There have been complex and diverse long-term historical, political, and social shifts that have contributed to the effects of globalization and glocalization on factors like culture and nationalism. A notable issue in these processes is states' security and their role in shaping security dynamics and reacting to security threats. In the case of Mali, the state has become entangled in complex glocalized security problems.

Glocalization, while more recent than globalization, has developed to explain more local outcomes globally that reflect diverse cultural, institutional, and political processes and may in certain cases differ from or even oppose the homogenizing impacts of globalization. These are highly pertinent to the Malian crisis, given the overlapping processes like armed actors, extremism, political instability, coups, multinational forces, peacekeeping, and ethnic grievances. Security in the Sahel, meanwhile, involves long-term processes that are largely shaped by external forces—including colonialism and the United States' (and its allies) Global War on Terror, initiated in the early 2000s in response to the September 11 attacks—but also various crises like political violence, wars like Libya, refugee and border crises, and ethnic grievances. In recent history, the Sahel region was quite stable in the 1980s and 1990s, when every country in the region experienced democratic elections and/or democratic transitions, low levels of violence and insecurity, and strong development and democratic indicators.[25] Thus, the deteriorating security, political instability, coups, and other outcomes in Mali and beyond did not emerge spontaneously and in a vacuum, nor were they inevitable, but rather emerged from regional and international processes alongside incomplete democratic transitions and consolidation and weak governance that plague the state.

Globalization and Glocalization

Globalization and glocalization were selected as frameworks for this analysis because they describe mutually constitutive and dependent processes—one local and one global—that are highly pertinent for tensions occurring in the context of Mali. The theories may be considered in certain respects to be twin processes that together explain the complex outcomes of global and local processes on institutions, culture, and politics, including cultural and institutional homogenization and heterogeneity, nationalism, modernization, migration, and other global processes.[26]

In certain conditions, globalization and glocalization may describe dialectical processes, but they are just as likely to be mutually dependent and synergistic. First, under globalization, there is a flattening or homogenization of institutions, trade, culture, and systems that increasingly connects and universalizes laws, institutions, nations, goods, and symbols. Simultaneously, these same places may be glocalized, in which the unique local customs, traditions, and identities are further preserved in contrast to globalized processes.[27] These two processes often overlap, and the tensions between these globalizing or homogenizing and unique localizing (glocalizing) processes help to explain some of the nature and implications of conflicts like Mopti, as is particularly evident with the role of international and regional interventions.

The long-term evolution of modernization gradually resulted in states as the universal form of political entities and territories.[28] Globalization, the phenomenon that countries are flattening, interconnected, and more homogenous, however, emerged as a threat to the concept of states. While globalization tends to involve homogenization and homogeneity, glocalization involves heterogeneity, albeit as often mutually constitutive and dependent processes that exist alongside each other. This dialectic is used to explain glocal processes: the former involves the homogeneity of national symbols and institutions (governance, institutions, laws, regulations, finance), while the latter creates or preserves heterogeneity via the intermix between unique cultural and national identities through more localized processes involving languages, histories, cultures, religions, traditions, and others—albeit within a world that has been persistently globalizing.[29] According to scholars like Roudometof and Robertson, globalization is considered "the particularization of universalism and the universalization of particularism."[30] These theorists contend that glocalization has not been sufficiently clarified to the point of an explicit definition, but instead is interpreted by scholars for specific applications to topics or processes. In a way, glocalization can take the form of some kind of resistance to hyperglobalization or a kind of effort to retreat from hyperglobalization.[31]

Modernization is an inherently global process and has been an important component of modern theories like globalization, under an assumption of a linear process whereby societies transform from tradition to modernity. International interventions and involvement in events like the Malian conflict often explicitly or implicitly integrate assumptions inherent to those powers (often wealthy and Western) coordinating the efforts, which tend to be neoliberal and "modern." There are two conceptual links for understanding nationalism's perseverance—universal adoption of statehood has created some homogeneity and isomorphism, while glocalization (through transnational nationalism) creates cultural heterogeneity and national specificity.[32]

The six waves of globalization have generated different periods and processes of change politically and economically,[33] with countries influenced by both modernity and modernization as well as globality and globalization.[34] While modernity is often treated as a homogenous and universal experience, there are multiple modernities that include both European and non-European. The process of globalization produced globality, which describes a post-1500 time-space compression, awareness of "Others," and cross-cultural comparison.[35] However, the process of globalization is complex, and the homogenizing effects are merely one potential outcome, and many scholars have illustrated the heterogeneous outcomes of globalization in space and time.

The origins of glocalization are heavily influenced by the recent theories involving globalization, though describing the other side of the dialectic in terms of uniqueness and localized processes. Glocalization's incipient use in the scholarship is from Appadurai's Fear of Small Numbers[36] and Robertson's 1992 article[37] and several subsequent articles, often working with Giulianotti or White.[38] Glocalization is a general and broad theory in which local processes and phenomenon are tied into larger and more global ones through networks, policies, regulation, trade, migration, and other processes. It differs from globalization—a theory with assumptions that all events and processes are truly global and that the world has become increasingly interconnected—by its emphasis on the uniqueness of local cities, states, and actors.

Unlike globalization, glocalization lacks a specific definition, but is rather a collection of various theories and applications.[39] In recent decades, globalization has been increasingly responsible for cultural uniformity of formal aspects of statehood, while glocalization accounts for the specificity and uniqueness of national and local experiences.[40] While examples of globalization are pervasive in the current era—with examples like ATMs, taxes, financialization, global institutions like the UN, education systems, legal systems, trade, and global transport—examples of glocalization are more nuanced and local, often context dependent and culturally dependent. There are three general interpretations to explain the process of glocalization: glocalization subsumed under globalization, globalization transformed into glocalization, or as an analytically autonomous concept.[41]

Power and temporality are fundamental concepts of glocalization.[42] Power often emerges in both global and regional (i.e., glocal) relations, with exercises of power also rendered alongside temporality. Local-global power dynamics come into play during local events, with local or glocal actors often viewed as having communal or social concerns, while the global is often perceived as having wider international interests such as corporatism, transnational capitalism, or other processes associated with homogenizing features of globalization.[43]

In the case of Mali's conflict, the local or glocal processes (local NGOs, politicians, traditional authorities, governance) were often subsumed or devalued relative to international actors, showing the inherent power dynamics of local-global binaries. While globalization and glocalization theories articulate dialectical and perhaps opposing processes, they are inevitably linked and intertwined through these processes. The global, for example, is not outside the local or glocal, but exists within them.[44] Various wars since WW II have also inherently involved power dynamics influenced by Western-centric modernization philosophies, often involving ideological divisions (communist/capitalist) or geographic (Global North/Global South). The United States' wars in Korea and Vietnam both involved support of anti-communist regimes against communist-supported regimes (North Vietnam, North Korea), while more recent invasions of Afghanistan, Iraq, and Somalia all involved vague concepts of Global War on Terror combined with proposed regime change, democratization, and elimination of extremist threats, often with unilateral (i.e., strictly American) or multilateral (i.e., "coalition of the willing" during the Iraq invasion that involved the United States, Australia, the UK, Italy, Japan, Spain, and others) forces that principally targeted Global South, poorer nations (Iraq, Somalia, Afghanistan, Libya, etc.). The "axis of evil"—describing "enemy" countries as first applied by President George W. Bush—also strictly included Global South countries: initially North Korea, Iran, and Iraq, but later expanded to include Syria, Libya, and Cuba. Both glocal and global processes are overlapping and interacting simultaneously: however, temporality of glocalization remains a dilemma to be resolved: how temporal variation shapes the relationship between the global and local.[45]

SECURITY IN THE SAHEL

Security in the Sahel has varied in space and time. Historically, it was influenced by local and regional factors like trade routes, political rivalries, empires, ethnic grievances, colonial exploitation, migration, and environmental scarcities.[46] In recent decades, the Sahel region has been the target and site for international actors like the United States, China, and Europe for two reasons: a) political and economic/energy interests and b) military, strategic, and security interests.[47] The threat of security has been increasingly exaggerated over time to justify attention to the former interests. The United States, for example, has not historically considered the region important in terms of bilateral development aid, trade, investment, or political/military allies. Rather, the United States and other major international actors have had more significant bilateral ties with Morocco and Tunisia and lucrative commercial relations in hydrocarbons with Algeria.

France, as the former colonial ruler of Mali, wielded significant influence and power over its economic and political conditions for decades and long remained the most important foreign power in terms of development, migration, and cultural ties. For these reasons, Mali's relations with France have always been strained and ambivalent. France remains one of the largest trading partners (along with South Africa, Switzerland, Senegal, and China) and destination countries for Malian immigrants, yet Malians likewise harbor grievances and hostility for both historical injustices but also the perceived contemporary power imbalances, exploitative nature of France's presence in the country, and lingering colonial attitudes and relations between the two.

The Global War on Terror in the early 2000s rapidly emphasized the Sahel as a zone of insecurity and a threat to global security despite the origins of the September 11 hijackers being exclusively North African and Middle Eastern (United Arab Emirates, Lebanon, Egypt, and Saudi Arabia), alongside the relative stability of most of the Sahel in the period of the 1980s to early 2000s and significant strides toward democratization.[48] Almost all Sahelian nations had democratic election in the 1980s and 1990s, for example.[49] Instead, the direct and indirect US strategies and interventions in Mali argued theoretically that the features of the Sahel predisposed it for fostering extremist and Islamist activity—because of its weak states, porous borders, vast expanses of sparsely populated territory, and lower security capacity than its North African neighbors under a concept of a security vacuum. The United States was highly concerned that such undergoverned spaces would inevitably be exploited as terrorist sanctuaries.[50] This motivation was sufficient to enable significant investment in missions, personnel, resources, and coordination. In more recent scholarship, parts of the Sahel, especially hinterlands and rural areas of Mali, reflect what has been described as areas of limited statehood, in which state institutions are weakly present.[51]

There are many diverse forms of international and regional interventions targeting governance and security in conflict and insecure zones, including military interventions, capacity building, regional intelligence, coordination, international policing operations, law enforcement, border security, training, and peacekeeping and/or stabilization. Several of these processes simultaneously overlap in the Sahel region, including Mali, such as the peacekeeping mission by the UN (MINUSMA) and the military interventions led by the French military (Barkhane and Serval). One commonality among many of these interventions is the link between regime change (toward neoliberal democratization) and humanitarian objectives, which rest on the assumed or actual problematic nature of the state and its capacity to deliver what is expected of states under global liberal governance.[52]

The intervention in Mali has been complex because it involves multiple and diverse actors at different scales (local, state, regional, international, multinational), requiring agreements between governments, military forces, multilateral organizations (UN), and others. The previous interventions in Sierra Leone shows the complexity of international interventions, in that while intervention was widely supported by most of the population, it still required authorization by the UN with permission and request by the state. Legitimacy in military operations is critical in discursive negotiations.[53] Another issue in international interventions is tensions in power dynamics between more powerful and less powerful states, related to the principal agent and alliance theories.[54] For example, in principal agent theory, a principal actor may incentivize another usually less dominant state to undertake tasks on the former's behalf, which tends to downplay the less dominant actor's volition, leadership, and decision-making capacity. This can be seen in the large-scale foreign investment in militarization and securitization (especially of borders and checkpoints) in the region from foreign countries, aimed at curtailing human trafficking, illicit trafficking, and migration to Europe.[55] These relationships tend to downplay and neglect the significance of the dependency of local partners and less powerful states (like Mali) in terms of sovereignty and decision-making on global powers in a postcolonial era.[56]

Various armed groups, extremists, and militias have formed in Mali since the 2012 civil war, with various interests and motivations like self-defense, pro- or anti-government grievances, protection, or ethnic grievances, often to protect the interests of various groups. Pro-Dogon and pro-Fulani militias are among the most important of these in Mopti, given the historical tensions between these groups and the significant populations of both groups within Mopti. The groups and actors involved in violence in Mopti are diverse but include Fulani-associated militias and Dogon-associated militias; however, they often feature members of other ethnic groups in the region (Bozo, Arab, Bambara, Songhai, etc.).[57] They also include pro-government militias or militias with tacit support from the government (in the case of several Dogon defense groups), extremist groups, such as Jama'at Nasr al-Islam wal Muslimin (JNIM), Islamic State West Africa (ISWA), Islamic State Sahel Province (ISSP), al-Qaeda in the Islamic Maghreb (AQIM), Ansar Dine, and Katiba Macina—and various ethnic militias.

These groups have complex relationships with the state, other groups, and extremist groups operating in the region, and there are also complex reasons for their formation—including lack of trust in the state, absence of state authorities and militaries in the region, high insecurity and threats from other groups, and access to weapons due to proliferation of arms trafficking in the region, principally through Niger and following the civil war in Libya.[58] There are now refugee and internal displacement camps in every region of Mali, with about half a million internally displaced, mostly because of the threats of extremism and ethnic violence.

The Case of Mopti and the Introduction of Wagner Group

Mali as a conflict zone provides an interesting case study for glocalized security. The Mopti region, located in Central Mali, has evolved into the main epicenter of violence in the Central Sahel region (along with northern Burkina Faso), involving overlapping conflicts sometimes described as hybridized violence. Actors engaged in violence in the region are diverse—including self-defense groups, pro-government militias, state and international forces, anti-government militias, extremist groups, criminal groups, communal militias, and non-aligned actors (bandits, criminals, gangs, etc.). The eruption of the war and insecurity in 2012 provoked a significant response from actors at various levels—domestic (Mali), regional (AU, ECOWAS, G5 Sahel, national militaries), and international (UN MINUSMA, French military, multilateral forces). These forces initially stopped the extremist groups and rebels from reaching Bamako and drove them back to the north before deteriorating security resulted in significant armed actors emerging in the country. The Wagner Group entered Mali in 2022 following the expulsion of France, further complicating the conflict by introducing an actor with ties to the Russian state that has ignored international human rights laws and conventions and has historically been implicated in abuses against civilians and flaunting international law.

Mopti conflict

In many ways, the Mopti conflict perfectly illustrates the glocalization process: the conflict there has clear international and regional links that demonstrate its homogenizing and globalized processes while simultaneously having highly localized and unique characteristics. For example, the UN's MINUSMA mission in Mali—the most fatal and second-largest operation in the world—is merely one project among many UN missions targeting security and peace. In this way, the Mopti conflict is both highly local and highly international. From an international perspective, the local problems of ethnic conflict, poverty, grievances, and political tensions produced a level of insecurity that provoked an international response of stabilization, peacekeeping, and maintaining security, yet this reductive and superficial interpretation ignored the regional and international factors inherent to the conflict (regional conflicts, borders, refugee crises, EU and US militarization/securitization, poverty, War on Terror, etc.).

Mali's Mopti region has been the site of complex and deteriorating security involving weak governance, state absence or neglect, poverty, communal violence, and the proliferation of numerous and diverse armed militias (including self-defense groups, extremists, communal and ethnic militias, and pro-government militias like Dan Na Ambassagou). While these tensions have been especially inflamed for the past several decades, there are long-term processes and histories involving these groups' power, economics, access to land, trade, and migration.[59] The role of the state and regional and international actors has been an important component of the conflict, given both the significant international missions and forces aimed at stabilization and the persistence of violence despite significant resources invested and active since 2012.[60] Often, the local, regional, and continental responses to the Malian conflict, despite their importance, were subsumed or less visible than the responses of major powers, which were frequently considered more effective or significant. Both ECOWAS and AU, for example, had separate missions to stabilize Mali (MICEMA and AFISMA, respectively) that were overshadowed by the larger international missions like the UN's MINUSMA and France's Serval and Barkhane (or, more recently, Wagner Group), which were also (perhaps unfairly) considered more effective.[61] The assumption that (mostly Western) global actors and multinational forces would be able to effectively and easily resolve the complex glocal issues in Mali relates to the power dynamics inherent in globalization like temporality and power and also a Western-centric modernization process in which Western countries are assumed to be more capable, democratic, and powerful. The ACLED data indicate that 588 different unique actors were involved in violent events in Mali from 1997 until June 2022 (author's calculations using ACLED data). This large set of diverse actors includes those on both sides of conflict—assailants and victims—with general categories including civilians, rebels, external forces, and others (table 5.1).[62] While the violence has certainly concentrated in certain areas—northern Mali shortly after the 2012 civil war and more recently in central Mali around Ségou and Mopti—violence has continued to spread throughout much of Mali and beyond its borders into neighboring Burkina Faso and Niger. The terror attack just outside Bamako, in Kati, was the first attack near Bamako since the 2015 Radisson Blu hotel attack, showing the potential dispersion of violence and deteriorating security.[63]

Table 5.1. Categories of ACLED actors in the dataset and examples from Mali.

Category of actor	Examples from Mali (in ACLED dataset)
State forces	Military forces of Mali
Rebel	JNIM: Group for Support of Islam and Muslims
Political militias	MSA: Movement for Azawad Salvation
Identity militias	Dan Na Ambassagou
Rioters	Rioters (Mali)
Protestors	Protestors (Mali)
Civilians	Civilians (Mali)
External forces	Wagner group

Source: Created by the author.

Many communities have accused the government of failing to protect them and their interests from extremists, armed groups, and communal and ethnic militias formed by other groups that may threaten them or for which there has been hostility or grievances in the past—prompting them to form militias to defend themselves.[64] Indeed, one of the major motivations provoking international interventions in Mali was to reduce human rights abuses and violence against civilians, yet this type of violence has risen to the most common form (fig. 5.1).

Various factors like government weakness, state neglect, and poverty all contributed to the formation of armed groups. Extremist groups have purportedly targeted their recruitment on certain marginalized communities, particularly Fulani, who may be more susceptible to the ideological rhetoric of the groups that emphasize anti-state grievance. Recruitment of Fulani and others into extremist groups has in turn inflamed the communal tensions between Fulani and other communities in the region like Bambara and Dogon. Mali now has the second-most violent events and fatalities in the North and West Africa region, after Nigeria, and violence against civilians is the most common form of violence in the country.[65] Temporally, violent events in Mali have increased significantly, and Mali remains one of the countries in the North and West Africa regions with the highest number of incidents of violent events and fatalities.[66] Violence against civilians has become the most common violent event (which include battles, remote violence, and violence against civilians), starting in 2016. This concerning trend mirrors those of much of the North and West Africa region.

Figure 5.1. Number of Violent Events by Event Category in Mali from 1997 to December of 2023. *Source*: Created by the author.

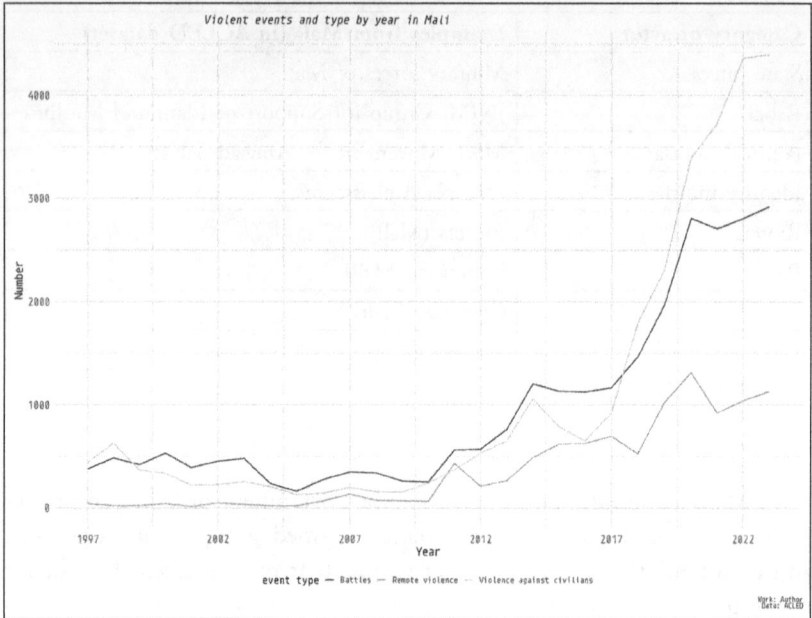

Interestingly, the original Organization for Africa Unity (OAU, predecessor of African Union) had such firm ideological commitment to state sovereignty that it was prevented from intervening in most conflicts, though it may have also lacked the capacity and resources to do so.[67] Cultural globalization has involved the elements of Africa's unique traditions and practices that have been transferred to and are matched with other globally identified cultures and norms.[68] There has been a concomitant shift from radical cultural relativism, as evidenced in OAU's policies, to radical universalism, as evidenced in the doctrine of Responsibility to Protect (R2P), which has been adopted by ECOWAS, UN, African Union, and other international organizations.[69] The African Union has adopted different security and governance frameworks and policies that promoted African agency and sovereignty on security and governance issues as embodied in the African Peace and Security Architecture (APSA) mechanisms and its doctrine of non-indifference. These complex and often contradictory mechanisms and policies complicate organizations like AU's intervention efforts while maintaining African agency. There has been an inherent tension between non-indifference to human security and efforts to promote governance, security, and democracy. These have had the unfortunate consequence of preventing the African Union from engaging in conflicts in Africa—either for lack of resources or lack of will.[70] Further, both national governments in Africa and continental institutions like the African Union have sought to avoid repeating Western global liberal governance mechanisms within Africa.

There has been deteriorating security across much of North and West Africa in past decades, although the hot spots or epicenters are centered around Lake Chad and the Central Sahel tri-border zone of Mopti, Niger, and Burkina Faso.[71] There are complex reasons producing this insecurity, including poverty, marginalization of groups like Tuareg or Fulani, drought, Islamic fundamentalism, state neglect or oppression, migrant/refugee crises, and political and economic grievances.[72] Violence in the region has the proclivity to disperse across borders, expand spatially and territorially, and resist defeat.[73] The highly political nature of the violence has widely resisted defeat or amelioration, instead evolving or shifting spatially and even taking more violent forms. The Boko Haram conflict in Lake Chad is one example in which the group seeks shelter and safety in border sanctuaries, safe havens, and peripheral areas in Niger, Cameron, and Nigeria. Groups like AQIM and Boko Haram have also succeeded in generating some community or host population support through recruitment, providing services, and their anti-government rhetoric that resonates with certain marginalized groups. Although they have suffered several defeats in battles and skirmishes, Boko Haram has a high capacity for regrouping, recruitment, fleeing to sanctuaries, and remaining viable. They have persisted in their sporadic attacks and operations despite heavy defeats, casualties, and regional opposition to them.[74]

Several factors and obstacles account for the continuing deterioration of security and complexities in curtailing insecurity. Three major obstacles to achieving peace and stability in northern Mali include lack of job opportunities, presence of armed groups, and exclusion of suspected jihadist and extremist groups from the peace process and various peace agreements.[75] The 2015 Agreement on Peace and Reconciliation involved agreements to disarm between two major umbrella organizations—Platform (pro-government) and Coordination (alliance of several militant groups fighting for self-determination and autonomy in the north). The proliferation of armed and violent non-state actors—typically armed militias, defense militias, and extremists—demonstrates the fragility of security and stability in Mali.[76] As security has deteriorated, these groups tend to form to protect interests, fill vacuums that a weak state has neglected, and agitate for power, resources, or other grievances. Furthermore, these groups continue to proliferate given the failure of the Malian state to address issues like lack of investment, poverty, social services, education, and inequality, particularly in northern and central Mali. The continued neglect of these regions and issues provokes groups to form militias given a perceived lack of protection and provision of services by the state.[77]

Wagner Group in Mali

After nearly a decade of active and direct intervention in Mali, consisting of two operations (Serval and Barkhane), training, coordination, cooperation, intelligence, and various associated activities, France and its operations were expelled by Mali in 2022 following criticisms by the French ambassador alongside increasing anti-French public sentiment.[78] Tensions in Mali toward France had been growing for years, with much of the population and government holding negative opinions stemming from the colonial history of France and perceived injustices.[79] Despite significant insecurity in the country, support for France's presence (and other international actors) and involvement declined over time. The 2020 military coup has challenged international outcry for restoration of democratic processes like elections and stifled decades of democratization in the country.

The Wagner group reflects an increasing Russian participation in African affairs, starting in 2017 in Sudan followed by Central African Republic (CAR) in 2018 and Libya (2019)—now renamed the Africa Corp following the transformation of Wagner.[80] The Wagner group is a military contractor that expanded into Africa following previous involvements in the Syrian Civil War supporting the Assad regime. Wagner has been active in Sudan, CAR, Mozambique, Libya, and Madagascar. Their typical set of activities while in African countries includes training exercises, fighting anti-government forces, private security, guarding facilities, and quelling protests or riots.[81] Wagner Group's activities overlapped with Russian foreign policy aims while giving Russia plausible deniability. Wagner Group provided Russia with a valuable tool in the ability to test new environments for military capabilities and cooperation, trade, or investment without appearing heavy-handed or colonial. Russian investment, military cooperation, and trade often corresponded with the presence and activities of Wagner Group. For example, Sudan has purchased more than 80 percent of its weapons from Russia since 2003.[82]

Throughout Wagner Group's missions and activities, it has cultivated ties to and within countries where it has been active that inevitably result, through gradual processes, to state-to-state ties between the African states and Russia. This was the long-term goal of both Russian foreign policy and the Wagner Group, which, despite its ostensible private status, had ties to state officials in Russia. Wagner Group used a three-tiered approach in the African countries where it operated: conduct misinformation and pro-government information warfare strategies (spurious polls and counterdemonstrations); secure payments for services via concessions in extractive industries and use a variety of organizations to oversee extraction projects; and become integrated and involved into a country's military via launching a relationship directly with Russia's military through training, advising, personal security, arms dealing, and anti-insurgency operations. The outcome of all of these has been closer political, trade, and state-to-state ties between the African and Russian states.[83]

In Sudan, Wagner Group gained access to mineral rights and extractions through its involvement in private security for guarding mines and politicians. These activities were leveraged to gain access to a large Russian project to establish naval facilities at Port Sudan. In CAR, 170 to 670 civilian advisors were present during the recent conflicts in advisory, intelligence, and training capacities. Entrepreneurial ventures and commercial ties by Wagner Group inevitably tied into state-state relations with the Russian state and were almost exclusively agreed on through mineral and mining concessions, rather than cash, through affiliate and subsidiary companies like Lobaye Invest, M Invest, Meroe Gold, or their affiliates.[84] In Mali, Wagner Group likewise used disinformation campaigns to enhance pro-government positions and pro-Russian and pro-Wagner positions through its propaganda unit called the Foundation for National Values Protection (FZNC), mirroring its activities in previous locations.

Wagner Group has encountered certain obstacles and challenges in Mali relative to other states of operation. There were diverse calls for its withdrawal, usually based on need for further support in the Ukraine conflict (where Wagner Group operated in highly trained units or to assassinate high-profile targets) or outcry against human rights violation claims. There were also funding issues for Wagner Group in Mali, given the relative difficulty in acquiring mining concessions and rights relative to previous locations in Sudan, CAR, and Mozambique. The recent regional and international sanctions against Mali complicated the group's efforts to exploit mineral resources (because of tighter regulation by Mali and Western nations), and some mines continued to be controlled by militias, armed groups, and jihadists like Coordination des mouvements de l'Azawad (CMA).

Wagner Group has been accused of several forms of human rights abuses and violations. Wagner Group, operating alongside Malian forces, killed more than 300 people in the central Malian town of Moura over a five-day period in March of 2022.[85] While many of Wagner's operations and activities targeted Islamists in the country (including the operation in Moura), accusations of collateral damage on civilians and directly targeting civilians (through extrajudicial torture, disappearance, and killings) occurred.[86] Interestingly, there is significant evidence of cooperation and coordination between different agencies and forces in Central Mali around Mopti that included Malian military forces, Wagner Group, and even the pro-government self-defense militia Dan Na Ambassagou, which started as a Dogon protection militia.

Responsibility to Protect: Regional and International Interventions in Mali

According to the US Department of Defense, military interventions are defined as the deliberate act of a state or group of state to introduce its military forces into the course of an existing controversy in another country.[87] Military interventions by foreign powers or militaries can be direct or indirect. Direct military interventions are sending forces to fight, occupy, or defend territory in other countries, including the use of missiles and air strikes. Indirect interventions provide security assistance or other support, such as intelligence or aerial refueling, to facilitate the use of military force by a third party, as the United States has been doing in Mali.[88]

Both R2P and the Global War on Terror (along with many other missions and programs) have humanitarian and state security objectives.[89] The goal is to ensure regional and international security and stabilization. Proponents of R2P contend that international interventions, including use of force, are fundamental and requisite moral imperatives to protect civilians and curtail violence.[90] R2P distinguishes between state and human security. The main critiques of R2P involve the misuse of humanitarian missions for economic or political interests of global powers like the United States or France. Further, while there are required legal frameworks for multinational and multilateral missions (like Serval or MINUSMA) between states and partner organizations, there are inevitably issues of power dynamics, strategies, authority, and leadership that may generate disputes or grievances. Examples of international interventions and long-term capacity building, including regime change, have occurred in African conflicts in the context of Libya, Sudan, and Côte d'Ivoire.

There are overlaps in interests and strategies between R2P and the Global War on Terror under global liberal governance. The United States has justified much of its military invasions and actions through the Global War on Terror as missions to protect civilians, prevent casualties, and tackle extremism and insecurity.[91] R2P and Global War on Terror missions abroad are both inherently accompanied by capacity and state building.[92] Both have also been consistently justified by the United States (and other countries) to protect civilians abroad and domestically from terrorist threats like Al-Qaeda and the Islamic State of Iraq and the Levant (ISIL).

Since 2018, violence has increased every year in Mali, and several were the most violent on record. A concerning impact of the increasing insecurity in Mali is civilian fatalities, often related to collateral damage (including by state forces of Mali and Burkina Faso), targeting by Wagner Group, and targeting by extremist groups active in the region (JNIM and ISIS Sahel being the two most deadly).[93] Mali also has the highest proportion of violence associated with pastoralist groups in the North and West Africa regions, alongside Burkina Faso.[94] Pastoralist-associated violence—which can be measured using ACLED data but is nondirectional, meaning victims and assailants can't be identified—was historically relatively low, yet began increasing after the 2012 Civil War. Since 2016 the violence has been not only very high, but also spatially dispersed across much of northern and central Mali (fig 5.2). Much of this stems from communal violence with other groups (like Dogon), but also some involvement with being victims of violence from state forces, self-defense militias, armed groups, and extremism.

REGIONAL INTERVENTIONS

Regional interventions and implications for the conflict in Mali have been important but perhaps overlooked relative to the more prominent actors like the French military and UN MINUSMA. The insecurity in Mali has dispersed into neighboring countries such as Côte d'Ivoire, Togo, Burkina Faso, and Niger.[95] This is consistent with modern conflicts being more intranational and transnational in nature rather than international. The potential for dispersion and transnationalism has been increasing given transnational links between

Figure 5.2. Overall and Pastoralist-Associated Violent Events in ACLED Dataset in Mali. *Source*: Created by the author.

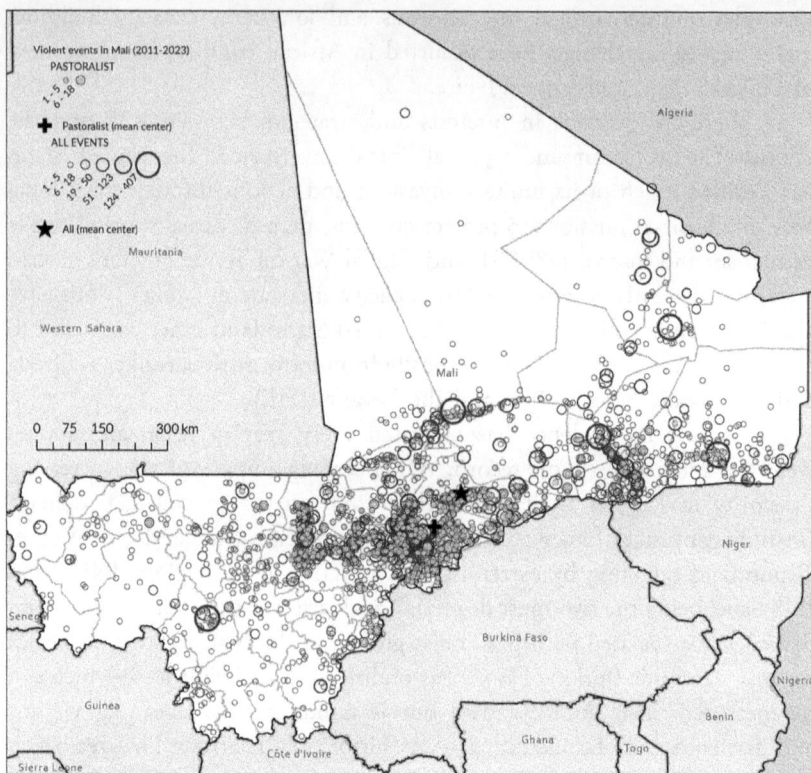

groups (ethnicities and groups), shared grievances, weak governance, and states and sanctuary areas where rebels, militias, and extremists can shelter and avoid capture.[96] This makes conflicts more intractable, susceptible to dispersion and/or transnationalism, and more difficult to stop. For example, few major extremist organizations across all of Africa have been definitively defeated because of strategies involving retreating and seeking sanctuary to enhance recruitment and resources.[97]

The Libyan conflict was likewise responsible for a domino effect of insecurity across the Sahel region, particularly as exiled or departing former soldiers brought arms and ammunition with them across the highly porous borders of the region.[98] The conflict dispersed spatially and triggered further conflicts in Niger, Chad, Mali, and elsewhere. The issue of insecurity in Algeria has likewise dispersed spatially, generating further insecurity, particularly in Mali. Until now, many rebel, militia, and extremist groups operating in the Central Sahel have Algerian leadership or ties to Algeria.

There are also several critical regional and continental forces involved in trying to achieve security and stability, such as G5 Sahel, ECOWAS missions, AU missions, and neighboring militaries (like Chad, Niger, and Nigeria). The goal of AU has been to universalize and integrate social, economic, political, institutional, and other aspects of pan-Africanism.[99] The African Union, unlike its predecessor, the OAU, has taken an active interventionist posture, yet still has largely failed to intervene in conflicts because it tries to avoid repeating Western-style pursuits of regime change and pressure along liberal governance and democracy ideologies.[100] ECOWAS, meanwhile, is guided by three principles: Responsibility to Prevent (actions taken to address the direct and root causes of intra- and interstate conflicts that put populations at risk); Responsibility to React (actions taken in response to grave and compelling humanitarian disasters); and Responsibility to Rebuild (actions taken to ensure recovery, reconstruction, rehabilitation, and reconciliation in the aftermath of violent conflict and humanitarian or natural disasters).[101] These reflect similar principles to those of UN interventions and R2P frameworks.

The regional response to the Malian conflict has been important but perhaps neglected in the scholarship and media attention to the conflict, which instead often overemphasize the international response in the form of UN MINUSMA, French armed forces, G5 Sahel, and other multilateral and multinational programs. For example, while France sent between 3,000 and 5,100 troops to Mali during its operations, UN MINUSMA reached a peak of 3,000. ECOWAS and the African Union sent contingents but were less reported and visible possibly because of their low prestige and smaller size.[102] On January 9, 2022, ECOWAS and UEMOA imposed economic and diplomatic sanctions on Mali. The sanctions severed financial aid to Mali and froze Malian assets within UEMOA commercial banks.[103] They also considered closing all borders between Mali and other ECOWAS countries, suspending transactions within Mali, and recalling ambassadors representing all member countries in Mali. This regional political and institutional response perhaps reflected global views on the Malian conflict yet simultaneously contradicted and belied common sentiment both within Mali and in wider West Africa, where people recognized the punitive harm and ineffectiveness of such sanctions, which mostly served to cripple individual households. In fact, in the first few months of 2024, ECOWAS was forced to reverse or soften some of the threats and sanctions on both Guinea and Mali—including blockades, economic ones, invasions, and others—because of increasing tensions in the region and threats by several countries to leave the association.

In principle, the policies targeted the ruling military junta for its decision to prolong its rule and delay presidential elections. The sanctions were supported by France, the United States, and the EU but strongly opposed by the Malian regime, the majority of Malians, and many political actors in the region.[104] Several large-scale protests have been mounted by Malians against ECOWAS for the sanctions, which have largely served to financially cripple typical Malians, the government, and other actors within Mali. Most ECOWAS countries are labeled as "hybrid or authoritarian regimes" in the 2020 Democracy Index, with only Ghana considered a "flawed democracy." Most Malians seem to support the junta's decision to postpone elections, fearing a rushed election may fail to deliver intended results, strengthen democracy, or bring a stable governance. Yet the international community and major powers viewed the delay in elections merely through the lenses of the democratization and state-building globalized ideologies inherent to R2P and the Global War on Terror.

ECOWAS, however, has largely failed to maintain security in Mali. Since 1960, Mali has faced five Tuareg rebellions, five coups, four transitions to civilian rule, and five unimplemented North-South agreements.[105] There has been a protracted conflict relating to the foundation of the state, process of state building, and institutionalization of liberal democracy.[106] Regional capacity building, state-building, governance enhancement, and democratization have had some successes—particularly in the 1990s when nearly all Sahelian countries had democratic elections. Yet the region is still suffering from political instability, coups, lack of proper democratic transitions, and consolidation of power among few hands and families.[107]

INTERNATIONAL INTERVENTIONS

There are different theories to account for the role of states and the relations among them under globalization. In many theories, the state is understood as the container of society, with the level of social organization mediating between the local and the global. The international interventions in Mali demonstrate the shifting dynamics and attitudes toward states, given the inevitable involvement of foreign states and multilateral forces in conflicts like Mali. A key element of this intervention is that of major powers.

The international connections to the security issue in Mopti have not been monolithic or static, but variable spatially and temporally. The US involvement in the Sahel region, for example, has shifted from an indirect military intervention (through advisement, intelligence, and resources) immediately after September 11 to more direct military interventions through personnel, military operations, drone strikes, and training. While the US Authorization for Use of Military Force voted on by Congress a few days after September 11 was initially restricted to targeting the responsible agents for the September 11 attack, it has quickly broadened to include emergent or potential threats, with proposed operations in more than eighty countries.[108] Specifically, the United States took a more active interventionist position in the Sahel region (and Mali) through operational support for French and Nigerien forces.[109] These cooperative and coordinating relationships were largely influenced by the previous relationships of the United States and coordination with militaries in other parts of the world like Afghanistan, Somalia, Sudan, and Iraq. There was significant criticism of the US intervention and strategies in Mali. Despite both indirect and then direct interventions in Mali—through support, intelligence, cooperation with France and neighboring countries, and training and funding—stability and security in Mali have continually deteriorated.

The US military has a "by, with, and through" approach for its foreign military interventions, implying that operations and missions are led by partners, state or non-state actors, with support by the United States and its coalitions, through US authorities and partner agreements.[110] Starting with the Pan Sahel Initiative in 2002 to build capacity for armed forces in Mali, Mauritania, Chad, and Niger, interventions later shifted to the Trans-Sahara Counter Terrorism Partnership, ultimately transitioning from indirect to more direct interventions following the termination of security assistance in 2012 due to US federal laws limiting international partnerships with countries with coups. The significant amount of personnel, training, resources, and funding (totaling $340 million from 2005 to 2013) did little to curtail extremism, address marginalization, or improve governance and security institutions and infrastructure. These failures, coupled with further crises in Mali (e.g., the consecutive coups, proliferation of armed groups, and spatial expansion of violence), show the limitations of international securitization under R2P or the Global War on Terror.

France's relationship with Mali through the conflict has also been strained. It was expected that France's status as a global power with an advanced military could quickly and easily tackle the extremist and insurgent threats posed by the various groups in the country. However, while France indeed curtailed the insurgent and extremist threat in 2013 and prevented it from reaching the capital,[111] it largely failed in its mission to tackle extremism and insecurity. Further, tensions between France and Mali escalated during the coups when the international community demanded an immediate return to democratic elections. The final point of contention involved the question of involving extremist groups in the peace process, which France has consistently repudiated.[112]

The international response to the conflict in Mali has had several accomplishments, but largely failed to overcome the systemic factors contributing to insecurity. There are three major limitations of the international intervention in Mali: incompatible agendas and assumptions of stakeholders; focus of international actors exclusively on security and governance over identity or underlying factors; and current state-centric international system despite increasing global connections with threats like terrorism and transnational conflict.[113] Namely, there are pervasive problems in the country, including poverty, ethnic grievances, political power, and infrastructural and historical marginalization, that have not been addressed through the many military, peacekeeping, and stabilization missions.[114] This demonstrates that despite significant international investment, resources, and attention to insecurity and conflict in Mali, underlying problems persist.

Conclusions: Glocalized Security and the State

Perhaps it is not surprising that the complex conflict in Mali involves both regional and international factors and implications. While in both scholarship and media reports Mali is often reductively presented as a weak state with weak governance and high levels of violence and corruption, there are clearly wider links to the conflict regionally and internationally. Despite the simplistic portrayal of Mali as an unstable and violent country in a violent region—consistent with the United States' assumptions of Mali and the wider Sahel as security vacuums and breeding grounds for insecurity and extremism—the recent history instead shows that much of the Sahel was stable, democratic, and stable until the early 2000s. Various regional crises over the past two decades—the Arab Spring, Libyan war, Nigerian conflicts, weak governance, and political coups—inevitably spilled across borders and provoked a crisis in Mali. The 2012 Tuareg rebellion was facilitated by returning Tuareg fighters trained in Libya under the Qaddafi regime and armed with weapons seized during the war.

The persistence of insecurity in Mali despite vast international responses typifies the failure of global processes like peacekeeping, multinational forces, and global and regional partnerships to address local conflicts. The Ogossagou massacre of Fulani in the Mopti region shows the dangers of neglecting local factors in conflicts. Several large-scale massacres of civilians in Mali (including by Wagner Group) have taken place despite advanced warning and civilians informing authorities at the time of the massacre, which were ignored. This creates cycles of grievances that inevitably result in persistent insecurity and distrust. One significant failure of the very international (i.e., globalized) response to the Malian conflict has been a significant neglect of local grievances and factors. Different parts of Mali have been severely neglected for decades by state institutions in terms of resources, trade, and investment—particularly the vast northern regions (Gao, Menaka, Timbuktu) and the poor central regions. In many ways, the conflict in Mali and the subsequent involvement of complex international and regional actors have only amplified the perception of neglect and even oppression by the Malian state. The consecutive coups in Mali over the preceding two years clearly exemplify the failure of the state to address lingering ethnic tensions, feelings of inequality, political marginalization, and lack of sufficient redress to insecurity and poverty.

Overall, intervention programs, militaries, and partnerships failed to sufficiently involve local actors and governments in consultation and engagement. This is a typical problem of Western development and political involvement in the Global South, in which "experts" at the international level of Western aid agencies tend to ignore local perspectives and knowledge. Moreover, the root factors driving insecurity and conflict in the country have not been addressed because of the complexity and local nature of these grievances. Local actors and Malians were not sufficiently engaged to the point that the major emphasis of interventions remained military in nature, rather than institutional, governmental, and political.

The international response and interventions to the Malian conflict proved successful in the short term (by preventing collapse of the entire state and fall of Bamako) but largely inadequate and insufficient in the long term. This is largely because trust and faith in the international response was so large, and the sheer size of the international response in terms of actors, funding, training, and personnel was so large. Meanwhile, the regional interventions in Mali were largely hamstrung by their own lack of will (because of fears of replicating colonial-style Western democratization and regime change policies) and resources. All of these failures ultimately facilitated the recent expulsion of French forces, along with many of their allies and partners (Germany, Denmark, Canada, and others), only to be replaced by the rather infamous Wagner Group. Unfortunately, the insecurity in Mali has increased since the late 2010s. None of the major extremist groups has been definitively curtailed, and much of the country remains unstable, weakly governed, poor, and insecure. Regional sanctions against Mali following its consecutive coups merely served to further cripple and persecute average Malians who are already struggling.

These events show a strong level of glocalization in the security processes of Mali. While there are significant local factors and causes of the current conflict, they exist alongside international and regional processes including neighboring conflicts and crises, *refugeeism* and migrations, political weakness, coups, and international and multilateral operations to conflicts. The expectation since WWII has been for international and multilateral processes and organizations like the UN to be able to resolve and mitigate crises and conflicts, yet in theaters across Africa (South Sudan, CAR, Mali, Chad, and Somalia) there remain local grievances, ethnic conflicts, tensions, and political violence, and weakness. The promises of the 1980s and 1990s toward democratic transition and consolidation and human rights have sadly eroded, and unfortunately significant international responses and actors could not assuage the insecurities, largely because they fail to address local problems, inequalities, and grievances. All of this goes to the heart of the state and its capacity.

In the end, glocalization provides a lens for examining the African state through its domestic and external drivers of conflict and the securitization that results from the failures of the state. Indeed, Mali faced significant challenges in maintaining order. Despite the domestic revolts and external interventions, Mali's security remains precarious. The Malian state has become an object of fixing through subversive domestic politics and revolts and external interventions that mostly serve the global security concerns of Western powers. This has created a significant mismatch between external resources and local needs, external preferences and domestic priorities, and the Malian vision of security and the interests of major powers. Even more, Malians and outsiders have developed different ways of seeing the state and what its primary role should be. All of these point to the ways in which the African states become entangled in glocalized security. This chapter goes back to the fundamental question of the context of state failure and the divergent interests in the securitization of the African state. This becomes very vivid in the human insecurity, absence of the state, and major power play in Mali, especially in the Mopti region. Mopti becomes a microcosm of state failure and global securitization of local spaces, which has created more glocalized security challenges for Mali and the powers and institutions vested in African security.

Notes

1. ACLED, "Political Violence Skyrockets in the Sahel According to the Latest ACLED Data"; ACLED, "The Sahel: Mid-Year Update."

2. Raleigh and Dowd, "The Sahel Crisis since 2012"; Walther, "Wars and Conflicts in the Sahara-Sahel."

3. In Africa, Wagner Group has been replaced by Africa Corps, which was created by the Russian government after Wagner Group's founders, Yevgeny Prigozhin and Dmitry Utkin, died in a plane crash in August 2023 in the midst of a conflict with the Russian government. See Lechner, "Is Africa Corps a Rebranded Wagner Group?"

4. Rupesinghe and Boas, "Local Drivers of Violent Extremism in Central Mali"; Raleigh et al., "The Sahel Crisis since 2012."

5. Pflaum, "Pastoralist Violence in North and West Africa"; OECD/SWAC, "The Geography of Conflict in North and West Africa," 2020.

6. Including United Nations Multidimensional Integrated Stabilization Mission in Mali (UN MINUSUMA), the former Operations Serval and Barkhane, Russian private security forces (like Wagner), regional and continental missions like African Union (AU) and the Economic Community of West African States (ECOWAS), G5 Sahel (involving militaries of five Sahelian nations), and, finally, the United States and other nations whose presence reflects Western interests related to a vague global War on Terror (WOT) implemented following September 11.

7. Bere, "Armed Rebellion, Violent Extremism, and the Challenges of International Intervention in Mali."

8. Bere, "Armed Rebellion, Violent Extremism, and the Challenges of International Intervention in Mali."

9. Sandor, *Insecurity, the Breakdown of Social Trust and Armed Actor Governance in Central and Northern Mali*; Baldaro, "A Dangerous Method: How Mali Lost Control of the North, and Learned to Stop Worrying"; FIDH, "In Central Mali, Civilian Populations Are Caught between Terrorism and Counterterrorism"; Eizenga, "Long Term Trends across Security and Development in the Sahel," 2019.

10. Bere, "Armed Rebellion, Violent Extremism, and the Challenges of International Intervention in Mali"; Elischer, "Populist Civil Society, the Wagner Group, and Post-Coup Politics in Mali."

11. Bere, "Armed Rebellion, Violent Extremism, and the Challenges of International Intervention in Mali."

12. Bere, "Armed Rebellion, Violent Extremism, and the Challenges of International Intervention in Mali."

13. Harmon, "Securitization Initiatives in the Sahara-Sahel Region in the Twenty-First Century"; Dowd, "Grievances, Governance and Islamist Violence in Sub-Saharan Africa"; Wing, "Combatting Insecurity in Mali."

14. Diao et al., "Senegal: Impacts of the Ukraine and Global Crises on Poverty and Food Security."

15. Andersson, "Europe's Failed 'Fight' against Irregular Migration: Ethnographic Notes on a Counterproductive Industry."

16. Lacher, "Libya's Fractious South and Regional Instability"; Eizenga, "Long Term Trends across Security and Development in the Sahel," 2019; Harmon, "Securitization Initiatives in the Sahara-Sahel Region in the Twenty-First Century."

17. Avoulete, "Should ECOWAS Rethink Its Approach to Coups?"

18. Brachet, "Manufacturing Smugglers: From Irregular to Clandestine Mobility in the Sahara"; de Tessières, "At the Crossroads of Sahelian Conflicts: Insecurity, Terrorism, and Arms Trafficking in Niger"; Boukhars, "Rethinking Security across the Sahara and the Sahel."

19. Haugegaard, "Sharia as 'Desert Business': Understanding the Links between Criminal Networks and Jihadism in Northern Mali."

20. D'Orsi, "An Outlook on the Conflict in Casamance with a Focus on the Legal Situation of the Mouvement Des Forces Democratiques ('Mouvement of Democratic Forces of Casamance') and Its Members."

21. Knoope and Buchanan-Clarke, "Central African Republic: A Conflict Misunderstood."

22. Elischer, "Populist Civil Society, the Wagner Group, and Post-Coup Politics in Mali."

23. Boeke and Schuurman, "Operation 'Serval': A Strategic Analysis of the French Intervention in Mali, 2013–2014"; Harmon, "Securitization Initiatives in the Sahara-Sahel Region in the Twenty-First Century"; Elischer, "Populist Civil Society, the Wagner Group, and Post-Coup Politics in Mali."

24. Parens, "The Wagner Group's Playbook in Mali."

25. Villalón and Idrissa, *Democratic Struggle, Institutional Reform, and State Resilience in the African Sahel*; Villalón, *The Oxford Handbook of the African Sahel.*

26. Roudometof, "Nationalism, Globalization and Glocalization."

27. Roudometof, "Nationalism, Globalization and Glocalization."

28. Roudometof, "Nationalism, Globalization and Glocalization."

29. Roudometof, "Nationalism, Globalization and Glocalization."

30. Roudometof, "Theorizing Glocalization: Three Interpretations"; Robertson, "Globality and Modernity"; Robertson, "Globalisation or Glocalisation?"

31. The five main elements of glocalization, according to Roudometof (2016): Diversity is the essence of social life; not all differences are erased; history and culture operate autonomously to offer a sense of uniqueness to the experiences of groups; glocalization removes the fear that globalization resembles a tidal wave erasing all differences; and glocalization does not promise a world free from conflict but offers a more historically grounded and pragmatic worldview.

32. Roudometof, "Nationalism, Globalization and Glocalization."

33. Six waves of globalization include the great dispersal, neolithic revolution, land-based globalization, ocean-based globalization, Anglo-American world, and New Globalization.

34. Roudometof, "Nationalism, Globalization and Glocalization"; Therborn, "Dimensions of Globalization and the Dynamics of (In)Inequalities"; Therborn, "Globalizations: Dimensions, Historical Waves, Regional Effects, Normative Governance."

35. Roudometof, "Nationalism, Globalization and Glocalization."

36. Appadurai, *Fear of Small Numbers: An Essay on the Geography of Anger.*

37. Robertson, "Globality and Modernity."

38. For example, see Robertson, "Globalisation or Glocalisation?"; Robertson, "Glocalization: Time-Space and Homogeneity-Heterogeneity," Robertson and Giulianotti, "The Globalization of Football: A Study in the Glocalization of the 'Serious Life'"; "Glocalization, Globalization, and Migration: The Case of Scottish Football Supporters in North America"; and Robertson and White, "What Is Globalization?"

39. Roudometof, "Theorizing Glocalization: Three Interpretations"; Roudometof, "Nationalism, Globalization and Glocalization."

40. Roudometof, "Nationalism, Globalization and Glocalization."

41. Roudometof, "Nationalism, Globalization and Glocalization"; Roudometof, "Theorizing Glocalization: Three Interpretations."

42. Roudometof, "Theorizing Glocalization: Three Interpretations."

43. Roudometof, "Theorizing Glocalization: Three Interpretations."

44. Roudometof, "Theorizing Glocalization: Three Interpretations."

45. Roudometof, "Theorizing Glocalization: Three Interpretations"; Robertson and White, "What Is Globalization?"; Robertson, "Glocalization: Time-Space and Homogeneity-Heterogeneity."

46. de Tessières, "At the Crossroads of Sahelian Conflicts: Insecurity, Terrorism, and Arms Trafficking in Niger"; Raleigh et al., "The Sahel Crisis since 2012."

47. Zoubir, "The United States and Maghreb-Sahel Security."

48. Bere, "Armed Rebellion, Violent Extremism, and the Challenges of International Intervention in Mali."

49. Villalón, *The Oxford Handbook of the African Sahel*; Villalón and Idrissa, *Democratic Struggle, Institutional Reform, and State Resilience in the African Sahel.*

50. Tankel, "US Counterterrorism in the Sahel: From Indirect to Direct Intervention."

51. Risse, *Governance without a State? Policies and Politics in Areas of Limited Statehood.*

52. Frowd and Sandor, "Militarism and Its Limits: Sociological Insights on Security Assemblages in the Sahel."

53. Bah, "The Contours of New Humanitarianism: War and Peacebuilding in Sierra Leone."

54. Tankel, "US Counterterrorism in the Sahel: From Indirect to Direct Intervention"; Bah, *International Security and Peacebuilding: Africa, the Middle East, and Europe.*

55. Andersson, "Europe's Failed 'Fight' against Irregular Migration: Ethnographic Notes on a Counterproductive Industry."

56. Tankel, "US Counterterrorism in the Sahel: From Indirect to Direct Intervention."

57. Benjaminsen and Ba, "Fulani-Dogon Killings in Mali: Farmer-Herder Conflicts as Insurgency and Counterinsurgency"; HRW, " 'How Much More Blood Must Be Spilled?' Atrocities against Civilians in Central Mali, 2019"; HRW, " 'We Used to Be Brothers': Self-Defense Group Abuses in Central Mali."

58. de Tessières, "Briefing Paper: Measuring Illicit Arms Flow (Niger)."

59. Benjaminsen and Ba, "Why Do Pastoralists in Mali Join Jihadist Groups? A Political Ecological Explanation."

60. Bere, "Armed Rebellion, Violent Extremism, and the Challenges of International Intervention in Mali."

61. Aning and Edu-Afful, "African Agency in R2P: Interventions by African Union and ECOWAS in Mali, Côte d'Ivoire, and Libya."

62. ACLED, "Armed Conflict Location & Event Data Project."

63. Bensimon, "Mali: Jihadists Attack the Army's Seat of Power."

64. Nnoko-Mewanu, "Farmer-Herder Conflicts on the Rise in Africa"; HRW, " 'How Much More Blood Must Be Spilled?' Atrocities against Civilians in Central Mali, 2019"; HRW, " 'We Used to Be Brothers': Self-Defense Group Abuses in Central Mali."

65. OECD/SWAC, "The Geography of Conflict in North and West Africa," 2020; ACLED, "The Sahel: Mid-Year Update."

66. OECD/SWAC, "The Geography of Conflict in North and West Africa," 2020; Pflaum, "Pastoralist Violence in North and West Africa"; ACLED, "The Sahel: Mid-Year Update."

67. Aning and Edu-Afful, "African Agency in R2P: Interventions by African Union and ECOWAS in Mali, Côte d'Ivoire, and Libya."

68. Aning and Edu-Afful, "African Agency in R2P."

69. Bah, "The Contours of New Humanitarianism: War and Peacebuilding in Sierra Leone."

70. Bah, *International Security and Peacebuilding.*

71. OECD/SWAC, "The Geography of Conflict in North and West Africa," 2020; Pflaum, "Pastoralist Violence in North and West Africa."

72. Ndem Okon, "Mali: ECOWAS Responses to the Conflict in Mali (2012–2021)"; OECD/SWAC, "The Geography of Conflict in North and West Africa," 2020.

73. Walther and Miles, *African Border Disorders: Addressing Transnational Extremist Organizations*; Lacher, "Libya's Fractious South and Regional Instability."

74. Curiel et al., "Uncovering the Internal Structure of Boko Haram through Its Mobility Patterns"; Dowd, "Nigeria's Boko Haram."

75. Haugegaard, "Sharia as 'Desert Business': Understanding the Links between Criminal Networks and Jihadism in Northern Mali."

76. Raleigh et al., "The Sahel Crisis since 2012"; Dowd, "Grievances, Governance and Islamist Violence in Sub-Saharan Africa."

77. Benjaminsen and Ba, "Why Do Pastoralists in Mali Join Jihadist Groups? A Political Ecological Explanation"; Wing, "Combatting Insecurity in Mali"; Raineri and Strazzari, "State, Secession, and Jihad: The Micropolitical Economy of Conflict in Northern Mali"; Diallo, "Ethnic Clashes, Jihad, and Insecurity in Central Mali."

78. Elischer, "Populist Civil Society, the Wagner Group, and Post-Coup Politics in Mali."

79. Elischer, "Populist Civil Society, the Wagner Group, and Post-Coup Politics in Mali."

80. Parens, "The Wagner Group's Playbook in Mali"; John A. Lechner, "Is Africa Corps a Rebranded Wagner Group?"

81. Parens, "The Wagner Group's Playbook in Mali."

82. Parens, "The Wagner Group's Playbook in Mali."

83. Parens, "The Wagner Group's Playbook in Mali."

84. Parens, "The Wagner Group's Playbook in Mali."

85. ACLED, "The Sahel: Mid-Year Update."

86. Elischer, "Populist Civil Society, the Wagner Group, and Post-Coup Politics in Mali"; ACLED, "The Sahel: Mid-Year Update."

87. Tankel, "US Counterterrorism in the Sahel: From Indirect to Direct Intervention."

88. Tankel, "US Counterterrorism in the Sahel: From Indirect to Direct Intervention."

89. Bah, *International Security and Peacebuilding*.

90. Bah, *International Security and Peacebuilding*.

91. Bere, "Armed Rebellion, Violent Extremism, and the Challenges of International Intervention in Mali"; Bah, *International Security and Peacebuilding*.

92. Bah, *International Security and Peacebuilding*.

93. ACLED, "The Sahel: Mid-Year Update."

94. Pflaum, "Pastoralist Violence in North and West Africa."

95. Forsberg, "Transnational Dimensions of Civil War: Clustering, Contagion, and Connectedness"; OECD/SWAC, "The Geography of Conflict in North and West Africa," 2020; OECD/SWAC, "Conflict Networks in North and West Africa."

96. Salehyan, "Transnational Rebels: Neighboring States as Sanctuary for Rebel Groups"; Walther and Miles, *African Border Disorders: Addressing Transnational Extremist Organizations*; Cilliers, "Violence in Africa: Trends, Drivers and Prospects to 2023."

97. Hansen and Bruce, *Horn, Sahel, and Rift: Fault-Lines of the African Jihad.*

98. Boukhars, "Rethinking Security across the Sahara and the Sahel"; Harmon, "Securitization Initiatives in the Sahara-Sahel Region in the Twenty-First Century"; Walther, "Wars and Conflicts in the Sahara-Sahel."

99. Aning and Edu-Afful, "African Agency in R2P: Interventions by African Union and ECOWAS in Mali, Côte d'Ivoire, and Libya."

100. Bah, *International Security and Peacebuilding.*

101. Aning and Edu-Afful, "African Agency in R2P: Interventions by African Union and ECOWAS in Mali, Côte d'Ivoire, and Libya."

102. Bere, "Armed Rebellion, Violent Extremism, and the Challenges of International Intervention in Mali"; Ndem Okon, "Mali: ECOWAS Responses to the Conflict in Mali (2012–2021)."

103. Avoulete, "Should ECOWAS Rethink Its Approach to Coups?"

104. Avoulete, "Should ECOWAS Rethink Its Approach to Coups?"

105. Ndem Okon, "Mali: ECOWAS Responses to the Conflict in Mali (2012–2021)."

106. Ndem Okon, "Mali: ECOWAS Responses to the Conflict in Mali (2012–2021)."

107. Villalón and Idrissa, *Democratic Struggle, Institutional Reform, and State Resilience in the African Sahel*; Villalón, *The Oxford Handbook of the African Sahel.*

108. Tankel, "US Counterterrorism in the Sahel: From Indirect to Direct Intervention."

109. Tankel, "US Counterterrorism in the Sahel: From Indirect to Direct Intervention."

110. Tankel, "US Counterterrorism in the Sahel: From Indirect to Direct Intervention."

111. Boeke and Schuurman, "Operation 'Serval': A Strategic Analysis of the French Intervention in Mali, 2013–2014."

112. BBC, "Why Are French Troops Leaving Mali, and What Will It Mean for the Region?"

113. Bere, "Armed Rebellion, Violent Extremism, and the Challenges of International Intervention in Mali."

114. Bere, "Armed Rebellion, Violent Extremism, and the Challenges of International Intervention in Mali."

References

ACLED. "Armed Conflict Location & Event Data Project," 2019.

———. "Political Violence Skyrockets in the Sahel According to the Latest ACLED Data." *Relief Web*, March 28, 2019. https://reliefweb.int/report/mali/political-violence-skyrockets-sahel-according-latest-acled-data.

———. "The Sahel: Mid-Year Update." *10 Conflicts to Worry about in 2022.* ACLED, 2022.

AMDH and FIDH. "In Central Mali, Civilian Populations Are Caught between Terrorism and Counterterrorism." Paris, 2018.

Andersson, Ruben. "Europe's Failed 'Fight' against Irregular Migration: Ethnographic Notes on a Counterproductive Industry." *Journal of Ethnic and Migration Studies*, 2016.

Aning, Kwesi, and Fiifi Edu-Afful. "African Agency in R2P: Interventions by African Union and ECOWAS in Mali, Côte d'Ivoire, and Libya." *International Studies Review* 18, no. 1 (2016): 120–33.

Appadurai, Arjun. *Fear of Small Numbers: An Essay on the Geography of Anger.* Durham, NC: Public Planet Books, 2006.

Associated Press. "France and EU to Withdraw Troops from Mali, Remain in Region." *Voice of America*, February 2022. https://www.voanews.com/a/france-and-eu-to-withdraw-troops-from-mali-remain-in-region-/6445606.html.

Avoulete, Komlan. "Should ECOWAS Rethink Its Approach to Coups?" *International Policy Digest*, January 2022. https://intpolicydigest.org/should-ecowas-rethink-its-approach-to-coups/.

Bah, Abu Bakaar. "The Contours of New Humanitarianism: War and Peacebuilding in Sierra Leone." *Africa Today* 60, no. 1 (2013): 3–26.

———. "Democracy and Civil War: Citizenship and Peacemaking in Côte d'Ivoire." *African Affairs* 109, no. 437 (2010): 597–615.

———. *International Security and Peacebuilding: Africa, the Middle East, and Europe.* Edited by Abu Bakaar Bah. Bloomington: Indiana University Press, 2017.

Baldaro, Edoardo. "A Dangerous Method: How Mali Lost Control of the North, and Learned to Stop Worrying." *Small Wars and Insurgencies* 29, no. 3 (2018): 579–603.

BBC. "Why Are French Troops Leaving Mali, and What Will It Mean for the Region?" *News*, April 26, 2022. https://www.bbc.com/news/world-60419799.

Benjaminsen, Tor A., and Boubacar Ba. "Fulani-Dogon Killings in Mali: Farmer-Herder Conflicts as Insurgency and Counterinsurgency." *African Security* 14, no. 1 (2021): 4–26.

———. "Why Do Pastoralists in Mali Join Jihadist Groups? A Political Ecological Explanation." *Journal of Peasant Studies* 46, no. 1 (2019): 1–20.

———. "Farmer-Herder Conflicts, Pastoral Marginalisation and Corruption: A Case Study from the Inland Niger Delta of Mali." *Geographical Journal*, 2009.

Bensimon, Cyril. "Mali: Jihadists Attack the Army's Seat of Power." *Le Monde Africa*, July 23, 2022. https://www.lemonde.fr/en/international/article/2022/07/23/in-mali-the-seat-of-power-attacked-by-jihadists_5991112_4.html.

Bere, Mathieu. "Armed Rebellion, Violent Extremism, and the Challenges of International Intervention in Mali." *African Conflict and Peacebuilding Review* 7, no. 2 (2017): 60–84.

Boeke, Sergei, and Bart Schuurman. "Operation 'Serval': A Strategic Analysis of the French Intervention in Mali, 2013–2014." *Journal of Strategic Studies*, 2015. https://doi.org/10.1080/01402390.2015.1045494.

Boukhars, Anouar. "Rethinking Security across the Sahara and the Sahel," no. 199 (April 2015).

Brachet, Julien. "Manufacturing Smugglers: From Irregular to Clandestine Mobility in the Sahara." *Annals of the American Academy of Political and Social Science* 676, no. 1 (2018): 16–35.

Cilliers, Jakkie. "Violence in Africa: Trends, Drivers and Prospects to 2023." Africa Report. Pretoria, 2018.

Curiel, R. P., O. Walther, and N. O'Clery. "Uncovering the Internal Structure of Boko Haram through Its Mobility Patterns." *Applied Network Science* 5, no. 28 (2020).

D'Orsi, Christiano. "An Outlook on the Conflict in Casamance with a Focus on the Legal Situation of the Mouvement Des Forces Democratiques ('Mouvement of Democratic Forces of Casamance') and Its Members." *Willamette Journal of International Law and Dispute Resolution* 23, no. 1 (2015): 1–60.

Diallo, Ousmane Aly. "Ethnic Clashes, Jihad, and Insecurity in Central Mali." *Peace Review* 29 (2017): 299–306.

Diao, Xinshen, Paul Dorosh, Josee Randriamamonjy, Jenny Smart, and James Thurlow. "Senegal: Impacts of the Ukraine and Global Crises on Poverty and Food Security." *Global Crisis: Country Series*. IFPRI, 2022.

Dowd, Caitriona. "Grievances, Governance and Islamist Violence in Sub-Saharan Africa." *Journal of Modern African Studies* 53, no. 4 (2015): 505–31. https://doi.org/10.1017/S0022278X15000737.

———. "Nigeria's Boko Haram." In *African Border Disorders: Addressing Transnational Extremist Organizations*, 1st ed., edited by Olivier J. Walther and William F. S. Miles, 21. New York: Routledge, 2017.

Eizenga, Dan. "Long Term Trends across Security and Development in the Sahel." West African Papers. Paris: OECD, 2019.

Elischer, Sebastian. "Populist Civil Society, the Wagner Group, and Post-Coup Politics in Mali." West African Papers. Paris: OECD, 2022.

EURACTIV.com with AFP and Reuters. "France, Allies Announce Mali Withdrawal, Plan Relocation." *EURACTIV*, February 2022.

Forsberg, Erika. "Transnational Dimensions of Civil War: Clustering, Contagion, and Connectedness." In *What Do We Know about Civil Wars?*, edited by David Mason and Sara McLaughlin Mitchell, 364. Lanham, MD: Rowan and Littlefield, 2016.

Frowd, Philippe M., and Adam J Sandor. "Militarism and Its Limits: Sociological Insights on Security Assemblages in the Sahel." *Security Dialogue* 49, no. 1–2 (2018): 13.

Giulianotti, Richard, and Roland Robertson. "The Globalization of Football: A Study in the Glocalization of the 'Serious Life.'" *British Journal of Sociology* 55, no. 4 (2004): 545–68.

———. "Glocalization, Globalization, and Migration: The Case of Scottish Football Supporters in North America." *International Sociology* 21, no. 2 (2006): 171–98.

Hansen, Stig Jarle, and Ronald Bruce. *Horn, Sahel, and Rift: Fault-Lines of the African Jihad. International Affairs.* London: Hurst & Company, 2019.

Harmon, Stephen. "Securitization Initiatives in the Sahara-Sahel Region in the Twenty-first Century." *African Security* 8, no. 4 (2015): 227–48. https://doi.org/10.1080/19392206.2015.1100503.

Haugegaard, Rikke. "Sharia as 'Desert Business': Understanding the Links between Criminal Networks and Jihadism in Northern Mali." *International Journal of Security and Development* 6, no. 1 (2017): 1–15.

HRW. "'How Much More Blood Must Be Spilled?' Atrocities against Civilians in Central Mali, 2019." Edited by Corinne Dufka. Human Rights Watch, 2020.

———. "'We Used to Be Brothers': Self-Defense Group Abuses in Central Mali." Edited by Corinne Dufka. Human Rights Watch, 2018.

Knoope, Peter, and Stephen Buchanan-Clarke. "Central African Republic: A Conflict Misunderstood." *Institute for Justice and Reconciliation.* Vol. 22. Occasional Paper. Cape Town: Institute for Justice and Reconciliation, 2017.

Lacher, Wolfram. "Libya's Fractious South and Regional Instability." *Security Assessment in North Africa*, 2014.

Lechner, John. "Is Africa Corps a Rebranded Wagner Group?" *Foreign Policy Magazine*, February 7, 2024. https://foreignpolicy.com/2024/02/07/africa-corps-wagner-group-russia-africa-burkina-faso.

Ndem Okon, Enoch. "Mali: ECOWAS Responses to the Conflict in Mali (2012–2021)." *Conflict Studies Quarterly*, no. 37 (2021): 18.

Nnoko-Mewanu, Juliana. "Farmer-Herder Conflicts on the Rise in Africa." *Inter Press Services (IPS) News Agency.* August 2018. https://www.hrw.org/news/2018/08/06/farmer-herder-conflicts-rise-africa.

OECD/SWAC. "Conflict Networks in North and West Africa." Edited by Marie Trémolières, Olivier J. Walther, and Steven M. Radil. West African Studies. Paris: OECD, 2021.

———. "The Geography of Conflict in North and West Africa." West African Studies. Paris: OECD, 2020.

———. "The Geography of Conflict in North and West Africa." Paris: OECD, 2020. https://doi.org/10.1787/862be517-en.

Parens, Raphael. "The Wagner Group's Playbook in Mali." *Foreign Policy Research Institute Eurasia Program*. Eurasia Program, 2022.

Pflaum, Matthew. "Pastoralist Violence in North and West Africa." West African Papers. Paris: OECD, 2021.

Raineri, Luca, and Francesco Strazzari. "State, Secession, and Jihad: The Micropolitical Economy of Conflict in Northern Mali." *African Security* 8, no. 4 (2015): 249–71. https://doi.org/10.1080/19392206.2015.1100501.

Raleigh, Clionadh, Héni Nsaibia, and Caitriona Dowd. "The Sahel Crisis since 2012." *African Affairs*, 2020.

Relief Web. "Internal Displacement in Mali since 2013." IDMC, 2022. https://reliefweb.int/map/mali/internal-displacement-mali-march-2013-1st-october-2013.

Risse, Thomas. *Governance without a State? Policies and Politics in Areas of Limited Statehood*. Edited by Thomas Risse. New York: Columbia University Press, 2011.

Robertson, Roland. "Globalisation or Glocalisation?" *Journal of International Communication* 1, no. 1 (1994): 33–52.

———. "Globality and Modernity." *Theory, Culture, and Society* 9 (1992): 153–61.

———. "Glocalization: Time-Space and Homogeneity-Heterogeneity." In *Global Modernities*. 1st ed., edited by Mike Featherstone, Scott Lash, and Roland Robertson, 24–44. London: Sage, 1995.

———, and Kathleen E. White. "What Is Globalization?" In *The Blackwell Companion to Globalization*, edited by George Ritzer, 54–66. Blackwell Publishing, 2007.

Roudometof, Victor. "Nationalism, Globalization and Glocalization." *Thesis Eleven* 122, no. 1 (2014): 18–33. https://doi.org/10.1177/0725513614535700.

———. "Theorizing Glocalization: Three Interpretations." *European Journal of Social Theory* 19, no. 3 (2016): 391–408.

Rupesinghe, Natasja, and Morten Boas. "Local Drivers of Violent Extremism in Central Mali." UNDP, 2019.

Salehyan, Idean. "Transnational Rebels: Neighboring States as Sanctuary for Rebel Groups." *World Politics* 59, no. 2 (2007): 217–42.

Sandor, Adam. *Insecurity, the Breakdown of Social Trust and Armed Actor Governance in Central and Northern Mali*, 2017.

Tankel, Stephen. "US Counterterrorism in the Sahel: From Indirect to Direct Intervention." *International Affairs* 96, no. 4 (2020): 875–93.

Tessières, Savannah de. *At the Crossroads of Sahelian Conflicts: Insecurity, Terrorism, and Arms Trafficking in Niger*, 2018. http://www.smallarmssurvey.org/fileadmin/docs/U-Reports/SAS-SANA-Report-Niger.pdf.

———. "Briefing Paper: Measuring Illicit Arms Flow (Niger)." Small Arms Survey. Geneva, 2017.

Therborn, Göran. "Dimensions of Globalization and the Dynamics of (In)Inequalities." In *The Ends of Globalization: Bringing Society Back In*, edited by Don

Kalb, Marco van der Land, Richard Staring, Bart van Steenbergen, and Nico Wilterdink, 416. Lanham, MD: Rowman & Littlefield, 2000.

———. "Globalizations: Dimensions, Historical Waves, Regional Effects, Normative Governance." *International Sociology* 15, no. 2 (2000): 151–79.

UNDP. "Radicalization, Violence, and (in)Security: What 800 Sahelians Have to Say." Edited by Reda Benkirane, 2016.

Villalón, L. A. *The Oxford Handbook of the African Sahel.* 1st ed. Edited by Leonardo A. Villalón. Oxford: Oxford University Press, 2021.

———, and Rahmane Idrissa, eds. *Democratic Struggle, Institutional Reform, and State Resilience in the African Sahel.* Lanham: Lexington Books, 2020.

Walther, Olivier. "Wars and Conflicts in the Sahara-Sahel." West African Papers No. 10. Paris: OECD/SWAC, 2017.

———, and William F. S. Miles, eds. *African Border Disorders: Addressing Transnational Extremist Organizations. Routledge Studies in African Politics and International Relations.* New York: Routledge, 2017.

Wiley, Stephen B. Crofts. "Rethinking Nationality in the Context of Globalization." *Communication Theory* 14, no. 1 (2004): 78–96.

Wing, Susanna. "Combatting Insecurity in Mali." *CHACR Global Analysis Programme Briefing.* Vol. 21. CHACR, 2020.

Zoubir, Yahia H. "The United States and Maghreb-Sahel Security." *International Affairs* 85, no. 5 (2009): 977–95.

6

Explaining Piracy

From State Failure to Glocalized Security

Keunsoo Jeong

When MV Faina was hijacked on September 25, 2008, by Somali piracy groups with more than 100 local pirates, international naval forces, including the US and Russian warships, were immediately dispatched. The Israeli-owned, Ukrainian-flagged vessel loaded with thirty-three Soviet-made T72 tanks and other munitions was officially headed to Mombasa, Kenya, but ultimately destined for South Sudan.[1] The implication of the incident resonated beyond East Africa by renewing worldwide attention on piracy. In Somalia, Al-Shabaab took a serious position by warning the pirate groups of the need to burn down the vessel. Regionally, Kenyan and Somali central and local governments, including the Himan and Heeb state of Tiiceey,[2] had to engage in the negotiation processes, though they had poor capacities for counterpiracy. Internationally, it led the United Nations (UN) to pass UN Resolution 1838 (October 7, 2008), which called for the active engagement of international naval forces, including NATO, in the fight against piracy. The incident starkly showed how a regional piracy incident became a glocalized security issue.

The piracy issue has perplexed security experts because it crosses fine boundaries of conventional international security. Contemporary piracy incidents involve multiple security areas. Piracy appears to be a global security issue because international commercial vessels are attacked. The targeted international vessels and crews also denote its global characteristics. However, it is a locally grown crime. Though the global factors open the opportunity for piracy, the local factors actually engender the occurrence of the crimes.[3] In other words, the Somali piracy incident indicated both global and local issues simultaneously. The incident patterns call for a glocalized security concept because present approaches have not been able to comprehend the deviant security issue. Yet most present piracy studies have remained in the conventional (inter)state-centered approach.

The concept of state failure has been a lynchpin in the primary causes of regional and global security threats. In the MV Faina hijacking incident, for an instance, there was no functioning central government to respond in Somalia. Interestingly, the September 11, 2001, terrorist attacks have been a momentous highlighter in finding connections between state failure and terrorism. Increasing piracy incident trends from 1996 have provided a possible link to state failure and terrorism because most piracy incidents, particularly hijacking and ransom gaining piracy, occurred in several troubled states, such as Somalia, Nigeria, and Indonesia. However, it is very rare to see actual empirical evidence between state failure and piracy. Thus, this study began with a research question of the real effectiveness of failed state and other state-centered concepts in explaining contemporary piracy while critically examining its drawbacks. This study examines whether failed state and other attributed factors are associated with piracy incidents. The study is based on an extensive dataset of 5,846 piracy incidents from 1996 to 2013. It analyzes the distribution of piracy incidents in major piracy-prone regions over the eighteen-year period using multiple statistical analyses. All the recorded maritime hijacking and relevant incidents are coded and compiled in a systematic data scheme.

Coggins already examined and concluded that the projected linkage between state failure and terrorism is overstated.[4] This study also identifies critical limitations in the failed state approaches as well as other macro factor-based approaches in explaining emerging piracy incidents. Based on binary logistic regression analyses, this study found very weak empirical grounds for the failed state approach. The results of the analyses also reveal the limits of the state-centered explanations. However, the results also give an interesting clue for alternative approaches based on glocalized security.[5] Therefore, this study argues that a glocalized security approach should be applied to contemporary piracy incidents to capture the real dynamics of the piracy incidents.

State Failure:
Global Piracy or Local Piracy?

Despite what might have been an optimistic forecast, anticipated changes due to globalization have not been accomplished.[6] Globalization has not meant the end of history, as one Hegelian scholar declared in an epic statement.[7] It has instead unleashed many unexpected issues such as terrorism, state failure, refugees, financial crises, and transnational crime—as if a Pandora's Box was mistakenly opened. The piracy-prone regions have mostly suffered from the uneven changes wrought by globalization in each different context of the regional security complex (see fig. 6.1).

As figure 6.1 shows, trends of world piracy incidents fluctuate along with the stability issues of the major piracy-prone regions, such as Southeast Asian, the Gulf of Aden, and the Gulf of Guinea. The overall frequency and distribution patterns of maritime piracy are segmented with periodic fluctuations across major piracy-prone regions. Notably, 70.8 percent of the total number of incidents occurred in the three main piracy hot zones. Furthermore, 95 percent of hijacking incidents out of a total of 559 occurred in those regions. This study also found that Somalia and the Gulf of Aden have witnessed 60.8 percent (340) of the total number of worldwide hijackings and 79.1 percent (185) of all ransom-seeking piracy incidents, while earning at least $380 million during that period. The two regions led the world piracy incident trends interchangeably. Until 2004,

Figure 6.1. World Piracy Incidents, 1996–2013. *Source*: Created by the author.

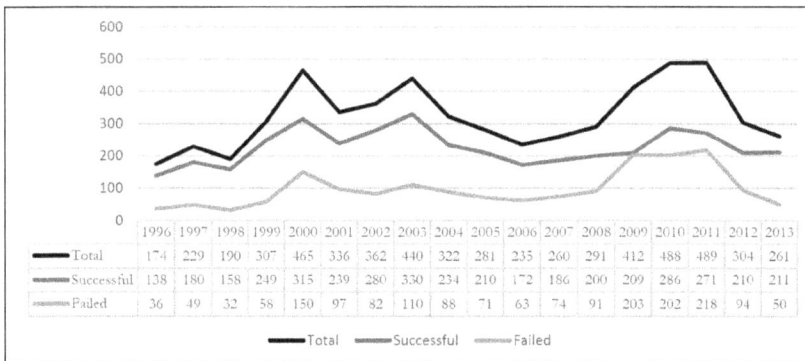

	1996	1997	1998	1999	2000	2001	2002	2003	2004	2005	2006	2007	2008	2009	2010	2011	2012	2013
Total	174	229	190	307	465	336	362	440	322	281	235	260	291	412	488	489	304	261
Successful	138	180	158	249	315	239	280	330	234	210	172	186	200	209	286	271	210	211
Failed	36	49	32	58	150	97	82	110	88	71	63	74	91	203	202	218	94	50

the trend was led by incidents in Southeast Asia. After 2005, the trend was led by incidents in East Africa.

In fact, piracy studies did not regard the maritime crime as a serious international issue (let alone global) until the 9/11 terrorist attacks in 2001. Moreover, two maritime terror incidents after the 9/11 terrorist attacks raised warnings about a possible conflation between piracy and terrorism. The 9/11 attacks shifted the scope of piracy studies to include the possible danger of maritime terrorism disrupting global commerce. This dangerous possibility was widely discussed and examined.[8] In this connection, the concept of the failed state gained significant traction with regard to the fundamental cause of piracy in regions such as in Southeast Asia, South Asia, the Gulf of Aden, and the Gulf of Guinea.

Yet state failure had not been regarded as a main cause of piracy before Somali piracy incidents gained international attention. As Somalia has been depicted as a quintessential case of the failed state, several issues in regard to the failed state concept have been critically discussed and examined.[9] The first is whether state fragility or state failure is connected to the increasing number of piracy incidents. Many piracy experts have shared the opinion that state failure is inherently connected to increasing piracy incidents.[10] The second issue is whether the failed state concept can be a crucial lever for understanding different types of piracy. Hastings, for example, argues that highly advanced piracy incidents hardly occurred in failed state conditions.[11] Though political motivation should not be overlooked,[12] the conflation possibility between piracy and terrorism is, realistically, hardly likely to occur for several reasons, including the difference in purposes, logistical difficulties, and indigenous resistance.[13] The third issue is whether the state-centered approaches can render a valid policy analysis.

Other studies of modern piracy have examined the issues in various aspects. As the linear relationship between political crisis and piracy was questioned, other macro factors, such as crime, economy, and business opportunity, have been applied.[14] Though those studies suggest possible causal links with piracy, the association could be at best indirect.[15] However, most studies did not take account of the effects of the long-term instability of the state.[16] For example, Somali piracy did not emerge as an international security threat until 2008, seventeen years after the Said Barre regime collapsed.

However, a critical question that has not yet been fully answered is whether state failure directly affects the emergence of piracy. This study examines empirical evidence between the state-centered factors and piracy incidents, particularly in the troubled states. Thus, the study is an empirical attempt to test whether state failure is a linearly direct factor on piracy. This study also examines the real validity of those state-centered macro factors, including the failed state factor.[17] Finally, it tackles the question of whether the failed state factor is a time-constrained effect or a timeless factor. Overall, the study suggests a glocalized security frame as an alternative to the state-centered approaches to understanding piracy.

The actual situation around the MV Faina incident demonstrates that homogenously measured factors tend to produce a confirmation illusion without explaining how the sophisticated hijacking incident could emerge in the failed state. The MV Faina incident was just one incident of many successful ransom gaining piracies between 2008 and 2010, a high time of Somali piracy. The total piracy incidents (621) in the Horn of African regions accounted for more than half of the world piracy incidents (1,191) during the time period. There were pirate stock markets in Haradheere and financial participation of the overseas Somali diaspora.[18] According to the UN Monitoring Group (2012), the groups were largely divided into two big umbrella groups: Puntland and Hobyo-Haradheere syndicates. The syndicates spawned many new pirate leaders, such as Yare, Yulux, Garfanje, and son of Afweyne, a representative Somali pirate kingpin.[19] The estimated ransom revenue was more than $166 million, which was enough to change local governance. Thus, Somali pirates enjoyed a golden age.

At the central state, the Transitional Federal Government in Somalia was formed as a coalition government while a violent resurgent group Al-Shabaab, an Islamist militia group loyal to the global terrorist group Al-Qaeda, rose to threaten the fragile government. Meanwhile, defunct governance in Puntland created an almost perfect soil for ransom piracy activity in 2008. The Puntland state was temporarily suspended because of the budget crisis caused by the resource drain of the civil war. Somali law enforcement employees could not receive their salary. With hyperinflation between 2006 and 2008, the living conditions became worse. Most of all, there were no working counter-piracy movements, either inside or outside Somalia, until 2009. The pirates did not have to worry about being arrested. Local coastal towns, such as Eyl, Hobyo, and Haradheere, became a piracy haven based on a symbiosis with the local community and authorities. The piracy activities also provided the important political and economic functions that conventional governance was supposed to perform.

Such local dynamics have not been well accounted for in the globalized security prism because the local responses were expected to be converged under the homogeneous globalization security frame. In other words, the globalized view "McDonaldized" the local security dynamics, to borrow a term from George Ritzer's McDonaldization.[20] The complicated dynamics as a mirrored McDonaldization are explained later in the chapter after analyses of statistical test results.

However, the globally standardized view does not explain the heterogenous incident patterns in Somali piracy and the relevant local dynamics. The telos of the globalized security frame ignores the embedded crime dynamics in the Somali local areas. The simultaneous processes in both globalization as a homogenous force and localization as a heterogenous response were invisible in the dominant security frame.[21] Therefore, this study seeks to reveal the limits of present state-centered approaches to the local piracy incidents, as the study results do not suggest any coherent connections between the globalized security factors and local piracy incidents. The results of this study provide an empirical bedrock for a glocalized security approach, which has not yet been fully developed and applied in mainstream international security studies.

Research Design and Variable Specification

This study poses research questions and research hypotheses relating to the macro factors, including state failure. The analyses ran binary logistic models with multiple time sets to determine whether certain time periods drove the effects of the macro factors, crucially failed state factors. If there is a coherent association between failed state and piracy incidents, it means that failed state is a valid explanatory factor and even could be a meaningful predictor for advancement of piracy incidents. If not, the state failure approach to local security issues needs to be critically reconsidered. Furthermore, if the state-centered factors, such as poverty and institutional strengths, turn out to be effective explanatory factors, then state-centered explanation and policy making are still useful methods.

Two binary logistic regression models are tested over multiple time sets. The models of this research examine the designated variables with 5,846 piracy incident cases from 1996 to 2013. Thus, the sample size is 5,846. Primary incident data were collected from the IMB Annual Piracy Report from 1996 to 2013. Other data sources, including global and local media sources, were also used for complementing missing incident data from the IMB reports, such as Federation of American Scientists (FAS) Anti-Shipping Activity Messages, BBC, AP, CNN, Al-Jazeera, Somalia Report, Garowe

Online, and Ecoterra International's piracy reports (a local NGO in Kenya). All the data were compiled and recorded for the statistical analyses.

The primary research question is: what factors are contributing to the success or failure of the different piracy incident types (successful piracy incident, hijacking piracy, and ransom gaining piracy)? Three binary categorical-dependent variables are tested in the logistic regression analysis: a) successful incident (1) versus failed incident (0); b) successful hijacking piracy incident (1) versus all other piracy incidents (0); and c) successful ransom gaining piracy incidents (1) versus all other piracy incidents (0).

The first model tests whether or not a failed state is a significantly coherent factor impacting the odds ratio of the three piracy incident types. Among the major macro factors, state failure has been regarded as a primary cause of piracy. Many studies have suggested that failed states provide a better opportunity for large-scale criminal activities such as terrorism and piracy.[22] These studies of piracy incidents have used failed state indexes from different sources such as the World Bank, Fund for Peace, and Ibrahim Index.[23] However, it is questionable whether these composite indexes can truly reflect the dynamic evolution of piracy. The failed state concept could be a glossy term that disregards a concrete analysis of actual security threat elements such as poor law enforcement, extreme poverty, and fragmentation.[24]

THE FIRST MODEL AND VARIABLE SPECIFICATION

The primary hypothesis is that successful piracy incidents, including hijacking and ransom piracy, are more likely to occur in failed states. The dependent variables are the types of piracy incident mentioned above. The model consists of the variables below.[25]

First is the main test variable, which is "failed state." The *World Governance Indicator* (WGI) from the World Bank was used as a primary proxy variable to represent the level of state failure because it covered the entire eighteen-year research period. The *Failed State Index* (FSI) from Fund for Peace was also used as a complementary variable because it only covers the nine-year period between 2005 and 2013. As Menkhaus argues, many piracy experts have applied the concept of failed states to their analyses of the causes of piracy.[26] State failure has been regarded as a rudimentary cause of piracy and its increase over time.[27] The indexes have been popularized through the media.[28] They are composite indices based on the combined calculation of various sub-indices. One criticism is that the indices do not facilitate a real understanding of local or regional state-level problems because they arbitrarily create a chaotic image.[29] This study tested the actual usefulness of the controversial term in understanding the real relationship between state failure and piracy.

Second are the control variables, notably location, success, and dummy variables. Location effect is a variable that is crucial in understanding the characteristics of an incident. Indonesia has a mix of neighboring states in terms of state strength. Singapore is a strong state, while Malaysia is a mid-level state. Every state adjacent to Somalia and Nigeria is categorized as a weak or even failed state. Experience of success in piracy is another important variable in determining whether piracy organizations have evolved over time. If previous success had a positive impact on piracy incidents, then piracy organizations would have attempted to target higher-value targets more often.[30] This means that piracy would be likely to occur more often.

The Second Model and Variable Specification

The failed state indexes are composite measurement with multiple sub-components in various aspects, such as political, institutional, economic, and social factors. WGI consists of six sub-indicators and FSI consists of twelve sub-indicators. This test used several key factors that indicate similar measures to the sub-components of the failed state indexes.

The second model consists of macro factor variables on institutional strength, fragmentation, unemployment, extreme poverty, police force size, and livestock and cereal yields. This model used the same dummy and control variables that the first model used. Here, the second model and its factors are a standard measurement used to gauge state stability. If the model and factors can deliver significant causal associations with piracy incidents, then the state-centered model and variables are useful in explaining contemporary piracy incidents while reflecting local status in the piracy-prone states. However, if not, the validity of the global security study frame is questionable.

In terms of the institutional strength variable, it should be noted that institutions are essential vehicles for modern state governance.[31] Many piracy experts attribute a significant increase in piracy to institutional weakness.[32] Somalia and Nigeria have suffered from low institutional strengths, which could be one of the causal factors for piracy incidents. Indonesia also had institutional problems until 2005, when its piracy incident number led the world piracy incident trends.

Fragmentation is another variable. Most postcolonial states have had integration issues regarding diverse ethnic groups within a state's boundaries. Most piracy hot zones are in highly fragmented societies. Even institutional strength does not always help social integration because of inherent differences between a modern state and ethnic boundaries.[33] Somali piracy groups take advantage of their clan networks, as do rebel groups in Nigeria and Indonesia. Thus, high fragmentation level might be a useful indicator for increasing piracy incidents.

Another variable is unemployment. Most weak and failed states have serious troubles due to a low level of economic activity. In determining economic effects on the micro level, either GDP per capita or the unemployment rate is used. Somalia is not the poorest country in terms of GDP per capita. Since 1995, it has done better than some of its neighboring countries in its overall level of wealth.[34] This ironic fact suggests that the unemployment rate is a better predictor of piracy. For example, piracy incidents have tended to increase after local law enforcement failed to pay salaries to officers in Somalia.[35]

Extreme poverty is the other variable. Poverty in general is not an accurate indicator of participation in criminal activity. The concrete level of poverty is a more helpful indicator. People often break moral codes in states suffering extreme poverty due to natural disaster, economic turmoil, or civil war. As indicated by captured pirates, extreme poverty provides physiological and psychological motivations to potential pirates.[36] It is also related to higher risk taking that could result in ransom piracy, which requires more daring behavior than simple robbery.

Police officers to population ratios is used as another variable. It is a very concrete indicator for examining whether law enforcement can handle criminal threats in a state. Indonesia suffered increased piracy incidents related to low levels of law enforcement until 2005.[37] With help from its neighboring states and outside forces, however, Indonesia began to control maritime crimes. Nigeria also has chronically low levels of law enforcement. Somalia is the worst case because even the local state of Puntland could not offer salaries to marine police officers for a time.[38]

Livestock and cereal are important daily staples for living in piracy-prone regions. They are also crucial bases of the regional economy. As such, changing cereal yield might be related to piracy incidents if hunger and desperate living conditions drive local people to participate in maritime crime.

Test Results

Three dependent variables are examined: successful piracy incidents, hijacking piracy, and ransom gaining piracy. Successful piracy incidents are a crime perpetrated by criminals against a vessel and crew on the sea. Total incident indicates all the recorded incidents, including those attempted and those that failed. Hijacking piracy is an incident in which pirates hijack and control a vessel and crew for a certain amount of time for criminal purposes. Ransom gaining piracy covers piracy incidents in which pirates acquired a ransom after hijacking a vessel and kidnapping its crew.

THE FIRST MODEL: FAILED STATE

The first model explores whether the failed state index is a coherently significant factor across different types of piracy incidents. The results suggest that improvement in state governance can be a significant predictor of an increase in hijacking piracy incidents. Concrete interpretations are below. The overall results provide very limited clues on the relationships between the designated independent variables and piracy incidents.

1) WGI

WGI as a failed state variable has significant odds on hijacking piracy incidents (see table 6.1). Notably, 1.428 odds means that each one-degree increase in WGI will increase the odds of hijacking piracy incidents 1.428 times after controlling for the other variables. However, it is a puzzle because a majority of hijacking incidents occurred in the three piracy-prone countries with very low governance indexes. In fact, hijacking piracy incidents decreased after failed state indexes worsened in Somalia (from 2011) and Indonesia (from 2004). These contradictory results initially pose a critical question about whether WGI as a failed state proxy variable can be a valid predictor for piracy incidents. Further, it also raises a fundamental question as to whether or not there is a universal yardstick for measuring globalized security issues.

2) FSI

This study also tested the FSI from the Fund for Peace. However, the direction is opposite compared with the WGI with a much smaller magnitude (see table 6.1). The direction is opposite from successful hijack incidents but a very small magnitude at 1.005 odds. The results add puzzling points. Considering the high time of Somali piracy between 2008 and 2010, the

Table 6.1a–b. Results of Failed State Models (Odds Ratio)

Table 6.1a. Model A WGI 1996–2013

	Outcome	Hijack	Ransom
WGI/FSI	1.008	1.428***	0.731
Success Rate	10.853***	0.584*	0.389*
Border Country	1.123***	0.945	0.96
Somalia	0.407***	15.058***	6.903***
Indonesia	0.774***	1.421**	1.587
Nigeria	0.758	3.084***	2.806**
_cons	0.417***	0.105***	0.023***

Table 6.1b. Model A FSI 2005–2013

	Outcome	Hijack	Ransom
WGI/FSI	1.005	0.990***	0.990
Success Rate	14.871***	0.667	0.043***
Border Country	1.148***	1.033	1.330**
Somalia	0.324***	13.702***	32.267***
Indonesia	0.928	1.154**	6.040***
Nigeria	0.499***	3.487***	11.309***
_cons	0.237***	0.124***	0.023***

(*indicates significance levels with following criteria: *< 0.1, **< 0.05, ***< 0.01.)
Source: Created by the author.

result provides no empirical ground of understanding the association between failed state index as a measuring variable of failed state and piracy incidents.

3) Controlling Variables

Success rate shows only high positive odds with successful piracy incidents (see table 6.1). It has negative odds with hijacking and ransom gaining piracy incidents. A one-unit increase in success rate will increase successful piracy incidents 10.853 times. However, the increase in success rate will also decrease the odds (41.6 percent) of hijacking piracy incidents and the odds (61.1 percent) of ransom gaining incidents. It means that the successful experience may facilitate advanced piracy incident types, as well as hijacking and ransom gaining piracy, though the latter two at lower success rates. The number of the border country, as a variable for location effect, in a state where piracy incidents occurred has a similar direction at the much lower magnitude. Among country dummy variables, only Somalia has significant odds ratios across piracy incident types. It appears that Somalia has higher positive odds with hijacking and ransom piracy incidents than other countries while having negative odds with successful piracy incidents. Significant associations in those piracy prone areas rather imply that piracy incidents and their unique evolving patterns might not be directly related to the failed state factor, but rather to regional contexts and conflict dynamics.

THE SECOND MODEL: MACRO FACTORS

The second model examines which macro factors are consistently associated with piracy incidents by type and at different time sets (see table 6.2).

Table 6.2. Results of the Second Model (18-Year Period)

1996–2013	Outcome	Hijack	Ransom
Institution	0.999	0.982	0.98
Unemployment	0.961**	0.921***	1.028
Poverty	0.992***	0.988***	0.984***
Fragmentation	0.85	1.266	2.866
Police Ratio	0.998***	1.001*	0.997***
Livestock	1.004*	1	0.97***
Cereal	1***	1	1
Success Rate	3.191***	0.306***	0.389*
Border Country	1.053*	0.952	0.819*
Somalia	0.365***	8.518***	19.603***
Indonesia	0.725*	2.27**	2.071
Nigeria	1.304	3.864***	7.533***
_cons	1.914	0.57	2.427

(* indicates significance levels with following criteria: *< 0.1, **< 0.05, ***< 0.01.)

Source: Created by the author.

1) Institutional Strength

Institutional strength does not have significant odds with piracy incidents. However, two nine-year period results in table 6.3 show significant odds with successful piracy incidents in both periods and hijacking piracy incidents in the latter period between 2005 and 2013. Regardless, the magnitude is very low. The results of the 2005-2013 period imply that increased institutional strength positively affects successful piracy incidents while negatively influence hijacking incidents.

2) Unemployment

Unemployment has negative odds ratios with successful piracy incidents (0.961) and hijacking piracy incidents (0.921). In contrast, the odds ratio with ransom gaining piracy indicates that increasing unemployment in one unit will increase by 1.028 odds of ransom gaining piracy incidents. Nevertheless, it is not statistically significant. Unemployment also does not show coherently significant odds with piracy incidents in the two periods, as shown in table 6.3. Even significant odds (hijacking between 1996-2004) and successful incidents (between 2005-2013) show very low negative odd ratios. They imply that increasing unemployment negatively affects piracy incidents.

3) Poverty

Poverty has significant odds ratios with piracy incidents in negative directions. However, it is also at a very small magnitude. An increase in one unit of extreme poverty will result in decreases of successful piracy incidents (0.008 odds), hijacking piracy incidents (0.012 odds), and ransom gaining piracy incidents (0.016 odds). Thus, increased extreme poverty negatively affects piracy incidents.

4) Fragmentation

Fragmentation has no significant odds except the latter period (2005-2013) with hijack and ransom piracy. However, it is difficult to use the odds ratios to interpret actual associations. The higher fragmented state has more than ten times odds (10.233***) than lower fragmented state whereas the direction is the opposite with very small negative odds (0.002**). Moreover, standard errors are too large to correctly interpret in the latter period hijacking (11.846).

5) Police Ratio

Police ratio has significant odds with piracy incidents. However, the degree is very small. For example, increasing one unit of police ratio results in decreasing piracy incidents at odds of 0.002 on successful piracy incidents. In contrast, the direction is opposite with hijacking piracy incidents at 0.001 odds. It is very difficult to interpret whether increasing police ratio decreases or increases piracy because of the contrasting odd ratios.

6) Livestock and Cereal

Though livestock and cereal have a few significant odds as shown in the results table, the magnitudes imply very small impacts or none (cereal). Interestingly, the latter period (2005~2013) shows that increasing livestock negatively affects ransom piracy.

7) Control Variables

Control variables show similar results with those of the failed state models. However, the magnitudes of the odds ratios are generally lower than those in the first models. For example, the success rate has lower odds ratios with successful piracy incidents and hijacking piracy incidents in the second model than those in the first models. Country dummy variables also show the same significant directions. The Somalia dummy variable shows a stronger odds ratio in the latter period of ransom piracy than one in the former period, whereas there is a relatively smaller odds ratio in the latter hijacking piracy than in the former period. The results indicate that the latter period has a strong association with Somali ransom gaining piracy. Two other country dummies (Indonesia and Nigeria) do not show a coherent base for clear direction interpretation in the results tables.

DIFFERENT TIME SETS

The research design is also to find meaningful clues for understanding the changing trends of piracy incidents over the eighteen-year period. The analyses also seek to identify whether or not a coherent direction exists in piracy incidents trends over time or whether there is a leading period that influences overall significant odds ratios across the time periods. The results of table 6.3 show that Somalia has a significantly higher odds ratio only for ransom gaining piracy in the latter period. But successful piracy

Table 6.3a–b. Results of the Second Model in Two Nine-Year Periods

Table 6.3a. 2nd Model 1996–2004

	Outcome	Hijack	Ransom
Institution	0.196***	1.073	0.961
Unemployment	0.978	0.894***	0.944
Poverty	0.998	0.981**	0.986
Fragmentation	1.103	0.241	0.615
Police Ratio	0.997***	1.002*	0.999
Livestock	1.000	1.025**	1.027
Cereal	1.000	1.000	1.000
Success Rate	2.528***	1.320	1.921
Border Country	0.993	0.993	0.799
Somalia	0.364***	16.353***	54.562***
Indonesia	0.613*	3.095**	2.555
Nigeria	2.678***	5.146***	11.024
_cons	9.639***	0.004***	0.008

Table 6.3b. 2nd Model 2005–2013

	Outcome	Hijack	Ransom
Institution	1.081***	0.896***	0.904
Unemployment	0.918***	0.930	1.168
Poverty	0.991**	0.986**	0.976**
Fragmentation	0.693	10.233**	0.002**
Police Ratio	0.998**	1.000	0.991
Livestock	1.001	0.993	0.937***
Cereal	1.000***	1.000***	1.000
Success Rate	3.063***	0.198***	0.283
Border Country	1.148**	0.910	0.791
Somalia	0.221***	12.145***	60.668**
Indonesia	0.871	2.015	2.416
Nigeria	0.892	3.928***	2.598
_cons	0.784	4.811	3.34e+07

(* indicates significance levels with following criteria: *< 0.1, **< 0.05, ***< 0.01.)

Source: Created by the author.

and hijacking piracy in Somalia show significantly lower odds ratios in the same period. In Nigeria, only hijacking piracy shows a significantly higher odds ratio in the former period between 1996 and 2004. Indonesia also does not show coherent significant ratios in all the piracy incidents types, though odds ratios for hijacking and ransom gaining piracy show a little higher in the former period.

Table 6.4 also shows that Somalia has a higher odds ratio for hijacking piracy in the latter period using the first failed state model (WGI as a failed state proxy variable). The results might imply that the effects of a failed state are larger in the latter period, especially for successful hijacking piracy incidents. It is also confirmed that the odds radio of a failed state is higher with hijacking piracy in the latter period than in the former period.

Table 6.4a–b. Comparing Failed State Model Between Different Time Sets

Table 6.4a. 1996–2004 Model A (WGI)

	Outcome	Hijack	Ransom
WGI	1.014	1.543**	0.962
Success Rate	5.073***	0.976	1.354
Border Country	1.071***	0.908*	0.853
Somalia	0.276***	9.540***	15.392***
Indonesia	0.670***	1.784**	1.396
Nigeria	1.095	2.461**	3.072**
_cons	0.864	0.080***	0.021***

Table 6.4b. 2005–2013 Model A (WGI)

	Outcome	Hijack	Ransom
WGI	0.913	1.664***	0.368*
Success Rate	18.537***	0.451**	0.044***
Border Country	1.214***	0.997	1.235
Somalia	0.406***	20.182***	2.775***
Indonesia	1.006	1.112	4.531***
Nigeria	0.559***	3.894***	4.084**
_cons	0.219***	0.112***	0.011***

(*indicates significance levels with following criteria: *< 0.1, **< 0.05, ***< 0.01.)

Source: Created by the author.

As figure 6.2 below shows, the frequency trends of hijacking piracy in the world for the eighteen-year period also support the projection that hijacking piracy rapidly increased in the latter period from 2005 to 2011. In the latter period, the total number of hijacking piracy incidents is 459. Most of the hijacking piracy was committed by Somali pirates (329 [71.68 percent]). Moreover, the world ransom gaining piracy (192) was mostly committed by Somali pirates (168 [87.5 percent]) during the same period. However, the test results show that the failed state has an opposite impact size on ransom piracy (0.368*), which indicates that the higher failed state index means lower probability of ransom piracy while the higher failed index is associated with higher hijacking probability (1.664***).

INTERPRETATION OF STATISTICAL TEST RESULTS

This study found no coherently significant factors on piracy incidents across different types and time sets. Such incoherent test results do provide few empirical grounds for understanding contemporary piracy. The test results show that none of the independent or control variables have a consistent association with piracy incidents. The odds ratios indicate that none of the failed state indicators, WGI and FSI, have any practically significant effects. Thus, the confusing results rather imply that the global standard measure cannot capture regional conflict dynamics because local variations have occurred in a refraction process of the global influence.[39] Then the results ironically imply that piracy matters might become a glocalized security issue.

Figure 6.2. World Hijacking Piracy Incidents, 1996–2013. *Source*: Created by the author.

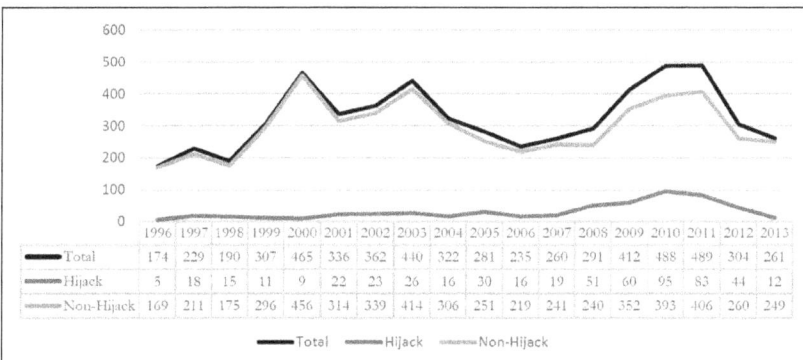

	1996	1997	1998	1999	2000	2001	2002	2003	2004	2005	2006	2007	2008	2009	2010	2011	2012	2013
Total	174	229	190	307	465	336	362	440	322	281	235	260	291	412	488	489	304	261
Hijack	5	18	15	11	9	22	23	26	16	30	16	19	51	60	95	83	44	12
Non-Hijack	169	211	175	296	456	314	339	414	306	251	219	241	240	352	393	406	260	249

The results reveal very limited clues regarding relations among several causal factors and piracy incidents across different time periods. First, the results imply that there are few meaningful relations between failed state and piracy incidents. Most of all, odd ratios are too small to interpret a meaningful effect. Thus, it is hard to determine whether failed states affect piracy incidents in a causally coherent direction. Although the status of a failed state has a significant relation to hijacking piracy, it is probably affected by the effects of incidents in the latter period (2005–2013). As the above frequency trends suggest in figure 6.2, the failed state effects are rather rendered mostly by Somali piracy than general piracy, specifically during the latter period when Somali piracy led the world hijacking and ransom piracy incidents. Then the results hardly support a general attribution that failed states or conditions of failed states affect the emergence of piracy, especially the advanced piracy incidents. The results rather imply that local piracy incidents in the piracy prone regions became a glocalized security matter, particularly from 2005.

The second model provides only partial clues about the relationship between macro sociopolitico-economic factors and piracy incidents in relative terms. First, institutional strength appears to be in reverse relation to piracy incidents, but the odds ratio is not valid with hijacking and ransom piracy. The odds ratios are also very small, which means institutional strength does not provide a meaningful association with piracy incidents. Second, economic factors such as unemployment and poverty are reversely associated with piracy incidents. It means that improving economic conditions increases the probability of piracy incidents. This is probably because participation in piracy activity could be expected to obtain greater gains in very poor institutional environments when economic situations are slightly improved in pastoral and agricultural states such as Somalia and Nigeria. The results could also be supported by the rational choice theory of economics, which is used to explain the motivations of pirate activities in some studies.[40] Nevertheless, the odds ratios at significant levels are not consistently high enough to be decisive factors.

Though effects of a few variables, such as success rate and Somalia dummy, on piracy incidents are significant, it is because the large sample size pushes the standard errors down to the point that odds ratios have significant effects, which is a simple artifact of measurement. However, those measures have no practical significance because of a validity problem. Thomas's study of WGI shows that a composite index's lack of construct validity always tends to produce practically insignificant results.[41] Thomas criticized the problem of construct validity with the WGI because of wrong data and a lack of empirical evidence.[42] The confusing results could be caused by the construct validity problems. Therefore, indexes on state failure, such as WGI and FSI, cannot be a meaningful predictor of piracy incidents in realistic aspects. The small variations in the piracy-prone regions, especially East and West African states, also may not be irrelevant to measurement reliability problems.

Limits of the State-Centered Approach to Glocalized Piracy

Somalia has been labeled as a prime example of state failure.[43] However, the label strongly implies that the disease should be cured or fixed in pathological and normative terms.[44] The stereotype of Somalia has also been applied to most African states, portraying them as deviant others of Western societies.[45] The scientifically packaged terms of the state failure, such as a failed state index and world governance indicator, have also contributed to the reification of the state reality as a perverted one.[46]

However, this study suggests that there are no universally applicable factor sets for piracy incidents across time, regions, and states. The highly skewed and uneven distributions of piracy incidents raise a question of the general observation's usefulness in understanding the regional maritime crime. Most of all the unevenly concentrated distributions of hijacking piracy incidents during the latter period (2005-2013) indicate that the failed state and its conditions have time-space conditional effects as long as majority incidents were committed by Somali pirates during the particular time period. It is a contextual periodic effect that might be securitized through the lens of the failed state concepts.[47]

On its surface, the piracy incident, such as MV Faina, is a simple casualty seemingly done by a group of sea thugs. It can simply be politically expedient to look the other way and ignore the root causes of the locally grown piracy. On the outlook of the incident, understanding the piracy incident as a simple byproduct of the failed state is a streamlined process of the security McDonaldization for securitizing agents, such as Western security agents and media. Then it is somewhat natural that the judgmental understanding of the troubled states has been construed on the vantage points of the securitizing participants who have handled the conflict issues with the wheel of one-way globalization or the McDonaldization security framing. But it underlies complex dynamics of the regional and local conflicts.

As Jeong demonstrates, the complex evolutionary process of the Somali piracy along with the prolonged civil wars, governance crises, and the architecture and criminal enterprise of the Somali piracy had successfully established a symbiosis with local governance and community through embeddedness of crime network. This went on until 2013 when the Somali piracy stopped gaining ransom revenue.[48] The main development of the Somali piracy activity was initiated by Hasan Abdi Afweyne, who hailed from the Habar-Gidir Saleeban clan in central Somalia Mudug region. He founded the "Somali Marine" based on clan associations between the sub-clans of Majerteen and Habar-Gidir. The maritime piracy group employed a mixed organization and management structure, somewhere between a military hierarchy and a business model.[49] Afweyne set the principle of the maritime piracy enterprise: keeping cost low while seeking maximum profit.

The criminal startup enjoyed a high time between 2008 and 2010. The total piracy incidents (621) in the Horn of African regions accounted for more than half of the world piracy incidents (1,191) during the period. A total of 112 ransom-gaining incidents and 188 hijack incidents occurred. The estimated ransom revenue was more than $173 million, which was enough to change local governance. Thus, Somali pirates enjoyed a golden age.

Interestingly, the Somali piracy industry offered government functions, such as coastal protection, the creation of service jobs, and provision of social welfare by sharing their ransom cuts with the local community. Therefore, Somali piracy became an entrenched part of local community affairs and governance by creating a powerful symbiosis, ironically through a capitalistic market system. From 2009, the fundraising channels became more diversified through the piracy stock market in Haradheere.[50] Roughly, seventy-two piracy companies were listed, and it was expected that local communities would benefit by promoting participation in investment channels.[51] The hijacking and ransoming of the tuna fishing vessel (FV) Alakrana provides a stark demonstration of the Afweyne's piracy business operation principle during the golden time of Somali piracy. The criminal operation was funded through the Somali piracy stock market. Alakrana was hijacked on October 2, 2009, at about 200 kilometers from the Somali coast by joint piracy syndication between Hobyo-Haradheere and the Puntland piracy syndicate. Somali pirates earned $3.5 million after forty-seven days of negotiation. A wedding party funded by the ransom revenue was held in Haradheere. Afweyne and Tiiceey, the governor of Himan and Heeb state, facilitated the operation.[52]

The overall operational architecture consists of three hierarchical layers. Top layer leader groups are local political and social leaders, investors, and pirate leaders, which is a critical form of network given the virtual absence of the Somali state. As a pirate leader, Afweyne had vast networks of local and even central state sponsors to safeguard the whole complex ransom acquiring operation. The leaders led a central committee to facilitate the ransom negotiation process. According to Bahadur's interview with pirate leader Boyah, the local elders and sponsors also participate in the committee meetings.[53] There is no orthodoxy of leadership because participants are concerned only with their own interests, based on their status, while pretending they are not participants in piracy crime.

In the second layer, various service groups, such as negotiators, loan providers, accountants, cooks and even medical aids, provide social and financial functions. The negotiations and hostage management are supported by multiple expert service groups such as negotiator (*dilals* in Somali) and holder groups (*illalo* in Somali). Most hostages are taken care of by the social service group under the custody of the leader group, which diligently keeps track of the cost of caring for hostages so that they get a proper ransom share. For them, a hostage is a valuable asset to ensure the ransom jackpot. However, in the worst case, the hostage could have become a tragic victim. For example, a hostage of MV Orna, hijacked on December 20, 2010, was shot to death as a warning sign to the shippers.[54]

In the bottom layer, pirate foot soldiers—a hunting team—bear the risk of exposure to international naval forces. Their preferred targets are big commercial vessels with a low freeboard moving at slow speed and with a large amount of cargo. A unit of the sea hijacking operations team is usually out for about one week, loaded with about ten days of supplies.[55] If the team is lucky enough to find prey within one week, the pirates do not have to worry about losing their way back home. Sea operations are quite dangerous. Often the supply is not enough to bring them back to their home base—say, from the Internationally Recommended Transit Corridor, where international commercial vessels often become prey for the sea hunter.

The targets of Somali piracy might have similar class structures. The shipping company, investor of the company, and counter-piracy commanders are in the leader class. The expert negotiator company, insurance company, law firm, and delivery agents work as middlemen. Those service companies ironically benefit from the piracy incidents through which they can exploit extra profit by imposing a war zone premium charge.[56] Finally, the crew members and their families reside at the bottom of the hierarchy, while enduring the most traumatic suffering from the hijacking ordeals. According to a report, 25.77 percent of the hostages have suffered from post-traumatic stress disorder.[57] The majority of the crew were from developing or poor countries such as the Philippines, Bangladesh, and Pakistan.

Similarly, most of the foot soldiers in Somali piracy who risked their lives on the open sea were recruited from poor urban and rural areas such as Galkayo, Eyl, Hobyo, and Haradheere. They are between twenty and forty years old with low literacy and maybe just an elementary education. Some of them have no formal educational background because of the prolonged civil war. Though they were recruited through clan ties, the clan lineage might make them blind to their lot in the hierarchy of Somali piracy. In the long-term war economy of Somalia, those illiterate and unemployed youths who hardly have had normal lives can be easily lured to risky ventures or into the Islamic military factions. In reality, they barely escape their vicious life cycles. At best, they are arrested and sent to a rich Western country where they can enjoy "hunger-free" daily life in prison. At worst, they simply drown in the open sea or are shot to death by law enforcement.

However, the leader group members mostly do not have to risk their lives. Pirate leaders like Afweyne, who is well connected to local governance and politics, have been able to thrive. Some of them, among leaders (such as Afweyne and Garfanje) in the Hobyo-Haradheere syndicates, even successfully transformed their activity into other legalized enterprises. In other words, Somali pirate leaders with the capacity for networking and using connections are like modern corporate CEOs, demonstrating their executive capabilities through the ransom business.

In a way, the structure and operations of Somali piracy may be quite similar to modern capitalism as it operates with the international system of states. The main purpose of the Somali piracy enterprise as a violence managing agency is to accumulate capital through the diverse social, political, and financial networks.[58] It is the very purpose of modern capitalistic companies listed in the stock markets. The overall operational dynamics between them resembles each other in a form of decalcomania of capitalism in spite of starkly different modus operandi, revealing quite similar hierarchical structure of food chains.

The piracy enterprise side mirrors the hierarchical food chain of the shipper side, which is quite similar to capitalistic sociopolitical economic relations in spite of its criminal practices. It is also interesting to note that this structure is tied to the state and people's relation to the state. In Somalia, prolonged war has rendered the state virtually nonexistent, resulting in international media and security agencies labeling it a failed state.

Yet systems of power do exist in Somalia through clan ties, capacities for violence, and entrepreneurialism. State authority is simply appropriated by other social entities and leaders, as the FV Alakrana incident exemplified. This localized reality of the Somali state presents the opposite of the state in the global term—a functional state with a recognized authority in the international system of states. That global sense of the state is what is sought under glocalized security. Hence, the absorption of Somali piracy under the Global War on Terror frame speaks to the way a state is expected to be under global liberal governance with globalized normative assumptions; the state must have a government, enforce domestic and international laws, and facilitate international trade. But, in reality, Somalia violated all these global notions of a state. For global powers and capitalist elites, Somalia must be securitized given the failure to fix it.

Conclusion:
Glocalization and Further Research on the State

The benefits of the Somali piracy began to erode from early 2011. The rate of ransom gaining incidents in relation to the total number of hijack incidents also continued to decrease from 2009 (from 86 percent in 2008 to 63.2 percent in 2009). Pelton described the incident in terms of several key declining features such as curbing profits from ransom, evacuating pirate enclaves as a result of an increasing anti-piracy stance in the local community, and the increasing difficulty of hijacking operations.[59] Externally, the international counter-piracy measures began to be more effective, at least from 2011. As piracy incidents have become a less critical international security issue, the UN Security Council stopped renewing its warning resolution from 2022.[60] So far, according to the IMB, 120 world piracy incidents were reported in 2023. Nevertheless, the real implications of the pseudo-causal connection between state failure and piracy incident patterns are not fully explicated.

Therefore, the capitalistic decalcomania rippling dynamics cannot be viewed on the simplified lens of the failed state concept. The statistical approaches without considering local factors cannot reflect the complex conflict dynamics on their static window. Perhaps the vague results of this study implicitly call for a new international security approach with glocalized lenses to comprehend the complicated incident patterns and causal mechanisms of piracy and its connection to the nature of the Somali state. The results of the analysis offer two implications. First, the causal connection between state failure and piracy is an illusory period effect that securitizes piracy under the troubled environments of regional states.[61] The second implication is about the limits of the state-centered approaches. As those state-based macro factors do not show a coherent interpretation ground, it is very difficult to make a valid relevance between major macro factors, such as poverty, institution, unemployment, and fragmentation, and piracy. Those state-centered approaches do not entail the local contexts in major piracy-prone regions even though piracy is locally engendered crime. Then the implications lead to a call for a glocalized security frame to illuminate the contextually glocalized security issue and thereby reveal the hidden complex dynamics behind the state failure scenes. Nevertheless, the test results provide several clues that ultimately call forth a region-specific, context-based qualitative analysis.[62] Then studying contemporary piracy requires a new prism of glocalization with the following considerations.[63]

First, it may be wrong to assume that failed states directly affect piracy incidents because the failed state and its conditional factors do not show a coherently general influence on piracy. Second, economic factors, such as unemployment and poverty, have only relative relations with trends and types of piracy incidents. In other words, there is no simple one-directional interpretation between them and piracy. Third, the effects of economic factors can be better understood with the combined effects of political and other social factors. Advanced piracy incidents are more likely to occur when relatively better conditions prevail related to political and economic factors. Fourth, only Somalia shows the most coherent associations with piracy incidents across different times and types as the uneven cluster of hijacking incidents during the particular time period indicates. It means that the particular contexts of the Somali state have more associations with the unique piracy patterns than other states. Then, interestingly, the Somali piracy is a representative case of glocalized contemporary piracy. Finally, the shortcomings of the "failed state" approach, with its stigma, could reveal the inherent weaknesses of globalization perspectives when taken as the default standpoint. As Goffman argued, stigmatization is essentially a result of the inherent imperfections within the concept of normality itself.[64]

According to Appadurai, globalization unfolds in terms of five "scapes": ethnoscape, technoscape, ideoscape, financescape, and mediascape.[65] Many current international security issues, including piracy, have occurred on the wide effects of the globalization as a key gravitational denominator. However, globalization has ironically increased instability and volatile responses from local contexts, which have, in turn, refracted and transformed the homogenous flows fit into local dynamics.[66] The actual security incidents and threats occur in local domains where local people bear the burden of the risk and damages on a daily basis.

The Somali pirate–led hijacking incidents starkly demonstrated the uneven rippling effects of globalization and the variant local responses. On the surface of the incidents projected through the global mediascape, the piracy incidents appear as major facets of globalization as pirates also use globalized technologies, such as weapons and GPS, and the US dollar as a universal financial currency. However, in actual encounters, there are fundamentally incommensurable claims clashing with each other between global actors and local reactors. The global media depicted the people involved in piracy activities as criminal and as a potential contributor to global terror incidents under the securitized lenses from the global metro centers. However, they were welcomed at home as a coastal defender and a key contributor to the local economy. At least there were no commensurable ethnoscape and ideoscape between the global and the local sides in Appadurai's term. Thus, the ambiguous natures of contemporary piracy imply that the violent maritime issue needs to be understood in a glocalized security frame, which incorporates the highly dynamic and nonlinear natures of context-specific security issues, such as contemporary piracy, at multidimensional levels from global to local.

In the end, glocalization provides a lens for examining the African state through the domestic and external drivers of violent conflicts and the international responses to such conflicts. Yet Somalia has not been a "real state," but a labeled "failed state," because of domestic and external conflict drivers necessitating more securitization. Works ranging from critiques of colonialism to liberal peace, collective security, and human security all find the African state to be peculiar and challenging to theorize. All of that is most vivid in the notion of failed state. This chapter takes on the issue of piracy as an entry point into understanding the glocal challenges and connections to the state in Africa, notably Somalia. It shows the limit of the notion of failed state in large part because of the overgeneralizations that have been made, especially in quantitative studies. Glocalization not only points to a theoretical frame, but also shows the kinds of methodological adjustments that may be needed to better gauge the local factors in relation to global measures of state stability and well-being.

Appendix: Statistical Models and Data Description

MODEL A

Figure 6.3. Equation for Model A.

$$\ln\left(\frac{\hat{y}}{1-\hat{y}}\right) = C + \beta_1 FI + \beta X + \alpha_1 T_1 + \alpha_2 T_2 + \varepsilon$$

Unit of analysis: Individual piracy Incident
Sample Size: 5846 World Piracy Incidents from 1996 to 2013.
C: Constant
Y1: Whether or not the piracy incident is the successful piracy incident (1) or not (0).
Y2: Whether or not the piracy incident is the successful hijacking piracy incident (1) or not (0).
Y3: Whether or not the piracy incident is the successful ransom gaining piracy incident (1) or not (0).
FI: Failed state index (WGI or FSI)
X: Control variables; country dummy, location effect (Number of neighbor state), previous success experience of piracy

MODEL B

Figure 6.4. Equation for Model B.

$$\Rightarrow \ln\left(\frac{\hat{y}}{1-\hat{y}}\right) = \beta_1 IS + \beta_2 FM + \beta_3 UE + \beta_4 EP + \beta_5 PC + \beta_6 LS + \beta_7 CR + \beta X +$$

$$\alpha_1 T_1 + \alpha_2 T_2 + \varepsilon$$

Unit of analysis: Individual piracy Incident
Y1: Whether or not the piracy incident is the actual incident (1) or not (0)
Y2: Whether or not the piracy incident is the hijack piracy (1) or not (0)
Y3: Whether or not the piracy incident is the ransom piracy (1) or not (0)
IS: Institutional strength of the country at the year of the piracy incident
FM: Fragmentation of the country at the year of the piracy incident
UE: Unemployment rate of the country at the year of the piracy incident
EP: Extreme poverty of country at the year of piracy incident
PC: Police officer to population ratio of the country at the year of the piracy incident
LS: Livestock yield of country at the year of the piracy incident
CR: Cereal yield of the country at the year of the piracy incident
X: Control variables: Same with Model A

Table 6.5. Description of Quantitative Variables

Variable	Measurement	Range	Data Source
Piracy Incident/ Type: outcome	Dummy variable (successful incident: 1, failed incident: 0)	0 or 1	IMB, IMO, Ecoterra International & Media Sources
Piracy Incident/ Type: hijack	Dummy variable (successful hijack: 1, the other: 0)	0 or 1	IMB, IMO, Ecoterra International & Media Sources
Piracy Incident/ Type: ransom	Dummy variable (ransom-gaining incident: 1, the other: 0)	0 or 1	IMB, IMO, Ecoterra International & Media Sources
Failed State Index (World Governance Indicator, WGI)	Continuous variable (Averaged Governance Indicator of 6 sub-indicators)	−2.5–2.5 (bigger= better)	The World Bank. (http://data. worldbank.org/ data-catalog/ worldwide-governance-indicators)
Failed State Index (FSI)	Continuous variable (Composite Index of 12 sub-indicators)	0–120 (bigger=worse)	the Peace for Fund (http://fsi. fundforpeace.org/)
Location Effect	Discrete variable (Number of Adjacent Country to Piracy Incident Country)	0–	The number of bordered countries.
Success Rate	Continuous variable (Successful Incident No./Total Incident No. in previous year)	0–1	Calculation from IMB, IMO, Ecoterra International & Media.
Institutional Strength	Continuous variable	0–25 (bigger=worse)	The Polity IV Project (http://www. systemicpeace. org/polity/polity4. htm)

continued on next page

Table 6.5. Continued

Variable	Measurement	Range	Data Source
Fragmentation	Continuous variable (Averaged Index of culture & Ethnicity diversity)	0~1 (bigger=more fragmented)	James Fearon (2003). "Ethnic and Cultural Diversity by Country." Journal of Economic Growth 8: 195–222.
Unemployment Rate	Continuous variable	0~100 (%)	The World Bank (http://data.worldbank.org/indicator/SL.UEM.TOTL.ZS)
Extreme Poverty	Continuous variable, Poverty headcount ratio at $2 a day (PPP) at 2005 international prices (% of population)	0~100 (%)	The World Bank. Data collected in Sept 2015.
Police Officer Rate	Continuous variable (Police Officer per 100,000)	0~1000 (‰)	UN Offices on Drug and Crime.
Livestock production index	Continuous variable (Weighted Average between 2004~2006 = 100)	0~	The World Bank (http://data.worldbank.org/indicator/AG.PRD.LVSK.XD)
Cereal yield	Continuous variable (kg per hectare)	0~	The World Bank (http://data.worldbank.org/indicator/AG.YLD.CREL.KG)
Country Dummy	Dummy variable. Country Dummy of Somalia, Nigeria, Indonesia	0 or 1	IMB, IMO, Ecoterra International & Media Sources

Source: Created by the author.

Notes

1. Knickmeyer, "U.S. Navy Bolsters Watch Over Ship Seized by Somali Pirates." *Washington Post*, http://www.washingtonpost.com/wpdyn/content/article/2008/09/29/AR2008092900541.html; Rice, "Somali Pirates Capture Ukrainian Cargo Ship Loaded With Military Hardware," *Guardian*. https://www.theguardian.com/world/2008/sep/27/3.

2. Tiiceey was the first governor of Himan and Heeb state in the Galmudug region of Somalia.

3. Jeong, "Diverse Patterns of World and Regional Piracy: Implications of the Recurrent Characteristics," 118–33.

4. Coggins, "Does State Failure Cause Terrorism? An Empirical Analysis (1999–2008)," 455–83.

5. Marfo and Arthur, "Beyond Classical Peace Paradigm: A Theoretical Argument for a 'Glocalized Peace and Security.' "

6. Friedman, *The World Is Flat: A Brief History of the Twenty-First Century.*

7. Fukuyama, "The End of History?," 3–18.

8. Hastings, "Geography, Globalization, and Terrorism: The Plots of Jemaah Islamiyah," 505–30; Hastings, "Geographies of State Failure and Sophistication in Maritime Piracy Hijackings," 1–11; Valencia, "The Politics of Anti-Piracy and Anti-Terrorism: Responses in Southeast Asia"; ISEAS; Dimitri Vlassis and Phil Williams, *Combating Transnational Crime: Concepts, Activities and Responses*, 157–94; Chalk, *The Maritime Dimension of International Security: Terrorism, Piracy, and Challenges for the United States.*

9. Hastings, "Geographies of State Failure and Sophistication in Maritime Piracy Hijackings"; Daxecker and Brandon, "The New Barbary Wars: Forecasting Maritime Piracy"; Murphy, *Contemporary Piracy and Maritime Terrorism*; Chalk, *The Maritime Dimension of International Security: Terrorism, Piracy, and Challenges for the United States*; Sörenson, "State Failure on the High Seas—Reviewing the Somali Piracy."

10. Murphy, *Contemporary Piracy and Maritime Terrorism*; Chalk, *The Maritime Dimension of International Security: Terrorism, Piracy, and Challenges for the United States*; Jablonski and Oliver, "The Political Economy of Plunder: Economic Opportunity and Modern Piracy"; Daxecker and Prins, "The New Barbary Wars: Forecasting Maritime Piracy."

11. Hastings, "Geographies Of State Failure and Sophistication In Maritime Piracy Hijackings," 1–11; Hastings, *No Man's Land: Globalization, Territory, and Clandestine Groups in Southeast Asia.*

12. Robert, *The Evolution of Piracy.*

13. Chalk, *The Maritime Dimension of International Security: Terrorism, Piracy, and Challenges For the United States*; Menkhaus, "Dangerous Waters"; Hastings, *No Man's Land: Globalization, Territory, and Clandestine Groups in Southeast Asia.*

14. Anderson, "Piracy and World History: An Economic Perspective on Maritime Predation"; De Groot and Anja, "Gov-arrrgh-nance. Jolly Rogers and Dodgy

Rulers"; Percy and Shortland, "The Business of Piracy in Somalia"; Jablonski and Steven Olive, "*The Political Economy of Plunder: Economic Opportunity and Modern Piracy*"; Vagg, "*Rough Seas? Contemporary Piracy in South East Asia.*"

15. Ravallion, "Growth, Inequality and Poverty: Looking Beyond Averages"; Hansen, *Piracy in the Greater Gulf of Aden: Myths, Misconception and Remedies.*

16. Menkhaus, *Somalia: State Collapse and the Threat Of Terrorism.*

17. Bah, "State Decay: A Conceptual Frame of Failing and Failed States in West Africa."

18. There were seventy-two registered pirate companies in the stock market. For example, the Spaniard fishing vessel Alakrana was financed through the stock market (Ahmed, "Somali sea gangs lure investors at pirate lair." Reuters, December 1, 2009, https://www.reuters.com/article/us-somalia-piracy-investors-idUSTRE5B01Z920091201).

19. He was arrested with his government partner Tiiceey at Brussels International Airport on October 13, 2013 (*The Independent*, October 15, 2013, http://www.independent.co.uk/news/world/africa/the-pirate-who-fell-into-a-movie-trap-kingpin-mohamed-big-mouth-abdi-hassan-arrested-in-belgium-8880645.html).

20. Ritzer, The *McDonaldization of Society.*

21. Robertson, "Globalisation or Glocalisation?"; Robertson, "Glocalization: Time-Space and Homogeneity-Heterogeneity."

22. Rotberg, *When States Fail: Causes and Consequences*; Menkhaus, *Somalia: State Collapse and the Threat Of Terrorism*; Sörenson, "*State Failure on the High Seas*—Reviewing the Somali Piracy"; Hastings, "*Geography, Globalization, and Terrorism*: The Plots of Jemaah Islamiyah; Ghani and Clare, *Fixing Failed States: A Framework For Rebuilding A Fractured World*; Kraska, James. *Contemporary Maritime Piracy: International Law, Strategy, and Diplomacy at Sea*; Marley, *Modern Piracy.*

23. Hastings, "Geography, Globalization, and Terrorism: The Plots of Jemaah Islamiyah"; Rice and Patrick, *Index of State Weakness In the Developing World*; Daxecker and Prins, "Insurgents of the Sea: Institutional and Economic Opportunities for Maritime Piracy."

24. Patrick, *Weak Links: Fragile States, Global Threats, and International Security*, 19–22.

25. Please see appendix for model equations and description of variable data and sources.

26. Menkhaus, "*Dangerous Waters*," 21–25.

27. Nincic, "State Failure and the Re-Emergence of Maritime Piracy."

28. For example, *Foreign Policy* has published the failed states index annually.

29. Beehner and Young. "The Failure of the Failed States Index."

30. Coggins, "Global Patterns of Maritime Piracy, 2000–09: Introducing a New Dataset"; Iyigun and Ratisukpimol, "Learning Piracy on the High Seas."

31. Rotberg, *When States Fail: Causes and Consequences*; Ghani and Clare, *Fixing Failed States: A Framework for Rebuilding a Fractured World.*

32. Hastings, "Geography, Globalization, and Terrorism: The Plots of Jemaah Islamiyah"; Hansen, *Piracy in the Greater Gulf of Aden: Myths, Misconception and Remedies*; Murphy, *Small Boats, Weak States, Dirty Money: Piracy and Maritime Terrorism in the Modern World*; Kraska, *Contemporary Maritime Piracy: International Law, Strategy, and Diplomacy at Sea*.

33. Bah, *Breakdown and Reconstitution: Democracy, the Nation-State, and Ethnicity in Nigeria*.

34. Leeson, "Better Off Stateless: Somalia Before and After Government Collapse," 698–99.

35. Hansen, *Piracy in the Greater Gulf of Aden: Myths, Misconception and Remedies*, 32–33; Bahadur, *The Pirates of Somalia*, 35–37.

36. Hirsi, "Somali Sea-Piracy: Business Model or Resource Conflict?," 14, 21.

37. Vagg, "Rough Seas? Contemporary Piracy in South East Asia"; Hastings, *No Man's Land: Globalization, Territory, and Clandestine Groups in Southeast Asia*, 27, 157.

38. Puntland declared independence on May 5, 1998, while remaining a part of Somali federal system. Because of poor capacity and longtime civil wars, Puntland failed to pay security forces in April 2008. The public security system was broken for a while. Some of the security forces turned to piracy; Puntland's law enforcement has been in chronic failure and at risk of a meltdown because of low funding (Bahadur, 2011:35; Hansen 2009).

39. Roudometof, *Theorizing Glocalization: Three Interpretations*.

40. Anderson, "Piracy and World History: An Economic Perspective on Maritime Predation"; Leeson, "Pirational Choice: The Economics of Infamous Pirate Practices"; Shortland, "Robin Hook: The Developmental Effects of Somali Piracy."

41. Thomas, "What Do the World Governance Indicators Measure?"

42. Thomas, "What Do the World Governance Indicators Measure?"

43. Lanford, "Things Fall Apart: State Failure and the Politics of Intervention," 61; Menkhaus, "Local Security Systems in Somali East Africa," 68.

44. Verhoeven, "The Self-Fulfilling Prophecy of Failed States: Somalia, State-Collapse and the Global War on Terror."

45. Young, *The African Colonial State in Comparative Perspective*.

46. Tilly, "Terror, Terrorism, Terrorists."

47. Buzan and Wæver, *Security: A New Framework For Analysis*.

48. Jeong "Piracy and Crime Embeddedness: State Decay and Social Transformation in Somalia."

49. Hansen *"Piracy in the Greater Gulf of Aden: Myths, Misconception and Remedies,"* 212–24.

50. Jorish, "Today's Pirates Have Their Own Stock Exchange."

51. Ahmed, "Somali Sea Gangs Lure Investors at Pirate Lair."

52. RT News, "Somali Pirates Waste Ransom Money on Weddings and Orgies."

53. Bahadur, *The Pirates of Somalia*, 13–24.

54. Associated Press, "Four American Hostages 'Killed by Pirates.'"
55. Bahadur, "*The Pirates of Somalia*, 232.
56. M Costello "Shipping Insurance Costs Soar With Piracy Surge Off Somalia."
57. Seyle, "After the Release: The Long-Term Behavioral Impact of Piracy on Seafarers and Families."
58. Volkov, *Violent Entrepreneurs: The Use of Force in the Making of Russian Capitalism.*
59. Pelton, "Pirate Fight Over MV Blida Ransom."
60. France 24, "UN Authorization to Fight Piracy in Somalia Waters Ends."
61. Buzan and Wæver, *Security: A New Framework for Analysis.*
62. Jeong, "Diverse Patterns of World and Regional Piracy: Implications of the Recurrent Characteristics."
63. Khondker, *Globalisation to Glocalization: A Conceptual Exploration*; Roudometof, Theorizing Glocalization: Three Interpretations."
64. Goffman, "Stigma: Notes on the Management of Spoiled Identity," 128.
65. Appadurai, *Modernity at Large: Cultural Dimension of Globalization.*
66. Khondker, *Globalisation to Glocalization: A Conceptual Exploration*; Roudometof, "Theorizing Glocalization: Three Interpretations"; Robertson, *Beyond the Discourse of Globalization.*

References

Associated Press. "Four American Hostages 'Killed By Pirates.'" *Independent*, February 22, 2011. http://www.independent.co.uk/news/world/africa/four-american-hostages-killed-by-pirates-2222570.html.

Anderson, John L. "Piracy and World History: An Economic Perspective on Maritime Predation." *Journal of World History* 6, no. 2 (1995): 175–99.

Ahmed, Mohamed. "Somali Sea Gangs Lure Investors at Pirate Lair." *Reuters*, December 1, 2009. http://www.reuters.com/article/us-somalia-piracy-investors/somali-sea-gangs-lure-investors-at-pirate-lair-idUSTRE5B01Z920091201?sp=true.

Appadurai, Arjun. *Modernity at Large: Cultural Dimension of Globalization*. Minneapolis: University of Minnesota Press, 1996.

Bah, Abu Bakarr. *Breakdown and Reconstitution: Democracy, the Nation-State, and Ethnicity in Nigeria*. Lanham, MD: Lexington Books, 2005.

———. "State Decay: A Conceptual Frame of Failing and Failed States in West Africa." *International Journal of Politics, Culture, and Society* 25, no. 1–3 (2012): 71–89.

Bahadur, Jay. *The Pirates of Somalia*. New York: Vintage Books, 2011.

Bateman, Sam. "Sea Piracy: Some Inconvenient Truths." *Maritime Security* (2010): 13–24.

Beehner, Lionet, and Joseph Young. *"The Failure of the Failed States Index."* World Policy Institution Blog. 2012. https://worldpolicy.org/2012/07/17/the-failure-of-the-failed-states-index/.

Burgess, Douglas R., Jr. "Hostis Humani Generi: Piracy, Terrorism and a New International Law." *University of Miami International and Comparative Law Review* 13, no. 1 (2006): 293–340.

Buzan, Barry, and Ole Wæver, et al. *Security: A New Framework for Analysis.* Boulder, CO: Lynne Rienner, 1998.

Chalk, Peter. *The Maritime Dimension of International Security: Terrorism, Piracy, and Challenges for the United States.* Santa Monica, CA: RAND, 2008.

Coggins, Bridget L. "Global Patterns of Maritime Piracy, 2000–09: Introducing a New Dataset." *Journal of Peace Research* 49, no. 4 (2012): 605–17.

———. "Does State Failure Cause Terrorism? An Empirical Analysis (1999–2008)." *Journal of Conflict Resolution* 59, no. 3 (2014): 455–83.

Costello, Miles. "Shipping Insurance Costs Soar with Piracy Surge off Somalia," *Times,* September 11, 2008. https://www.thetimes.co.uk/article/shipping-insurance-cost-soars-with-piracy-surge-off-somalia-dnrrcgpwx9k.

Daxecker, Ursula, and Brandon Prins. "Insurgents of the Sea: Institutional and Economic Opportunities for Maritime Piracy." *Journal of Conflict Resolution* 57, no. 6 (2013): 940–65.

———. "The New Barbary Wars: Forecasting Maritime Piracy." *Foreign Policy Analysis* 11 (2015): 23–44.

De Groot, Olaf J., and Anja Shortland. "Gov-arrrgh-nance. Jolly Rogers and Dodgy Rulers." *DIW Discussion Papers* 1063 (2010).

De Wijk, Rob. "The Evolution of Piracy." *Somalia and the Pirates.* European Security Forum Working Paper 33 (2009): 9–18.

France 24. "UN Authorization to Fight Piracy in Somalia Waters End." November 3, 2022. https://www.france24.com/en/live-news/20220311-un-authorization-to-fight-piracy-in-somali-waters-ends.

Friedman, T. L. *The World Is Flat: A Brief History of the Twenty-First Century.* New York: Farrar, Straus and Giroux, 2005.

Fukuyama, Francis. "The End of History?" *National Interest* 16 (1989): 3–18.

Ghani, Ashraf, and Lockhart, Clare. *Fixing Failed States: A Framework for Rebuilding a Fractured World.* New York: Oxford University Press, 2008.

Goffman, Erving. *Stigma: Notes on the Management of Spoiled Identity.* New York: Prentice Hall, 1963.

Gourevitch, Alex. "The Unfailing of the State." *Journal of International Affairs* 58, no. 1 (2004): 255–60.

Hansen, Stig Jarle. *Piracy in the Greater Gulf of Aden: Myths, Misconception and Remedies.* Oslo: Norwegin Institute for Urban and Regional Research. NIBR. 2009. http://estaticos.elmundo.es/documentos/2009/11/12/piratas.pdf.

Hastings, Justin V. "Geographies of State Failure and Sophistication in Maritime Piracy Hijackings." *Political Geography* 30 (2009): 1–11.

———. "Geography, Globalization, and Terrorism: The Plots of Jemaah Islamiyah." *Security Studies* 17, no. 3 (2008): 505–30.

———. *No Man's Land: Globalization, Territory, and Clandestine Groups in Southeast Asia*. Ithaca: Cornell University Press, 2010.

Hirsi, Ahmed. "Somali Sea-Piracy: Business Model or Resource Conflict?" *Wardheer News*, September 15, 2011.

Iyigun, Murat, and Watcharapong Ratisukpimol. "Learning Piracy on the High Seas." *Mimeo*. January 2011.

Jablonski, Ryan S., and Steven Oliver. "The Political Economy of Plunder: Economic Opportunity and Modern Piracy." *Journal of Conflict Resolution* 57, no. 4 (2012): 682–708.

Jeong, Keunsoo. "Diverse Patterns of World and Regional Piracy: Implications of the Recurrent Characteristics." *Australian Journal of Maritime & Ocean Affairs* 10 (2018): 118–33.

———. "Piracy and Crime Embeddedness: State Decay and Social Transformation in Somalia." *African Conflict & Peacebuilding Review* 9 no. 1 (2019): 72–99.

Jorisch, Avi. "Today's Pirates Have Their Own Stock Exchange." *Wall Street Journal*, June 16, 2011. https://www.wsj.com/articles/SB10001424052702304520804576341223910765818.

Kleemans, Edward R., and Christianne J. de Poot. "Criminal Careers in Organized Crime and Social Opportunity Structure." *European Journal of Criminology* 5, no. 1 (2008): 69–98.

———, and Hank G. van de Bunt. "The Social Embeddedness of Organized Crime." *Transnational Organized Crime* 5, no. 2 (1999): 19–36.

Khondker, Habibul Haque. *Globalisation to Glocalization: A Conceptual Exploration*. *Intellectual Discourse* 13, no. 2 (2005): 181–99.

Kraska, James. *Contemporary Maritime Piracy: International Law, Strategy, and Diplomacy at Sea*. Santa Barbara, CA: Praeger, 2011.

Leeson, Peter T. "Better Off Stateless: Somalia Before and after Government Collapse." *Journal of Comparative Economics* 35, no. 4 (2007): 689–710.

———. "Pirational Choice: The Economics of Infamous Pirate Practices." *Journal of Economic Behavior & Organization* 76, no. 3 (2010): 497–510.

Langford, Tonya. "Things Fall Apart: State Failure and The Politics of Intervention." *International Studies Review* 1, no. 1 (1999): 59–79.

Marfo, Samuel, Halidu Musah, and D. D. Arthur. "Beyond Classical Peace Paradigm: A Theoretical Argument for a 'Glocalized Peace and Security.'" *African Journal of Political Science and International Relations* 10, no. 4 (2016): 47–55.

Marley, David F. *Modern Piracy*. Santa Barbara, CA: ABC-CLIO, 2011.

Menkhaus, Ken. 2004. *Somalia: State Collapse and the Threat of Terrorism*. Oxford: Oxford University Press, 2011.

Menkhaus, Ken. "Dangerous Waters." *Survival* 51, no. 1 (2009): 21–25.

———. "Local Security Systems in Somali East Africa." In *Fragile States and Insecure People? Violence, Security and Statehood in the Twenty-First Century,* edited by Louise Andersen, Bjørn Møller, and Finn Stepputat, 67–97. New York: Palgrave, 2007.

Murphy, Martin N. *Contemporary Piracy and Maritime Terrorism.* New York: Routledge, 2007.

———. *Small Boats, Weak States, Dirty Money: Piracy and Maritime Terrorism in the Modern World.* London: Hurst, 2010.

———. *Somalia, the New Barbary? Piracy and Islam in the Horn of Africa.* New York: Hurst, 2011.

Nincic, Donna. "State Failure and the Re-Emergence of Maritime Piracy." Paper presented at the 49th Annual Convention of the International Studies Association; March 26–29, 2008; San Francisco, CA.

Ong-Webb, Graham. "Piracy in Maritime Asia: Current Trends." In *Violence at Sea: Piracy in the Age of Global Terrorism,* edited by Peter Lehr, 37–94. New York: Routledge, 2007.

Paris, Roland. *At War's End: Building Peace after Civil Conflict.* Cambridge: Cambridge University Press, 2004.

Patrick, Stewart. *Weak Links: Fragile States, Global Threats, and International Security.* New York: Oxford University Press, 2011.

Percy, Sarah, and Anja Shortland. "The Business of Piracy in Somalia." DIW Discussion Paper 1033. Berlin: DIW Berlin, 2011.

Ravallion, Martin. "Growth, Inequality and Poverty: Looking Beyond Averages." *World Development* 29, no. 11 (2001): 1803–15.

Reuter, Peter. *Disorganized Crime: The Economics of the Visible Hand.* Cambridge, MA: MIT Press, 1983.

Rice, Susan E., and Stewart Patrick. *Index of State Weakness in the Developing World.* Washington, DC: Brookings Institution, 2008.

Richardson, Michael. *A Time Bomb for Global Trade: Maritime-Related Terrorism in an Age of WMD.* Singapore: Institute of South East Asian Studies, 2004.

Ritzer, George. *The McDonaldization of Society.* Thousand Oaks, CA: Pine Forge, 2000.

Robert De Wijk. *The Evolution of Piracy.* ESF Working Paper No. 33. December 2009.

Robertson, Roland. "Beyond the Discourse of Globalization." *Glocalism: Journal of Culture, Politics and Innovation,* no. 1 (2015). https://doi.org/10.12893/gjcpi.2015.1.6.

———. "Globalisation or Glocalisation?" *Journal of International Communication* 1, no. 1 (1994): 33–52.

———. "Glocalization: Time-Space and Homogeneity-Heterogeneity." In *Global Modernities.* 1st ed., edited by Mike Featherstone, Scott Lash, and Roland Robertson, 24–44. London: Sage, 1995.

———. "Glocalization: Self-Referential Remembrances." *Glocalism: Journal of Culture, Politics and Innovation* 3 (2020). https://doi.org/10.12893/gjcpi.2020.3.17.

Rotberg, Robert I., ed. *State Failure and State Weakness in a Time of Terror*. Cambridge, MA: World Peace Foundation, 2003.

———, ed. *When States Fail: Causes and Consequences*. Princeton, NJ: Princeton University Press, 2004.

Roudometof, Victor. "Theorizing Glocalization: Three Interpretations." *European Journal of Social Theory* 19, no. 3 (2016): 291–408.

RT News. "Somali Pirates Waste Ransom Money on Weddings and Orgies." *RT News*, November 19, 2009. https://www.rt.com/news/somali-pirates-waste-ransom/.

Seyle Conor. "After the Release: The Long-Term Behavioral Impact of Piracy on Seafarers and Families." One Earth Future Foundation, 2016.

Shortland, Anja. "Robin Hook: The Developmental Effects of Somali Piracy." *CEDI Working Paper* 07 (2011).

Sörenson, Karl. "State Failure on the High Seas—Reviewing the Somali Piracy." FOI Somalia Papers, Report 3 (2008).

Thomas, Melissa A. "What Do the World Governance Indicators Measure?" *European Journal of Development Research* 22 (2010): 31–54.

Tilly, Charles. "Terror, Terrorism, Terrorists." *Sociological Theory* 22, no. 1 (2004): 5–13.

Vagg, Jon. "Rough Seas? Contemporary Piracy in South East Asia." *British Journal of World Development* 29, no. 11 (1995): 1803–15.

Valencia, M. J. "The Politics of Anti-Piracy and Anti-Terrorism: Responses in Southeast Asia. In *Piracy, Maritime Terrorism and Securing the Malacca Straits*, edited by Graham Gerard Ong-Webb. Singapore: ISEAS Publishing, 2006.

Verhoeven, Harry. 2009. "The Self-Fulfilling Prophecy of Failed States: Somalia, State-Collapse and the Global War on Terror." *Journal of Eastern African Studies* 3, no. 3 (2009): 405–25.

Vlassis, Dimitri, and Phil Williams. *Combating Transnational Crime: Concepts, Activities and Responses*. London: Routledge, 2001.

Volkov, Vadim. *Violent Entrepreneurs: The Use of Force in the Making of Russian Capitalism*. Ithaca, NY: Cornell University Press, 2002.

Young, Crawford. *The African Colonial State in Comparative Perspective*. New Haven, CT: Yale University Press, 1994.

Young Pelton, Robert. "Pirates Fight over MV Blida Ransom." Somalia Report. November 7, 2011.

Zachary, Abuza. "Terrorism in Southeast Asia: Keeping Al-Qaeda at Bay." *Terrorism Monitor* 2, no. 9 (2004). https://jamestown.org/program/terrorism-in-southeast-asia-keeping-al-qaeda-at-bay-2/.

Foreign Military and Security Bases

Implications for the Practice of Peace and Security in Africa

Sebastian Angzoorokuu Paalo and
John-Paul Safunu Banchani

As key contemporary global phenomena, foreign military and security bases have become a topical theme in academic and policy circles in recent decades. This is largely because of the increasing complexity of security challenges and the apparent lack of capacity of the affected states, coupled with competition among external powers for spheres of influence to establish military bases abroad as an extension to their foreign policies rooted in cultural, economic, political, and overseas national and security interests.[1] This chapter adopts the definition of a foreign military base as "an extraterritorial unit with an external actor's sovereign or semi-sovereign rights."[2] "Foreign military bases" is used here interchangeably or in connection with associated terms such as "foreign security bases," "overseas security bases," "foreign security arrangements," "foreign security/military posts," "foreign military alliances," or "foreign security installations."[3] While these terms have slight differences, they are used in this chapter to broadly mean Africa-based external military establishments or posts that form part of global partnerships with African states with the claim to address security challenges in Africa.

While the exact number of military-related bases globally is not fully established in the literature (because of conceptual/definitional contentions), the continent of Africa is considered to be hosting the most foreign military-related posts established by various Western powers as well as Russia and China. Presently, the African continent hosts more than sixty military-related bases established by at least thirteen different foreign countries, mostly competing global powers such as the United States, France, China, the UK, Japan, Germany, the United Arab Emirates, Russia, Belgium, Italy, Saudi Arabia, Turkey, and India.[4] This phenomenon continues to grow because of increasing bilateral agreements between some African Union (AU) member states and foreign powers as part of economic and state stabilization support to African states in lieu of increasing economic challenges and security dilemmas across the continent.[5] Within this framing, military-related bases in Africa are largely a response by foreign partners to specific local security challenges in their operations while simultaneously serving as instruments to pursue the interests of states that establish these military bases.

Yet this foreign influence on Africa's security architecture appears to be in contrast with the AU's aim to offer "African solutions to African problems," including homegrown policies to address security concerns.[6] The AU through its Peace and Security Council (PSC) expresses concerns about possible consequences of this growing development on peace and security on the continent and admonishes member states to be circumspect when engaging in bilateral relations leading to the setting up of foreign military posts and other matters relating to peace and security. In this regard, the AU warns that the intense "external military deployment in the region, which is driven by geopolitical, commercial, and military competition, largely with negative effects on regional stability," is problematic.[7] This issue has implications for both African security and the independence of African states, especially because military bases raise issues of sovereign decision-making. Despite the potential consequences of the proliferation of foreign security bases, many African governments see these foreign countries as important trading and security partners and engage in such related agreements with them as a result.[8]

Africa has become increasingly important in the discourses and practices on global security for some economic and political reasons. The continent is host to 16 percent of the world's population and about 60 percent of Africa's population is under the age of twenty-five. Besides, by 2050, Africa's population is projected to be around two billion people.[9] These statistics have implications for a mix of important issues, including market potential, human resource development, (un)employment, and migration-related issues, which together could seriously influence world order. This barrage of potential issues vis-à-vis the limited capacity of many African states and regional bodies has attracted competing interests from external powers to establish bases for military and other security operation centers across Africa. For example, Russian mercenaries are a notable force operating in Central African Republic, Mali and the Sahel, while China has a base in Djibouti. While it is obvious that this military presence is aimed at increasing the sphere of influence of Russia and China, the usual discourse of contributing to stabilizing the fragile security situation in the region and fighting terrorism and drug trafficking has mostly overwhelmed justifications for such military presence.

Besides these rationales, Linnéa Gelot and Adam Sandor raise other concerns, indicating that increasing cross-border crimes and insurgencies, regime-sponsored election violence, and other security dilemmas have attracted international military interventions and establishments in Africa as part of attempts to stabilize African polities and support security sector capacity-building.[10] Foreign interventions are therefore becoming normal in the African contexts because respective states have not significantly addressed these concerns, largely because of the lack of state capacity and the complicity of regimes, especially those that use violence to remain in power.[11] Notably, many African countries face state security and human security challenges. These complexities exacerbate the economic and political dilemmas in Africa that attract external interest and action, generally to support transitions to stability, democracy, and economic development on the continent.[12]

Some accounts suggest that the proliferation of foreign military activities forms part of the glocalization of the understanding and practice of security and related matters of political and economic importance.[13] Formally a common usage in business and international communication from the mid-twentieth century,[14] the notion of localizing global norms, practices, and events and the reflection of local peculiarities in global spheres has also come to be used prominently in cognate disciplines within the social sciences. For instance, Roland Robertson argues that globalized security suggests the co-penetration of the so-called "global" and "local" in ways that the global is not seen predominantly as universal from elsewhere, while the local is not understood as contrasting global issues.[15] This indicates that African countries' embracement of foreign military bases is a consequence of the continued deterioration of world peace in the last decade and the attendant increase in military spending and militarized security in recent years, especially in the wake of the coronavirus pandemic, Russia's invasion of Ukraine, and the Israel-Palestine war.[16] Thus, foreign military bases form part of the increasing search for collaborative solutions to solve local security concerns in Africa as part of the attempts to combat global security challenges such as conflicts, insurgencies, terrorism, and the general deterioration of the liberal order. This glocalized way of addressing security challenges in Africa is particularly compelling because of the manifest nested, transborder, and trans-scaler nature of contemporary security dilemmas.[17]

However, other bodies of literature have offered critical appreciations of the growing phenomenon of foreign security presence and installations in Africa, including concerns of colonial/neocolonial posturing of foreign bases and related military arrangements that sometimes undermine the sovereignty of the state,[18] foreign policy proxies for Western governments in Africa,[19] the promotion of hegemonic world order thus power imbalances,[20] intense geopolitical competition among external powers for agreements and bases in the era of multipolarity in global politics with attendant problems of more insecurity and instability in affected areas,[21] and the promotion of illiberal regimes and sustenance of state-sponsored violence.[22]

This chapter contributes to the debates on the increasing glocalization of security by examining how the phenomenon of foreign military installations has affected the idea of African peace and security through the regional organizations in charge of peace and security in the continent, using the statement "African solutions to African problems"—African-centered Solutions (AfSol). This is insightful for understanding both security issues and state sovereignty in Africa. This chapter thus attempts to address one broad question: how do the establishment and operation of foreign military bases affect the performance of regional organizations and collaborative networks of institutions and actors in terms of peace and security in Africa? To address this question, we examine the relevant scholarship and policy frameworks on peace and security, regionalism, politics, and international relations—all in conjunction with the issue of state sovereignty. We focus on the related debates on foreign military bases, rooted in the interaction between emergent global and local concerns and approaches to peace and security, and the implications for peace and security and state sovereignty in Africa. The chapter concludes that the phenomenon of foreign military establishments and operations affects the pursuit of African regional security by distorting the challenging idea of "African solutions to African problems" in two important ways: it increases the overlaps and redundancy of structures in charge of peace and security and limits the potential to localize continental security policies at the state and substate levels. All of this not only poses more security challenges, but also undermines the sovereignty of African states in an increasingly contentious global system.

In addressing these issues, the rest of the chapter is presented as follows. The chapter first provides background information about military bases and operations in Africa, followed by a section on the African Peace and Security Architecture (APSA) as the vehicle for attaining stability through Africa's initiative; solving Africa's security problems through the APSA in collaboration with the respective subregional organizations, and how it contributes to peace and stability in Africa. Following this is a discussion of how the intersection between the peace and security architecture within Africa's regional bodies and foreign military installations affects the discourse and practice of African security.

Foreign Military Bases in Africa

The idea and practice of having military bases overseas date back to ancient Greece and its city-states.[23] However, it was only in the twentieth century, from the late 1930s that overseas military bases in sovereign states gradually became a more accepted reality.[24] The history of modern military bases is traced to the hegemonic engagements by organizations such as NATO and the European Union (EU), whose overseas military installations partly provoked the current development regarding Russia and Ukraine. The Cold War between the two great powers, the Soviet Union (Russia) and United States, spurred a mass race for regional power from 1945 through 1991. When the Soviet Union disintegrated, the United States became a global hegemon in foreign military installations with little competition.[25] However, the contemporary rise to prominence of some historically nontraditional superpowers such as China, Brazil, India, and the Gulf states among others has increased competition for strategic geopolitical and economic partnership (which involves military bases in some cases), and most of such attention is drawn to Africa.

As indicated before, Africa attracts most of the foreign military bases largely because of the region's strategic proximity to the Middle East and Asia as well as the emergence of regional security complexity along the Red Sea among other economic and political reasons.[26] Historically, two foreign powers (the United States and France) have dominated the spaces of military bases and activities in Africa. As Himanshu Dubey notes, the

United States and France are in vanguard of operations on African soil.[27] These foreign militaries operate in crisis zones all over Africa, the most recent instance being in northern Mozambique. However, the first phase of US military bases in Africa ended in the 1970s, largely because of changes in government and public pressure, which resulted in mass opposition as the continent was undergoing the process of decolonization.[28] Before this, however, the French had operated a similar model of security in the continent in the nineteenth century. The idea of French military bases in Africa could be traced back to the former French Interior Minister Charles Pasque, who said, "European security strategy relies on three rings, namely, the Mediterranean, the European continent and the Atlantic. France is the only country that could play an active part in all the three rings."[29] Later, when France's former colonies in Africa began to gain their independence, notably during the 1960s, it started to sign bilateral treaties with its former colonies, with a variety of degrees of military cooperation and support. One of the commitments made in these treaties was to establish French military bases, especially in former French colonies. Therefore, most of the operations involved in protecting French nationals and their allied governments in Africa during the twentieth century used such bases.[30]

Leaving aside the colonial period, foreign military and mercenaries first appeared in Africa during the post-colonial/post-independence era. The African continent embarked on a new phase of state formation and national integration, with different external partners, where security support became key in the stability of the modern state.[31] As Pierre Englebert and Kevin Dunn indicate, political instabilities, civil strife, and the rise of low-intensity violence as well as the emergence of warlords in post-independence Africa resulted in the expansion and proliferation of foreign troops and mercenaries.[32] The period between 1960 and 1990 has been relevant in this context of statehood and foreign military support because of the political transformation that occurred at the time and the resulting sociopolitical realities.[33] Specifically, 1960 is known as the "Year of Africa" because of the many events that occurred at that time—most notably the independence of seventeen African countries—that emphasized the continent's determination for autonomy to address important domestic political and economic matters. However, the promise of solving Africa's problems through African efforts became a significant failure. In the aftermath of independence, many civil disputes and political instabilities pushed the region's socioeconomic development into grave difficulties, attracting more foreign, global interests, which rather compounded the continent's security dilemmas resulting from complexly entwined global and local politics.[34]

Reflecting on the immediate post-colonial era, Robert Lloyd indicates that the African continent beheld two conflicting realities: the euphoria of independence and emancipation, and the difficulties for independent states to forge their future, in particular, in preventing significant threats to the authority of the state.[35] The latter has resulted in the emergence of foreign military or mercenaries on the continent, where individual states have signed various agreements with different foreign powers to boost the security of the state. For instance, during the Year of Africa, Belgium, like Britain and France, intended to flee Africa as soon as possible and granted Congo independence (now the Democratic Republic of the Congo).[36] However, after gaining independence, Congo was soon consumed by political instability, secessionism, and violence.[37] In response to the Congolese conflicts, the United Nations (UN) established its first enormous peacekeeping mission, UN Operations in the Congo (Opération des Nations Unies au Congo, or ONUC), in 1960.[38] When the UN agreed to send peacekeeping forces to Congo, for instance, India played a key role by sending 4,700 personnel. As a result, the number of mercenaries on the continent increased, and now the continent hosts more than thirteen foreign countries that have a considerable presence, especially in the Horn of Africa—not counting UN missions.[39]

Africa is witnessing an increasing number of foreign military missions and outposts. With around eleven foreign military bases, the Horn of Africa has become the epicenter of foreign mercenaries. By 2021, forty-eight foreign military bases were in Africa, with France and the United States having the most bases.[40] While France took the lead in the early days of post-colonial Africa, the United States has currently expanded its bases across the continent.[41] Owing to the phenomenon of rising powers in the global political and market economy linked with foreign bases, so-called nontraditional superpowers such as China, Turkey, Japan, Belgium, and Saudi Arabia each has a military base in Africa, all situated in East Africa, except Belgium, whose military base was in West Africa, precisely in Mali. Presently, most of these military bases are concentrated in East Africa and West Africa, with each region having nineteen and sixteen foreign military bases, respectively. Central Africa follows with eight bases, while North Africa and South Africa host the fewest number of foreign military bases, with two bases and one base, respectively. In terms of individual countries' statistics, Djibouti hosts the highest number of bases with seven, followed by Niger with four. Somalia and Chad also host three bases each, while Kenya, Eritrea, Seychelles, Burkina Faso, Senegal, Central African Republic (CAR), Gabon, and Libya each hosts two bases. Ghana, Somaliland, Cameroon, Uganda, South Sudan, Côte d'Ivoire, Mauritania, the Democratic Republic of the Congo (DRC), and Botswana each has one foreign military base or installation.

As indicated earlier, these military corporations have been hailed as successful in meeting key political and economic needs that domestic governments and international organizations no longer adequately fulfill.[42] Along the political line, the international system, which revolves around the realist atmosphere where states are considered the major actors, and the potential internal and external threats to the authority of the state largely inform the setting up of foreign military and security bases in Africa to prevent crime and create a peaceful coexistence. In line with this, the Horn of Africa and the Red Sea regions have forged the most foreign military installation and operation agreements across the continent because of the strategic geography of these regions that connects the African and Asian continents and because the Gulf is prone to security threats such as terrorism, human trafficking, piracy, and cyberattacks, among others. Also, because of the large scale of terrorist attacks or activities by weak tribal populations all over the continent, the United States established several other bases across the continent in a single voice of maintaining peace and stability on the continent. Similarly, Russia expanded its military influence by providing training programs and security agreements, and sales of arms to fragile states.[43] Thus, the territorial integrity and the desire to ward off threats to internal security lie centrally in the rationale of bilateral agreements that sometimes guarantee foreign military installations in many parts of Africa.

On the economic front, foreign military presence in Africa is deemed to be driven by the fact that some AU member states lease their territories to foreign powers for military bases, mainly for domestic economic gains as well as the strategic economic potential of the host country to the external partner. For instance, Djibouti's hosting of Chinese military base generates more than $300 million annually for the East African country.[44] Besides, Himanshu Dubey argues that China's military base in Djibouti should be viewed as a means of China's economic interest and a ground for conducting naval diplomacy by the Chinese government. Thus, the establishment of a military base in Djibouti took place to strengthen diplomatic relations between Djibouti, China, and Ethiopia, intending to construct the Ethio-Djibouti Railway, the Ethiopia-Djibouti water pipeline, and Chinese investment in Doarleh Multipurpose port.[45]

However, some scholars have pointed out four potential negative implications of these broad economic and political rationales for the increasing militarization of security globally and the corresponding local effect of the presence of foreign military bases across Africa. These concerns touch on related matters: interference in domestic governance spaces, resource exploitation, colonial and neocolonial posturing and correspondent activities against the African partners, and the view of foreign security installations as an illegal practice being endorsed by global governance bodies such as the UN and partner regional organizations.

On the point of governance interference, a case is advanced that some foreign military bases in Africa usually interfere with host-country governance as a result of the oft-extensive military influence from foreign security partners who partly use foreign aid as baits as well. For instance, France had a military presence in Niger that was intimately related to the country's energy sector, and one in every three French light bulbs is fueled by uranium mines in Niger, where the foreign forces were stationed. Also, the US military serves as the world's gendarme, not for the benefit of the global community but for the benefactors of capitalism. For instance, the United States has 7,000 military personnel on rotational deployment housed in military outposts around Africa, including in Uganda, South Sudan, Senegal, Niger, Gabon, Cameroon, and, most importantly, DRC around the oil reserves.[46] In this context, Africa's history with colonial interference in domestic governance raises serious concerns about the sovereignty of African states in such security-related deals with external partners. Not surprisingly, we have seen hardline military regimes in the Sahel ask France and the United States to leave their countries.

Further, the increased attention on Africa by foreign mercenaries is also linked with the rising global competing interests in exploiting natural resources in the continent, where emerging global superpowers such as China, India, and the Gulf states have all demonstrated strong desires to influence domestic policies in foreign lands. In this instance, mercenaries are deemed to be the new face of neocolonialism in Africa in terms of resource exploitation, as the subsoil of Africa contains 98 percent of the world's chromium and 90 percent of the world's cobalt and other precious minerals such as bauxite, diamonds, tantalum, tungsten, and tin.[47] The failure of most African state governments to effectively harness resources that contribute between 30 percent and 50 percent of the continent's total wealth and drive people-centered development programs largely contributes to the constant dependency on foreign capital for development projects.[48] This attracts the interest of foreign geostrategic powers such as the United States and France to integrate military bases as part of foreign support agreements in many parts of Africa. Thus, the leasing of territories by African governments for military bases is mainly influenced by domestic economic gains as well as some member states' proclivity to request external assistance in dealing with serious security challenges.[49]

Besides, some scholars posit that foreign military activities in Africa have made the continent a battleground for hegemonic competition for spaces of influence by foreign powers, with negative implications for the security and stability of the continent, especially in the Sahel and the Horn of Africa. For instance, the growing competition among these foreign governments, particularly relating to their military bases and economic relations with Africa, is transforming into a neo–Cold War on the continent. For example, the intense competition between China and the United States for territories for overseas military installations in Africa is central to their battle for global hegemony.[50] In line with this view, some scholars have criticized foreign military bases for using Africa as a battleground for hegemony and not for the maintenance of peace and security.[51] The general concern here, thus, is that each external power uses foreign military bases as a way of gaining influence and building global hegemony by gaining more possession and alliance with African countries. From this dimension, foreign aid has largely been used as payment for the right to establish military bases across the continent to control its mineral resources. This partly explains why the presence of US military bases in strategically significant regions such as those bordering the Red Sea and the Gulf of Guinea is intensifying.

A final criticism of foreign military bases in Africa concerns the legitimacy of the practice. The prohibition on the use of force, as enshrined in the UN Charter and customary international law, has been used to justify the illegality of foreign military bases in Africa.[52] When it comes to military involvement, one of the most serious issues is legality, and one of the cornerstones of the modern international legal order is the prohibition of the threat or use of force. In fact, Article 2(4) of the UN Charter expressly prohibits UN member states from using force against another state's territorial integrity or political sovereignty, or in any other way that is incompatible with the UN's objectives.[53] For instance, in 2018, intellectuals, academics, and social activists criticized the US-Ghana Status of Forces Agreement (SOFA) as a threat to state integrity. This atmosphere of resistance is reflected, for instance, in most West African countries, where the public is becoming increasingly hostile to the expansion of foreign military bases in the subregion.[54] Large crowds took to the streets in Accra in March 2018 to protest the proposed SOFA, a twenty-million-dollar agreement that would allow the US military to expand its presence in Ghana. Opposition parties, concerned about the possibility of the United States establishing a military base in the country, took part in these protests in parliament. Many described it as a threat to state sovereignty, a roadmap to the collapse of the state.[55] A key concern of the protesters is that many of these foreign establishments have contributed to more security dilemmas in some countries, like Somalia and DRC, pushing them further into states of fragility and collapse.[56] Relatedly, such military installations and operations are also regarded as invasive, which is illegal per international laws about the sovereignty of the state.[57]

The African Peace and Security Architecture

The APSA represents the overarching framework for approaching issues of security and governance in Africa. As captured by the AU Peace and Security Department, "APSA is built around structures, objectives, principles and values, as well as decision-making processes relating to the prevention, management and resolution of crises and conflicts, post-conflict reconstruction and development in the continent."[58] APSA is under the AU's PSC, which was adopted in July 2002 in Durban and came into force in 2003. It is the PSC that serves as the link between the AU on the one hand and the UN and other stakeholders and external partners on the other hand on matters of continental peace and security. As its main pillar, the PSC outlines the various functions of the APSA, which are performed under the Commission, the Panel of the Wise (PoW), the Continental Early Warning System (CEWS), the African Standby Force (ASF), and the Peace Fund. The key functions of the APSA, as mandated under the PSC protocol, include (i) early warning and conflict prevention; (ii) peacemaking, peace support operations, peacebuilding, and post-conflict reconstruction and development; (iii) promotion of democratic practices, good governance, and respect for human rights; and (iv) humanitarian action and disaster management.[59] These functions are performed under the AU in collaboration with the continents' five main subregions, namely the Economic Community of West African States (ECOWAS), the Intergovernmental Authority on Development (IGAD), the Southern African Development Community (SADC), the Economic Community of Central African States (ECCAS), and the Arab Maghreb Union (AMU).[60]

As the embodiment or directorate of Africa's formula for continental peace and security, therefore, the APSA is deemed to be at the center of the discourses and practices about peace, security, and development in the African continent. APSA and other AU mechanisms such as the New Partnership for Africa's Development (NEPAD), Elections and Governance (ACDEG), and the African Charter on Democracy (ACD), established for the promotion of good governance and democracy, are "driven not only by the genuine need to promote human security, democracy, and good governance in African countries, but also by the strategic desire of African leaders to assert African agency in African affairs and thereby thwart the application of Western global liberal governance in Africa."[61] This means that the related activities surrounding foreign military bases pose important implications for African agency, thus the discourses and practices of peace and security in Africa.

The discourses on African peace and security are reflected in three broad themes. First is the state-centered, largely liberalist view, which favors the state and regional and multistate organizations and Western models in the pursuit of a stable Africa. Here, the focus is on restructuring and strengthening liberal-oriented institutions such as state military and security apparatuses, capacity building for modern law courts, democratization, and liberal economic policies among other related ideals.[62] In contrast, the second theme is a broad understanding of the African philosophy of peace and security, mainly through so-called long-standing indigenous or traditional African approaches. This view argues for the maintenance of peace and order using the African knowledge systems through indigenous institutions such as chieftaincy, community cultural representations, and other indigenous settings and procedures as against liberal ideals, which are believed to be largely incongruent with African traditional practices of peace.[63] On the third theme, hybridity is encouraged, involving the embracing of both liberal and traditional approaches in the pursuit of peace and security and a fusing of African regional peace operations and external forces through the UN and other partner states for peace operations.[64]

While all these dimensions of the discourses and associated practices have reflected in Africa, the decades of deteriorating security in the continent have piled immense pressure on the AU and allied subregional organizations and member states as the primary providers of peace in the modern international governance sphere, which involves modular and multidimensional approaches.[65] Thus, like the traditional philosophy on peace and security, the regional bodies through the APSA have upheld the idea of "African solutions to African problems," for instance, as captured in Article 3(b) of the Constitutive Act of the AU (2003),[66] which indicates that the AU is mandated to "defend the sovereignty, territorial integrity and independence of its Member States."[67] This "implies that this is the time for Africans to take things into their own hands and make use of their resources to solve Africa's troubles," especially for "African states to take personal responsibility for preserving peace and stability."[68]

While the idea of African solutions to African problems emerged as part of a strong consensus among African leaders (since the formation of the Organisation of African Unity) and policy and academic actors to reverse the trend of marginalization and exploitation of the continent through centuries-old issues of slavery, colonialism (and neocolonialism), oppression, war, and hunger among other hindrances caused by asymmetric global forces,[69] this self-help idea and associated practices have attracted varying reactions in academic and policy discussions on peace and security in Africa, most of which are critical about the capacity of the AU and subregional bodies to autonomously or with little external support ensure peace and stability in the continent.[70] While the AU and especially Regional Economic Communities (RECs) have contributed significantly to stability in many parts of the continent, many scholars are concerned about key long-standing flaws of the AU, such as limited resource capacity due to poor and weak economies.[71] Besides, the weak political/structural and cultural integration of member states, due to colonial legacies, ideological and related differences, as well as the challenge of hegemonic regional players all hinder the AU's potential to effectively promote peace and stability.[72]

These conditions, therefore, paved the way for the influx of foreign mercenaries into the continent to boost the capacity of state and regional organizations.[73] However, Paul Williams and Arthur Boutellis further argue that the embracing of foreign military activities in Africa seems to weaken or erode the capacity of the AU and RECs to maintain peace and security on the continent, with such foreign-local security collaborations partly compounding insecurities within the region. Such glocalized security concerns in Africa, for instance, were witnessed in November 1970 when Guinea experienced an attempted invasion by Portuguese mercenaries in the country.[74] Although foreign troops are targeted at fighting security dilemmas such as terrorism, which poses a threat to international peace and security (especially after the 9/11 attacks), some of those local-international military operations have been cited for establishing links with terrorists in some parts of the continent.[75] This has partly made it very difficult for the AU and RECs to fight security threats and provide peace, thus the increasing reliance on foreign security establishments with local collaboration, mostly linked with economic support for respective African states and organizations.

Yet there are concerns about the economic dangers of Africa's reliance on foreign military support in Africa. For instance, in 2017 more than ten

African countries, including Senegal, Morocco, Tunisia, Egypt, Liberia, Ghana, Nigeria, South Africa, Kenya, Ethiopia, and Djibouti, received US Foreign Military Financing (FMF). The FMF, to be paid either as grants or loans, was "to provide means for stabilization, counter-terrorism, counternarcotics, coalition operations, interoperability and military relations" and enable partner countries to purchase "U.S. defense articles, services and training."[76] Yet such military-related financing and the associated foreign military bases in Africa have harmed the ability of the AU and RECs to find solutions to both economic and security issues by putting the continent under an unending reliance on foreign aid for economic recovery and peacekeeping activities. The AU is still significantly reliant on outside funding and resources for its peacekeeping activities.

However, the reliance of the AU on outside money and resources for its operations, especially peacekeeping, has hampered the organization's ability to make independent, strategic, and tactical decisions, which raises African state sovereignty issues. For example, African states contribute only 2 percent of the cost of the AU's peace and security operations, whereas outside donors such as the EU provide 98 percent. Consequently, the PSC's ability to establish its agenda has been weakened by the expanding presence of foreign military bases and their participation in political and security matters on the continent.[77] Therefore, the AU's role in maintaining peace and security has been hampered and, in some cases, taken over by these foreign military outposts, while the agency of African states remains weak. However, foreign military bases have largely failed to reflect positively in terms of contributing to successful peacekeeping missions and a sustained peaceful political atmosphere, the primary reasons for African countries' embracing of foreign military bases in their territories.[78] Adding to the important implications of foregoing discussions on security, development, and broadly regional integration, this chapter calls further attention to how foreign military bases affect the discourses and practices associated with this idea of a self-help approach to African peace and security.

Foreign Military and Security Bases and Peace and Security in Africa

Despite the burgeoning literature on the potential and manifest effects of foreign security bases on African countries, the related debates have not adequately addressed how the idea of homegrown solutions to African security challenges is shaped by the increasing external interests in Africa's security affairs. As we argue, external military bases impede the African solutions to African problems approach to African security. This problem is reflected in the compounding overlaps and redundancy of peace and security structures and the hindering of effective localizing of continental security policies at the state and substate levels.

OVERLAPS AND REDUNDANCIES OF PEACE AND SECURITY STRUCTURES

The growing interest by African countries in hosting foreign military bases as part of global partnerships to combat emerging complex security challenges has important implications for the effective functioning of the existing peace and security structures in Africa. Thus, the increasing number of actors—mainly state, multistate, international, and civil society players—and the corresponding institutional, normative, and associational leanings is a compelling topic in contemporary discussions on African politics, security, and development because this phenomenon causes overlapping bureaucracies, structures, and procedures that stifle effective security operations.[79] As we demonstrate subsequently, the various foreign security pacts and establishments in strategic and sensitive jurisdictions in Africa creates disharmonies and structural overlaps in AU and RECs partnerships, RECs and state partnerships, AU and/or RECs, and UN and other multinational organizations' partnerships. For instance, APSA's two main levels of operationalization, continental and subregional, reflect challenging structural arrangements that breed competition, non-correspondence, duplications, and ambiguities in the structures and functions of the AU and RECs. These are further challenged by the individual nations' signing of various security pacts with different global powers, with some conditions not in the full interest of the regional and subregional statutes.

On the aspect of competition, while there exist some examples of complementarity, unhealthy competitions also characterize the interactions between the AU and UN Security Council, the AU and RECs, and among member states within the respective RECs in peacekeeping operations and other security and political arrangements.[80] Besides, the multiple structures with similar tasks from continental to subregional organizations create duplications, non-correspondence, and ambiguities in the roles to be performed. Alex Vines exemplifies this structural non-correspondence between the APSA and at least five of the eight existing RECs within the AU. He observes that, for instance, while ECOWAS and SADC both have a security arm integrated within its structure, each of the Common Market for East and Southern Africa (COMESA) and the East African Community (EAC) does not have security elements or a comprehensive regional membership. Consequently, the responsibility to coordinate the East Africa Brigade (EASBRIG) was ceded to IGAD. Yet Rwanda, Seychelles, and Madagascar are not members of IGAD, leading to the establishment of a new EASBRIG mechanism to address the lapses.[81] Alex Vines stresses that such related matters cause a subsidiary mismatch, underperformance, and noncommitment of member states and RECs to regional or continental duties among others.[82] Therefore, the expansion of foreign military agreements, thus AU's security alliances with NATO, China, and the United States among others, and member states' different external security pacts, for instance, Mali and Niger's military agreements with France and Russia's military pacts with Nigeria and Ethiopia,[83] pose negative implication for continental and subcontinental security structures. That is, these collaborations invariably contribute to the structural tensions and overlaps that negatively impact on the effectiveness of peace and security structures in the continent. A recent, key example of the structural overlaps and tensions is reflected in how the Biden administration prioritizes a strengthening of twenty-seven US outposts in Africa, while the US Africa command (Africom) sees counterterrorism in the Horn of Africa and the Sahel regions as Africa's topmost concern.[84]

Similarly, structural overlaps and tensions also create ambiguities in APSA's mandate on security operations with member states and RECs. For instance, international law grants RECs autonomy in their relationship with the AU in terms of peace and security operations. However, AU's Constitutive Act also grants the continental body the powers to first sanction such operations of the RECs. Yet there is no provision of a caveat in international law concerning under what conditions, for instance, RECs could act without consent from the AU in terms of peace and security operations. Although these ambiguous operations have brought some compliance over the decades, they have also led to cases where the RECs have acted ahead of and without sanction from the AU. For example, the AU only played a catch-up role in ECOWAS efforts during the crisis in Mali in 2012.[85] Similarly, the failure of ECOWAS to act decisively on Mali's controversial agreements with the Wagner group of mercenaries linked with Moscow, for instance, also indicates the ambiguousness of RECs' role in dealing with such related security agreements and operations within existing regional peace and security structures.

These prevalent structural tensions and incoherence have two broad serious implications in the era of growing foreign military establishments in Africa. First, foreign military agreements in Africa could exacerbate RECs' different stances on matters of security. As most of such partnerships are linked with economic benefits, coupled with other factors such as ideological, cultural, and political differences, host countries will increasingly have inconsistent stances within the respective RECs. Besides, volatile regions, for instance within IGAD and ECOWAS, would most likely adopt different positions from relatively stable regions within SADC and the Maghreb region concerning the nature of agreements with external partners in terms of security installations and operations. Second, the foreign security bases are invariably adding to the bureaucratic overlaps that characterize the AU and RECs. This follows the intense glocalization of militarized human security in Africa, coupled with the fact that member states and regional actors taking part in such security arrangements face potential dilemmas of enabling those agreements to rival or usurp juridical powers of the existing regional organizations or add more challenging bureaucracy to the structures in charge of peace and security. These compound the tensions, ambiguities, redundancies, and ineffectiveness in the collaborations between RECs and the AU and related multinational organizations on peace and security in Africa.

LIMITED LOCALIZATION OF CONTINENTAL SECURITY POLICIES

The growing phenomena of foreign security agreements in Africa could further promote the prevalent situation of the limited reflection of regional security frameworks at the local level and national and subnational arenas.[86] In other words, foreign military agreements will potentially embolden the predominantly elite and state-centric view of security that has produced minimal results on the ground in contemporary times.[87] With the US-led global stabilization mission (post-9/11), which involves the militarization of security, including in Africa,[88] the mandates of foreign military bases usually target so-called threats to the authority of the state and territorial integrity. Indeed, some key nontraditional security issues, such as the liberalization agenda on democracy, human rights and human security,[89] civil society's roles in peace and security,[90] and climate and environmental security have been reflected in regional peace and security arrangements.[91] However, the largely traditional view and practice of security in foreign security arrangements in Africa could compound the already failed attempts to translate regional and subregional norm regimes and thus peace and security frameworks to the ground, where the impact is usually felt the most.[92]

This top-down, elite-centered, and state-oriented nature of foreign security operations in Africa poses a further challenge to the long-standing difficulty of reflecting regional norms on the ground. This means that with the promise of foreign security arrangements to address security crises, especially in the Horn of Africa and the Sahelian regions of the continent,[93] more concentration is likely to be on external models, strategies, and views of security being forged with local elites, as already being witnessed, which is usually not in synch with local realities.[94] This further reduces the potential of African citizens' understanding and practice of "African solution to African problems" as framed and diffused through APSA's collaboration with RECs. The bottom line here is that while there is an increasing realization of local realities, for instance, in China's strategic reframing of established norms on security and development to gain legitimacy in its security operations in Africa,[95] the elite-centered and interest-based engagements of foreign security-related activities pose a serious threat to the efforts to localize the discourses and practices of African peace and security by African citizens. While Emmanuel Bombande suggests that the growing civil society contribution to regional security matters indicates some intent by regional and national actors to translate such norms to the masses,[96] Christian Ani asserts that conscious efforts are not made to localize regional and global security norms and practices because of local elites' co-option of peace and security programs and the RECs and AU's overreliance on international support.[97] Therefore, foreign security arrangements in Africa could potentially weaken the promise of bottom-up peace and security in the continent.

Conclusion: Glocalized Security, State Sovereignty, and the Practice of Security

The chapter sets out to examine how the rising number of foreign security bases on the continent—a reflection of glocalized militarization of security—affects the discourse and practice of African security through the famous phrase "African solutions to African problems," which raises issues of state sovereignty in Africa. Indeed, Africa has become an epicenter of global attempts to localize the US-led stabilization mission to fight contemporary security dilemmas. In this move to apply and reconcile external norms to the African terrain to address political instability in the continent, one of the key partnerships that are usually formed involves the establishment of foreign military and security bases in strategic parts of the continent through bilateral agreements with African states. The establishment of foreign military bases has become a growing phenomenon characterized by the competition among traditional and emerging global powers for territories. While potentially contributing to global order, in the predominant claim to address security volatilities in Africa, foreign security bases also become strategic spheres of global political and economic influence. This trend of competition among foreign powers for security alliances in the continent may keep increasing, given the resource endowment, market potential, and geostrategic location of Africa, especially the eastern and western parts of the continent. Consequently, the establishment and operations of foreign security bases have added to the existing bureaucracies in charge of peace and security on the continent. At the same time, the sovereignty of African states becomes increasingly precarious without necessarily adding to the efficacy of pan-African peace and security mechanisms.

This chapter shows that the glocalized view and practice of security, which embrace foreign military bases in Africa, further complicate the existing difficulty in reconciling global and continental norms of peace and security to local realities in Africa. This poses serious implications for the pursuit of African regional security, as it distorts the challenging idea of "African solutions to African problems" in two important ways. First, the corresponding security arrangements further increase the overlaps and redundancies of structures in charge of peace and security. This exacerbates the weaknesses of the AU and subregional bodies in providing coordinated, committed, and proactive peace and security support in the continent. Second, external security arrangements in Africa limit the potential to localize continental security policies at the state and substate levels. This is caused by the militarized and elite-centered approach to peace and security through such agreements with foreign governments, which reduces genuine engagements with the masses to promote endogenous norms on African peace and security as captured in AU's Agenda 2063 and other regional peace and security frameworks. Therefore, foreign military bases pose a grave potential to further hinder the proper functioning of African-owned security structures and processes, increasing the dilemmas surrounding the continent's prevalent security threats, and in worse cases undermining the sovereignty of African states.

In the end, glocalization provides a lens for examining the African state through the domestic and external drivers of securitization and the implications for state sovereignty. Indeed, African states have faced significant challenges in maintaining peace. Despite the AU efforts, the pan-African and regional security mechanisms still lack full capacity, especially because of poor logistics and funding. These deficits in African security, coupled with the growing domestic and external threats to state security and human security in Africa, have reinvigorated the external military involvement in Africa, notably through the establishment of military bases under bilateral agreements that feed into geopolitical competition among major powers and elite economic and political interests in African states. All of these point to how the sovereignty of African states becomes even more vulnerable under dubious neocolonial and geopolitical agendas. This chapter goes back to the fundamental question of pan-African security through the APSA and how bilateral agreements by African states to host foreign military bases may effectively undermine the effort to have African solutions to African problems and assert African agency in security matters within Africa. This becomes a problem not only for the AU and the RECs, but also for the states that are hosting foreign military bases, especially as domestic political and economic calculations of those states change. Once foreign military bases are fully entrenched, state sovereignty becomes increasingly vulnerable and human security remains a major challenge.

Notes

1. Sun, "Outpost for Power Projection," 53–69; CSIS, *Africa's Security Challenges*.

2. Klin, "The Significance of Foreign Military Bases as Instruments of Spheres of Influence," 120–44, 124.

3. Vines, "A Decade of African Peace and Security Architecture," 89–109; Young and Khan, "Extended States," 99–126.

4. CSIS, *Africa's Security Challenges*.

5. Atta-Asamoah, *Proceed with Caution*.

6. AU, "The Constitutive Act of African Union," 1–21.

7. Dubey, "Africa's Growing Foreign Military Bases," 1–8.

8. CSIS, *Africa's Security Challenges*.

9. Statistica (2023), "Forecast of the Total Population of Africa from 2020 to 2050," https://www.statista.com/statistics/1224205/forecast-of-the-total-population-of-africa/#:~:text=According%20to%20the%20forecast%2C%20Africa's,as%20the%20most%20populous%20countries.

10. Gelot and Sandor, "African Security and Global Militarism," 521–42.

11. Ashaba et al., "State Fragility, Regime Survival and Spoilers in South Sudan," 77–99.

12. dos Santos Lersch and Sarti, "The Establishment of Foreign Military Bases and the International Distribution of Power," L14–115.

13. Ramutsindela, "Scaling Peace and Peacemakers in Transboundary Parks," 69–82; Marfo et al., "Beyond Classical Peace Paradigm," 47–55.

14. Robertson, "Globalisation or Glocalisation?" 33–52.

15. Robertson, "Globalisation or Glocalisation?" 33–52.

16. Gpi, "Measuring Peace in a Complex World," 1–100.

17. Marfo et al., "Beyond Classical Peace Paradigm," 47–55; Bah, "African Agency in New Humanitarianism and Responsible Governance," 148–69.

18. Gerson, "US Foreign Military Bases and Military Colonialism," 44–70; dos Santos Lersch and Sarti, "The Establishment of Foreign Military Bases and the International Distribution of Power," 114–15; Stergiou, "The Exceptional Case of the British Military Bases on Cyprus," 285–300.

19. Francis, "Mercenary Intervention in Sierra Leone," 319–38; Shearer, *Private Armies and Military Intervention.*

20. dos Santos Lersch and Sarti, "The Establishment of Foreign Military Bases and the International Distribution of Power," 114–15; Bitar, *US Military Bases, Quasi-Bases, and Domestic Politics in Latin America.*

21. Elmahly and Sun, "China's Military Diplomacy towards Arab Countries in Africa's Peace and Security," 111–34; Lob, "Iran's Foreign Policy and Developmental Activities in Africa," 68–98; Young and Khan, "Extended states," 99–126.

22. Packenham, *Liberal America and the Third World*; Klin, "The Significance of Foreign Military Bases as Instruments of Spheres of Influence," 120–44; Ylönen, "Engaging Foreign Powers for Regime Survival," 249–71.

23. Harkavy, *Strategic Basing and the Great Powers, 1200–2000.*

24. dos Santos Lersch and Sarti, "The Establishment of Foreign Military Bases and the International Distribution of Power," 114–15; Conversino, "Embattled Garrisons," 994.

25. Dubey, "Africa's Growing Foreign Military Bases," 1–8.

26. Dubey, "Africa's Growing Foreign Military Bases," 1–8.

27. Dubey, "Africa's Growing Foreign Military Bases," 1–8.

28. Tricontinental, "Defending Our Sovereignty," 1–39.

29. Keiger, *France and the World since 1870.*

30. Hansen, *The French Military in Africa.*

31. Klin, "The Significance of Foreign Military Bases as Instruments of Spheres of Influence," 120–44; Melvin, "The Foreign Military Presence in the Horn of Africa Region," 7–8.

32. Englebert and Dunn, *Inside African Politics.*

33. Ng'Oma, "Challenges of Democratic Consolidation in Africa," 107–19.

34. McDonnell and Fine, "Pride and Shame in Ghana," 121–42.

35. Lloyd, "Conflict in Africa," 171–86; Odhiambo, "The Origins and Evolution of Anglo-Kenyan Military Diplomatic Relations since 1963," 1–44.

36. Kamais, "Military Integration of Armed Groups as a Conflict Resolution Approach in Africa," 1–16.

37. Kamais, "Military Integration of Armed Groups as a Conflict Resolution Approach in Africa," 1–16.

38. Johansson and Larsson, "A Model for Understanding Stress and Daily Experiences among Soldiers in Peacekeeping Operations," 124–41; Kamais, "Military Integration of Armed Groups as a Conflict Resolution Approach in Africa," 1–16.

39. Melvin, "The Foreign Military Presence in the Horn of Africa Region," 7–8.

40. Dubey, "Africa's Growing Foreign Military Bases," 1–8; Odhiambo, "The Origins and Evolution of Anglo-Kenyan Military Diplomatic Relations since 1963," 1–44.

41. Campbell, "The United States and Security in Africa," 45–71.

42. Dubey, "Africa's Growing Foreign Military Bases," 1–8; Shearer, *Private Armies and Military Intervention.*

43. Aluwaisheg, *Why Red Sea Security Is a Global Concern.*

44. Atta-Asamoah, *Proceed with Caution.*

45. Dubey, "Africa's Growing Foreign Military Bases," 1–8.

46. Melvin, "The Foreign Military Presence in the Horn of Africa Region," 7–8.

47. Olanrewaju and Olanrewaju, "Natural Resources, Conflict and Security Challenges in Africa," 552–68.

48. Bah, "People-Centered Liberalism," 989–1007.

49. Hahn, *Two Centuries of US Military Operations in Liberia.*

50. Shearer, *Private Armies and Military Intervention*; Dos Santos Lersch and Sarti, "The Establishment of Foreign Military Bases and the International Distribution of Power," 114–15.

51. Kitio, "The Rising Security Cooperation of Turkey in Africa," 17–36; Borshchevskaya, *The Role of Russian Private Military Contractors in Africa*; Matisek, "International Competition to Provide Security Force Assistance in Africa," 102–13.

52. Amouri, "An Examination of Unlawful Foreign Military Operations in Africa," 298.

53. Amouri, "An Examination of Unlawful Foreign Military Operations in Africa," 298.

54. dos Santos Lersch and Sarti, "The Establishment of Foreign Military Bases and the International Distribution of Power," 114–15.

55. Dubey, "Africa's Growing Foreign Military Bases," 1–8; Hahn, *Two Centuries of US Military Operations in Liberia*; Odhiambo, "The Origins and Evolution of Anglo-Kenyan Military Diplomatic Relations Since 1963," 1–44.

56. Lloyd, "Conflict in Africa," 171–86.

57. Hahn, *Two Centuries of US Military Operations in Liberia.*

58. AU Peace and Security Department, *The African Peace and Security Architecture (APSA).*

59. AU Peace and Security Department, *The African Peace and Security Architecture (APSA)*.

60. Møller, "Africa's Sub-Regional Organisations," 1–31, 1.

61. Bah, "African Agency in New Humanitarianism and Responsible Governance," 148–69, 149.

62. Zwanenburg, "Regional Organisations and the Maintenance of International Peace and Security," 483–508; Atuobi and Aning, "Responsibility to Protect in Africa," 90–113; Tom, *Liberal Peace and Post-Conflict*.

63. Murithi, "African Indigenous and Endogenous Approaches to Peace and Conflict Resolution," 16–30; Arthur et al., "An Analysis of the Influence of Ubuntu Principle on the South Africa Peace Building Process," 63–77; Hakorimana and Busingye, "The Concept of Peace," 15–34.

64. Boege et al., "Building Peace and Political Community in Hybrid Political Orders," 599–615; Belloni, "Hybrid Peace Governance," 21–38; Paalo and Issifu, "De-Internationalizing Hybrid Peace," 406–24; Prinsloo, "The AU/UN Hybrid Peace Operation in Africa," 218–96; Tardy, "Hybrid Peace Operations," 95.

65. Laakso, "Beyond the Notion of Security Community," 489–502; Brosig and Sempijja, "What Peacekeeping Leaves Behind," 21–52.

66. AU, *The Constitutive Act of African Union*.

67. The OAU Charter, *OAU Charter*; AU, *Agenda 2063*.

68. Lipman, "African Solutions for African Problems?" 4.

69. Solomon, "African Solutions to Africa's Problems?" 45–76; Tlałka, "Between High Hopes and Moderate Results—A Decade of the African Peace and Security Architecture," 309–41.

70. Tlałka, "Between High Hopes and Moderate Results—A Decade of the African Peace and Security Architecture," 309–41.

71. Williams, "The African Union's Peace Operations," 97–118; Pugh, "Peace Operations," 415–30; Jentzsch, "Opportunities and Challenges to Financing African Union Peace Operations," 86–107.

72. Tlałka, "Between High Hopes and Moderate Results—A Decade of the African Peace and Security Architecture," 309–41.

73. Williams and Boutellis, "Partnership Peacekeeping," 254–78.

74. Williams and Boutellis, "Partnership Peacekeeping," 254–78.

75. Young and Khan, "Extended States," 99–126.

76. MSS Defence, *Foreign Military Financing—Africa*.

77. Campbell, "The United States and Security in Africa," 45–71.

78. Gelot and Sandor, "African Security and Global Militarism," 521–42.

79. Vines, "A Decade of African Peace and Security Architecture," 89–109; Tlałka, "Between High Hopes and Moderate Results—A Decade of the African Peace and Security Architecture," 309–41.

80. Vines, "A Decade of African Peace and Security Architecture," 89–109.

81. Vines, "A Decade of African Peace and Security Architecture," 101.

82. Vines, "A Decade of African Peace and Security Architecture," 101.

83. Smith, *Russia Is Building Its Military Influence in Africa, Challenging U.S. and French Dominance.*

84. Smith, *Russia Is Building Its Military Influence in Africa, Challenging U.S. and French Dominance.*

85. Vines, "A Decade of African Peace and Security Architecture," 89–109, 104.

86. Croese et al., "Bringing the Global to the Local," 435–47; Paalo, "A Systemic Understanding of Hybrid Peace," 1–31.

87. Obi, "The African Union and the Prevention of Democratic Reversal in Africa," 60–85.

88. Campbell, "The United States and Security in Africa," 45–71; Conteh-Morgan, "Militarization and Securitization in Africa," 77–94.

89. Bah, "African Agency in New Humanitarianism and Responsible Governance," 148–69.

90. Tieku, "African Union Promotion of Human Security in Africa," 26–37; Olonisakin, "ECOWAS and Civil Society Movements in West Africa," 105–12; Bah, "Civil Non-State Actors in Peacekeeping and Peacebuilding in West Africa," 313–36.

91. Abiodun, "Securitization of Non-Traditional Security Threats by the Economic Community of West African States (ECOWAS), 1999–2009," 1–7.

92. Paalo, "A Systemic Understanding of Hybrid Peace," 1–31.

93. Dagne, *Africa.*

94. SIRADAĞ, "Understanding French Foreign and Security Policy towards Africa," 100–22; Campbell, "The United States and Security in Africa," 45–71; Jowell, "The Unintended Consequences of Foreign Military Assistance in Africa," 102–19.

95. Alden and Large, "On Becoming a Norms Maker," 123–42.

96. Bombande, "The Role of WANEP in Crafting Peace and Security Architecture in West Africa," 119–42.

97. Ani, "The Rationale for Afsol in Peace and Security," 4.

References

Abiodun, Adams Isiaka. "Securitization of Non-Traditional Security Threats by the Economic Community of West African States (ECOWAS), 1999–2009" (2013): 1–7.

Alden, Chris, and Daniel Large. "On Becoming a Norms Maker: Chinese Foreign Policy, Norms Evolution and the Challenges of Security in Africa." *China Quarterly* 221 (2015): 123–42.

Aluwaisheg, Abdel Aziz. "Why Red Sea Security Is a Global Concern." *Arab News*, April 1 2019. https://www.arabnews.com/node/1476051.

Amouri, Baya. "An Examination of Unlawful Foreign Military Operations in Africa." *African Human Rights Yearbook* (2020): 298.

Ani, Ndubuisi Christian. "The Rationale for AfSol in Peace and Security: The Global, National and Regional Precipitants." *AfSol* 2 (2018): 4.

Arthur, Dominic Degraft, Abdul Karim Issifu, and Samuel Marfo. "An Analysis of the Influence of Ubuntu Principle on the South Africa Peace Building Process." *Journal of Global Peace and Conflict* 3, no. 2 (2015): 63–77.

Ashaba, Ivan M., Sebastian A. Paalo, and Samuel Adu-Gyamfi. "State Fragility, Regime Survival and Spoilers in South Sudan." *International Journal of Afro-Asiatic Studies* 23, no. 1 (2019): 77–99.

Atta-Asamoah, Andrews. "Proceed with Caution: Africa's Growing Foreign Military Presence, *ISS.* 2019. https://issafrica.org/iss-today/proceed-with-caution-africas-growing-foreign-military-presence.

Atuobi, Samuel, and Kwesi Aning. "Responsibility to Protect in Africa: An Analysis of the African Union's Peace and Security Architecture." *Global Responsibility to Protect* 1, no. 1 (2009): 90–113.

AU. The Constitutif Act of African Union: The Constitutive Act 2003. https://au.int/sites/default/files/pages/34873-file-constitutiveact_en.pdf.

———. "Agenda 2063: The Africa We Want." African Union. February 2020. https://au.int/agenda2063/overview.

AU Peace and Security Department. "The African Peace and Security Architecture (APSA)." October 2012. https://www.peaceau.org/en/topic/the-african-peace-and-security-architecture-apsa.

Bah, Abu Bakarr. "African Agency in New Humanitarianism and Responsible Governance." *International Security and Peacebuilding* (2017): 148–69.

———. "Civil Non-State Actors in Peacekeeping and Peacebuilding in West Africa." *Journal of International Peacekeeping* 17, no. 3–4 (2013): 313–36.

———. "Introduction: The Conundrums of Global Liberal Governance." *International Security and Peacebuilding. Africa, the Middle East, and Europe* (2017): 1–25.

———. "People-Centered Liberalism: An Alternative Approach to International State-Building in Sierra Leone and Liberia." *Critical Sociology* 43, no. 7–8 (2017): 989–1007.

Belloni, Roberto. "Hybrid Peace Governance: Its Emergence and Significance." *Global Governance* (2012): 21–38.

Bitar, Sebastian E. *US Military Bases, Quasi-Bases, and Domestic Politics in Latin America.* New York: Springer, 2016.

Boege, Volker, Anne Brown, Kevin Clements, and Anna Nolan. "Building Peace and Political Community in Hybrid Political Orders." *International Peacekeeping* 16, no. 5 (2009): 599–615.

Bombande, Emmanuel. "The Role of WANEP in Crafting Peace and Security Architecture in West Africa." *Civil Society, Peace, and Power* (2016): 119–42.

Borshchevskaya, Anna. "The Role of Russian Private Military Contractors in Africa." *Foreign Policy and Research Institute.* 2020. https://www.fpri.org/article/2020/08/the-role-of-russian-private-military-contractors-in-africa/.

Branca, Eleonora. "Complicity of States in Partnered Drone Operations." *Journal of Conflict and Security Law* 27, no. 2 (2022): 253–78.

Brosig, Malte, and Norman Sempijja. "What Peacekeeping Leaves Behind: Evalu-ating the Effects of Multi-Dimensional Peace Operations in Africa." *Conflict, Security & Development* 17, no. 1 (2017): 21–52.

Campbell, Horace G. "The United States and Security In Africa: The Impact of the Military Management of the International System." *Africa Development* 42, no. 3 (2017): 45–71.

Conteh-Morgan, Earl. "Militarization and Securitization in Africa." *Insight Turkey* 21, no. 1 (2019): 77–94.

Conversino, Mark J. "Embattled Garrisons: Comparative Base Politics and American Globalism." *Journal of Military History* 74, no. 3 (2010): 994.

Croese, Sylvia, Michael Oloko, David Simon, and Sandra C. Valencia. "Bringing the Global to the Local: The Challenges of Multi-Level Governance for Global Policy Implementation in Africa." *International Journal of Urban Sustainable Development* 13, no. 3 (2021): 435–47.

CSIS. "Africa's Security Challenges: A View from Congress, the Pentagon, and USAID." Centre for Strategic and International Studies. 2021. https://www.csis.org/analysis/africas-security-challenges-view-congress-pentagon-and-usaid.

Dagne, Ted. *Africa: US Foreign Assistance Issues*. Collingdale, PA: Diane Publishing, 2009.

dos Santos Lersch, Bruna, and Josiane Simão Sarti. "The Establishment of Foreign Military Bases and the International Distribution of Power." *UFRGS Model United Nations* 2 (2014): 114–15.

Dubey, Himanshu. "Africa's Growing Foreign Military Bases." *CSS Issue Brief* (January 2021): 1–8.

Englebert, Pierre, and Kevin C. Dunn. "Inside African Politics." In *Inside African Politics*. Boulder, CO: Lynne Rienner, 2022.

Elmahly, Hend, and Degang Sun. "China's Military Diplomacy towards Arab Countries in Africa's Peace and Security: The Case of Djibouti." *Contemporary Arab Affairs* 11, no. 4 (2018): 111–34.

Francis, David J. "Mercenary Intervention in Sierra Leone: Providing National Security or International Exploitation?" *Third World Quarterly* 20, no. 2 (1999): 319–38.

Gelot, Linnéa, and Adam Sandor. "African Security and Global Militarism." *Conflict, Security & Development* 19, no. 6 (2019): 521–42.

Gerson, Joseph. "US Foreign Military Bases and Military Colonialism: Personal and Analytical Perspectives." *The Bases of Empire: The Global Struggle against US Military Posts* (2009): 44–70.

GPI. "Measuring Peace in a Complex World." *Institute of Economics & Peace* (2022): 1–100. https://www.economicsandpeace.org/wp-content/uploads/2022/06/GPI-2022-web.pdf.

Hahn, Niels S. *Two Centuries of US Military Operations in Liberia: Challenges of Resistance and Compliance*. Montgomery, AL: Air University Press, 2020.

Hakorimana, Desire, and Godard Busingye. "The Concept of Peace: An African Perspective." In *Palgrave Handbook of Sustainable Peace and Security in Africa*, 15–34. London: Palgrave Macmillan, 2022.

Hansen, Andrew. "The French Military in Africa. Council on Foreign Relations Backgrounder." *Council on Foreign Relations.* 2008. https://www.cfr.org/backgrounder/french-military-africa.

Harkavy, Robert E. *Strategic Basing and the Great Powers, 1200–2000.* London: Routledge, 2007.

ISS-Africa. "African Solutions to African Problems." *Institute for Security Studies.* September 2008. https://issafrica.org/iss-today/african-solutions-to-african-problems.

Jentzsch, Corinna. "Opportunities and Challenges to Financing African Union Peace Operations." *African Conflict and Peacebuilding Review* 4, no. 2 (2014): 86–107.

Johansson, Eva, and Gerry Larsson. "A Model for Understanding Stress and Daily Experiences among Soldiers in Peacekeeping Operations." *Journal of International Peacekeeping* 5, no. 3 (1998): 124–41.

Jowell, Marco. "The Unintended Consequences of Foreign Military Assistance in Africa: An Analysis of Peacekeeping Training in Kenya." *Journal of Eastern African Studies* 12, no. 1 (2018): 102–19.

Kamais, Cosmas Ekwom. "Military Integration of Armed Groups as a Conflict Resolution Approach in Africa: Good Strategy or Bad Compromise?" *Open Access Library Journal* 6, no. 6 (2019): 1.

Keiger, John FV. *France and the World since 1870.* London: Hodder Arnold, 2001.

Kitio, Alexe Kenfack. "The Rising Security Cooperation of Turkey in Africa: An Assessment from the Military Perspective." *American Journal of Economics and Business* Management 3, no. 4 (2020): 17–36.

Klin, Tomasz. "The Significance of Foreign Military Bases as Instruments of Spheres of Influence." *Croatian International Relations Review* 26, no. 87 (2020): 120–44.

Laakso, Liisa. "Beyond the Notion of Security Community: What Role for the African Regional Organizations in Peace and Security?" *The Round Table* 94, no. 381 (2005): 489–502.

Lipman, Elyse. "African Solutions for African Problems? The Philosophy, Politics and Economics of African Peacekeeping in Darfur and Liberia." *Penn Journal of Philosophy, Politics & Economics* 5, no. 1 (2010): 4.

Lloyd, Robert B. "Conflict in Africa." *Journal of the Middle East and Africa* 1, no. 2 (2010): 171–86.

Lob, Eric. "Iran's Foreign Policy and Developmental Activities in Africa: Between Expansionist Ambitions and Hegemonic Constraints." In *The Gulf States and the Horn of Africa*, 68–98. Manchester: Manchester University Press, 2022.

Marfo, Samuel, Halidu Musah, and D. D. Arthur. "Beyond Classical Peace Paradigm: A Theoretical Argument for a 'Glocalized Peace and Security.'" *African Journal of Political Science and International Relations* 20, no. 4 (2016): 47–55.

Matisek, Jahara. "International Competition to Provide Security Force Assistance in Africa." *PRISM* 9, no. 1 (2020): 102–13.

McDonnell, Erin Metz, and Gary Alan Fine. "Pride and Shame in Ghana: Collective Memory and Nationalism among Elite Students." *African Studies Review* 54, no. 3 (2011): 121–42.

Melvin, Neil. "The Foreign Military Presence in the Horn of Africa Region." *International Peace Research Institute (SPRI)* (April 2019): 7–8.

Møller, Bjørn. "Africa's Sub-Regional Organisations: Seamless Web or Patchwork?" *Crisis States Working Papers Series* no. 2 (2009): 1–31.

MSS Defence. FMF–Foreign Military Financing–Africa (2022). https://www.mss-defence.com/fmf-foreign-military-financing-africa/.

Murithi, Tim. "African Indigenous and Endogenous Approaches to Peace and Conflict Resolution." *Peace and Conflict in Africa* (2008): 16–30.

Neethling, T. "Why Foreign Countries Are Scrambling to Set Up Bases in Africa." *The Conservation.* 2020. https://globelynews.com/africa/foreign-bases-africa/#:~:text=But%20there%20are%20other%20motivations,focus%20of%20rising%20global%20competition.

Ng'oma, Alex Mwamba. "Challenges of Democratic Consolidation in Africa: Implications for India's Investment Drive." *India Quarterly* 72, no. 2 (2016): 107–19.

The OAU Charter. "OAU Charter." Addis Ababa, May 25, 1963. https://au.int/sites/default/files/treaties/7759-file-oau_charter_1963.pdf.

Obi, Cyril. "The African Union and the Prevention of Democratic Reversal in Africa: Navigating the Gaps." *African Conflict and Peacebuilding Review* 4, no. 2 (2014): 60–85.

Odhiambo, Elijah O. S. "The Origins and Evolution of Anglo-Kenyan Military Diplomatic Relations Since 1963." *Open Access Library Journal* 8, no. 9 (2021): 1–44.

Olanrewaju, Faith Osasumwen, Segun Joshua, and Adekunle Olanrewaju. "Natural Resources, Conflict and Security Challenges in Africa." *India Quarterly* 76, no. 4 (2020): 552–68.

Olonisakin, 'Funmi. "ECOWAS and Civil Society Movements in West Africa." *IDS Bulletin* 40, no. 2 (2009): 105–12.

Paalo, Sebastian Angzoorokuu. "A Systemic Understanding of Hybrid Peace: An Examination of Hybrid Political Orders in African Peace Governance." *African Conflict & Peacebuilding Review* 11, no. 1 (2021): 1–31.

———, and Abdul Karim Issifu. "De-Internationalizing Hybrid Peace: State-Traditional Authority Collaboration and Conflict Resolution in Northern Ghana." *Journal of Intervention and Statebuilding* 15, no. 3 (2021): 406–24.

Packenham, Robert A. "Liberal America and the Third World." In *Liberal America and the Third World.* Princeton, NJ: Princeton University Press, 2015.

Prinsloo, Barend Louwrens. "The AU/UN Hybrid Peace Operation in Africa: A New Approach to Maintain International Peace and Security." PhD diss.,

The North-West University, South Africa, 2012. https://repository.nwu.ac.za/bitstream/handle/10394/11076/Prinsloo_BL_Chapter_6.pdf?sequence=7.

Pugh, Michael. "Peace Operations." In *Security Studies*, edited by Paul D. Williams and Matt McDonald, 415–30. London: Routledge, 2012.

Ramutsindela, Maano. "Scaling Peace and Peacemakers in Transboundary Parks: Understanding Glocalization." *Peace Parks: Conservation and Conflict Resolution* (2007): 69–82.

Robertson, Roland. "Globalisation or Glocalisation?" *Journal of International Communication* 1, no. 1 (1994): 33–52.

Sarkozy, Nicolas. *The French White Paper on Defence and National Security*. Paris: Odile Jacob, 2008.

Shearer, David. *Private Armies and Military Intervention*. London: Routledge, 2020.

SIRADAĞ, Abdurrahim. "Understanding French Foreign and Security Policy towards Africa: Pragmatism or Altruism." *Afro Eurasian Studies* 3, no. 1 (2014): 100–22.

Smith, Elliot. "Russia Is Building Its Military Influence in Africa, Challenging US and French Dominance." *CNBC*, September 13, 2021. https://www.cnbc.com/2021/09/13/russia-is-building-military-influence-in-africa-challenging-us-france.html.

Solomon, Hussein. "African Solutions to Africa's Problems? African Approaches to Peace, Security and Stability." *Scientia Militaria: South African Journal of Military Studies* 43, no. 1 (2015): 45–76.

Statistica. "Forecast of the Total Population of Africa from 2020 to 2050." 2023. https://www.statista.com/statistics/1224205/forecast-of-the-total-population-of-africa/#:~:text=According%20to%20the%20forecast%2C%20Africa's,as%20the%20most%20populous%20countries.

Stergiou, Andreas. "The Exceptional Case of the British Military Bases on Cyprus." *Middle Eastern Studies* 51, no. 2 (2015): 285–300.

Sun, Degang. "Outpost for Power Projection: A Chinese Perspective of French Military Bases on African Continent." *Journal of Cambridge Studies* 6, no. 4 (2011): 53–69.

Tardy, Thierry. "Hybrid Peace Operations: Rationale and Challenges." *Global Governance* 20 (2014): 95.

Tieku, Thomas Kwasi. "African Union Promotion of Human Security in Africa." *African Security Review* 16, no. 2 (2007): 26–37.

Tlałka, Krzysztof. "Between High Hopes and Moderate Results—A Decade of the African Peace and Security Architecture." *Politeja-Pismo Wydziału Studiów Międzynarodowych i Politycznych Uniwersytetu Jagiellońskiego* 13, no. 42 (2016): 309–41.

Tom, Patrick. *Liberal Peace and Post-Conflict Peacebuilding in Africa*. New York: Springer, 2017.

Tricontinental. "Defending Our Sovereignty: US Military Bases in Africa and the Future of African Unity." *Tricontinental: Institute for Social Research* 42 (2021): 1–39.

Turse, Nick. "Pentagon's Own Map of US Bases in Africa Contradicts Its Claim of 'Light' Footprint." *Intercept*, February 27, 2020.

Vine, David. "The United States Probably Has More Foreign Military Bases Than Any Other People, Nation, or Empire in History." *The Nation*, September 14, 2015, 14.

Vines, Alex. "A Decade of African Peace and Security Architecture." *International Affairs* 89, no. 1 (2013): 89–109.

Williams, Paul D. "The African Union's Peace Operations: A Comparative Analysis." *African Security* 2, no. 2–3 (2009): 97–118.

———, and Arthur Boutellis. "Partnership Peacekeeping: Challenges and Opportunities in the United Nations–African Union Relationship." *African Affairs* 113, no. 451 (2014): 254–78.

Ylönen, Aleksi. "Engaging Foreign Powers for Regime Survival: The Relative Autonomy of Coastal Horn of Africa States in Their Relations with Gulf Countries." In *The Gulf States and the Horn of Africa*, 249–271.

Young, Karen E., and Taimur Khan. "Extended States: The Politics and Purpose of United Arab Emirates Economic Statecraft in the Horn of Africa." In *The Gulf States and the Horn of Africa*, 99–126.

Zwanenburg, Marten. "Regional Organisations and the Maintenance of International Peace and Security: Three Recent Regional African Peace Operations." *Journal of Conflict and Security Law* 11, no. 3 (2006): 483–508.

About the Contributors

Abu Bakarr Bah is presidential research professor and chair of the Department of Sociology at Northern Illinois University. He is also editor-in-chief of *African Conflict & Peacebuilding Review*, African editor for *Critical Sociology*, and founding director of the Institute for Research and Policy Integration in Africa (IRPIA). Bah has been an invited speaker at more than forty major institutions globally. His works include *International Statebuilding in West Africa* (with Nikolas Emmanuel, Indiana University Press, 2024); *Post-Conflict Institutional Design* (Zed Books, 2020); *International Security and Peacebuilding* (Indiana University Press, 2017); and *Breakdown and Reconstitution: Democracy, the Nation-State, and Ethnicity in Nigeria* (Lexington Books, 2005). His articles have been published in top journals such as *African Affairs*, *Administrative Theory & Praxis*, and *Critical Sociology*. For more, see www.niu.edu/bah.

John-Paul Safunu Banchani is a lecturer in international politics and American foreign policy at the Department of History and Political Studies of the Kwame Nkrumah University of Science and Technology, Kumasi Ghana. He is presently an associate of Democracy Without Borders. He received his PhD at the University of Bamberg, Germany, and holds two master of arts degrees in international affairs and conflict, security and development from the University of Ghana, Legon and King's College, London, respectively. His research interests include international organizations, global governance, security and development, and Africa in world politics.

Mary-Jane Fox (PhD) is an independent researcher and editor with previous teaching positions and guest lecturing at Georgetown, St. Andrews, and Uppsala Universities. Topics of interest include issues around democracy, political culture, child soldiers, violent non-state actors, and international humanitarian law. Publications include *The Roots of Somali Political Culture* (Lynne Rienner, 2015) and articles in peer-reviewed journals on the topics listed above.

Kassandra Gonzalez is a doctoral student in sociology at University of Illinois Urbana-Champaign and managing editor for *African Conflict & Peacebuilding Review*. She holds a master's degree in sociology from Northern Illinois University. Her research interests include issues of sustainability, climate change, environmental degradation, international relations, and globalization.

Keunsoo Jeong completed his PhD at the University of Pittsburgh Graduate School of International and Public Affairs. His publications include "Diverse Patterns of World and Regional Piracy: Implications of the Recurrent Characteristics" (*Australian Journal of Maritime & Ocean Affairs*, 2018) and "Piracy and Crime Embeddedness: State Decay and Social Transformation in Somalia" (*African Conflict & Peace Building Review*, 2019). He is currently a freelance independent research scholar in international security issues.

Sebastian Angzoorokuu Paalo is a lecturer at the Department of History and Political Studies, KNUST. He is also the assistant director for research at the Institute for Research and Policy Integration in Africa (IRPIA). Sebastian obtained his PhD in political science and international studies from the University of Queensland (Australia). He serves as a reviewer for many reputable journals and grant applications in his multidisciplinary fields of governance, peace and conflict, international relations, and development studies. His publications and research interests cut across peace and conflict, governance and politics in Africa, and Africa in international relations. He has worked on several independent and collaborative projects, the latest being his collaborative policy research with Chatham House on Forest Governance in Africa and the African Peacebuilding Network (APN) Fellowship of the Social Science Research Council (SSRC).

Matthew Pflaum completed his PhD in geography at the University of Florida. He is interested in heterogeneities of insecurities across groups in the Sahel, violence against civilians, and marginalized communities. More broadly, he is interested in dimensions of insecurity including borders, urbanization, governance, gender, extremism, mobility, and livelihoods. He holds a master's degree in African studies and international development from the University of Edinburgh and an MPH in global health and infectious disease from Emory University.

Walters Tohnji Samah is a conflict resolution and governance expert. He currently works as peace and development advisor in Guinea, where he provides strategic analysis and advisory support to the United Nations system. He served in the same capacity in Eritrea and Chad. Walters previously worked as African Union political affairs coordinator in the CAR, chief analyst of the African Union Mission in Somalia, mediator and dialogue facilitator for the Danish Refugee Council in the CAR, parliamentary strengthening specialist (USAID/DAI Haiti), and UN civil affairs officer (Haiti). He holds a *Maitrise* in political science and a doctorate in history of international relations from the University of Yaoundé I, Cameroon.

Ian S. Spears is associate professor of political science at the University of Guelph. His research interests focus on the obstacles to the resolution of violent conflict. Ian Spears is the author of *Believers, Skeptics and Failure in Conflict Resolution* (Palgrave, 2019) and *Civil War in African States: The Search for Security* (Lynne Rienner, 2010). He is co-editor, with Paul Kingston, of *States Within States: Incipient Political Entities in the Post-Cold War Era* (Palgrave 2004). He has published numerous book chapters as well as articles in scholarly journals including *Global Change, Peace & Security*, *The Journal of Democracy*, *Third World Quarterly*, *Review of African Political Economy*, *African Security Review*, *African Conflict and Peacebuilding Review*, *The International Journal*, and *Civil Wars*.

Index